Plate I.

From a Photograph.

P.S. Duval, Son & Co. Phila

AMERICAN BEAVER.

THE
AMERICAN BEAVER

A Classic of Natural History and Ecology

by

LEWIS H. MORGAN

With a New Introduction by
ROBERT J. NAIMAN
National Resources Research Institute
University of Minnesota, Duluth

DOVER PUBLICATIONS, INC.
NEW YORK

Published in Canada by General Publishing Company, Ltd., 30 Lesmill
Road, Don Mills, Toronto, Ontario.
Published in the United Kingdom by Constable and Company, Ltd., 10
Orange Street, London WC2H 7EG.

This Dover edition, first published in 1986, is an unabridged republication
of the work originally published by J. B. Lippincott & Co., Philadelphia, in
1868 under the title *The American Beaver and His Works*. A fold-out map
following p. 82 in the original edition appears as a two-page spread following
p. 83 in this edition. A new Introduction has been written by Robert J.
Naiman especially for the Dover edition.

Manufactured in the United States of America
Dover Publications, Inc., 31 East 2nd Street, Mineola, N.Y. 11501

Library of Congress Cataloging in Publication Data

Morgan, Lewis Henry, 1818–1881.
The American beaver.

Reprint. Originally published: The American beaver and his works. Philadelphia : J.B. Lippincott, 1868.
1. Beavers.   I. Title.
[QL737.R632M67   1986]   599.32'32   85-12848
ISBN 0-486-24995-6 (pbk.)

INTRODUCTION TO THE
DOVER EDITION

When Lewis Henry Morgan (1818–1881) published *The American Beaver and His Works* in 1868, he clearly did not suspect that it would become a classic. The Preface to the original edition, besides being an outstanding introduction, lays bare his humility: ". . . although it falls much below the dignity and completeness of a monograph, [this book] is offered as an experiment in this special undertaking of collecting and systematizing our knowledge of the habits and mode of life of the inferior animals." Further, he writes, "A treatise overdone is as distasteful to the reader as one imperfectly executed; and since this [book] is liable to both objections, it is submitted, not without misgivings, to the public judgment." Yet for over a hundred years this book has been judged to be one of the most important writings available on the beaver.

More than the animal itself, the constructions of beavers—their lodges, dams, and canals—have fascinated naturalists for over two hundred years. Beavers are rodents, the largest in North America, but their ability to modify the environment has allowed us to imagine them as somehow better, smarter, or more civilized than other animals. Morgan was the first to study the North American beaver in detail. He writes of their "complicated and extended process of reasoning" and then, in a single and revealing sentence, suggests the reason for his fascination with them: "The results of the persevering labors of the beaver were suggestive of human industry." Beavers shape their environment and, in that way, they are like us. By the time Morgan encountered his first beaver, the population throughout North America was substantially reduced and declining rapidly. Fortunately, Morgan was able to observe beavers in a region that had been subjected only to minor and recent anthropogenic disturbance, and where beaver population and structures had been unchanged for centuries.

These statements mask the fact that the beaver was probably the single most important factor in the early exploration of North America. Early penetrations into western and northern lands were often made solely for the purpose of discovering new trapping areas, not for gold or other purposes. The exploration of Meriwether Lewis and William Clark was primarily an expedition to find a route that would capture the fur trade from Canada. Lewis and Clark, Alexander Mackenzie, Simon Fraser, and David Thompson all made substantial explorations in the quest for beavers, as the Pacific Fur Company, the Hudson's Bay Company, and the American Fur Company established numerous outposts to facilitate the movement of pelts to market.

The magnitude and value of this market can be seen in the records of these companies and the prices paid. The Hudson's Bay Company alone sold nearly three million beaver skins in London between 1853 and 1877. The American naturalist Thomas Seton estimated that the annual carnage by trappers and Indians between 1860 and 1870 was close to five hundred thousand. Different annual totals can be found in different sources, but the end result never varies. By 1900 the beaver, whose North American population prior to the arrival of Europeans was estimated by Seton at sixty million, was nearly exterminated.

Today, with laws for its protection and a virtual lack of natural predators, the North American beaver population has increased substantially throughout its former range. As a result, the beaver's widespread and significant impact on aquatic ecosystems is becoming evident again. This impact, both historically and currently, has important implications for nutrient cycling, hydrology, geomorphology, and the dynamics and structure of aquatic ecosystems throughout North America. Through their activities, beavers sequester huge amounts of sediment and nutrients high up in the watersheds. They are responsible for the creation and maintenance of vast regions of wetlands. They increase habitat diversity and enhance ecosystem stability through the alteration of stream channels. And they significantly alter the cycling of essential nutrients (such as nitrogen and phosphorus), creating an ecosystem where these elements are efficiently utilized. Inasmuch as the beaver is the mediator of these enormous alterations in the environment, an understanding of its natural history is essential.

Ironically, Lewis Henry Morgan was not primarily a naturalist in the strict sense. He is best known as an ethnologist for his researches among American Indians at a time when anthropology in America had scarcely reached the stage of infancy. In later years this work earned him the title of "Father of American Anthropology."

Morgan graduated from Union College in Schenectady, New York, in 1840 before studying law and being admitted to the bar. In 1855 Morgan became legal adviser to a railroad being constructed between Marquette, Michigan, and the iron region of Lake Superior. Later he devoted much attention to political affairs and served in the New York Assembly and Senate for several years. Morgan's initial interest in Indian life was rather casual, but he was soon drawn into a serious investigation of Iroquois institutions and customs. This eventually led him to further investigations among other American tribes and finally to the field of world anthropology, to which he contributed the broadly theoretical work, *Ancient Society or Researches in the Lines of Human Progress* (1877). His first book, *League of the Ho-dé-no-sau-nee, or Iroquois* (1851), has been considered the world's first scientific account of an Indian culture.

During his visits to Michigan in the interest of the railroad, he not only pursued his ethnological studies, but, following up one of his earlier interests—that in the manifestation of mind by lower animals—studied the beaver. The result is the book being republished here.

Morgan was active and energetic in all aspects of life. For his contributions to ethnology he was elected a member of the National Academy of Sciences in 1875. In 1879 he became president of the American Association for the Advancement of Science. Although not immensely wealthy, he bequeathed a good share of what money he did possess to the University of Rochester for the education of women.

The main value of *The American Beaver and His Works* lies in its historical, rather than its zoological, content. It was published at a time when the beaver in North America was rapidly approaching extinction. Morgan's work gives us a vivid and detailed glimpse into the habitat, constructions, natural history, and methods of environmental exploitation of an animal that had an enormous impact on the landscape of North America. The book's sketches, photographs, maps, and in-depth descriptions of beavers and their habitat allow the modern biologist to reconstruct and attempt to understand the nature of unaltered aquatic ecosystems. Without such aid, an understanding of this kind is virtually impossible to attain anywhere in the world today. Morgan's insights into natural history are remarkable in that he envisioned biogeochemical processes that scientists are rediscovering only today.

As a contribution to zoology, this book provides detailed accounts of beaver anatomy and habits. However, since the time of its publication, hundreds of more advanced papers have appeared on beaver zoogeography, evolution, anatomy, physiology, reproduction, ecology, behavior, and genetics. Nonetheless, Morgan wrote of beaver populations that had undergone little modification until the arrival of the railroad. Morgan saw and described beaver populations as they had existed for centuries, and for this reason alone his work is a classic that can be used to place current studies of wetlands and stream ecosystems in historical perspective.

ROBERT J. NAIMAN

THE
AMERICAN BEAVER

Lewis Henry Morgan in his library. Photograph from the Lewis Henry Morgan Papers; courtesy of the Rush Rhees Library, The University of Rochester, Rochester, New York.

TO

SAMUEL P. ELY, Esq.,

OF MARQUETTE, MICHIGAN,

This Volume is inscribed

AS A SLIGHT MEMENTO

OF THE LONG AND UNINTERRUPTED FRIENDSHIP

WHICH HAS SUBSISTED BETWEEN HIM AND

THE AUTHOR.

ROCHESTER, NEW YORK,
November 21, 1867.

"Natural History, then, should be based on what is called a *System of Nature;* or a great Catalogue, in which all beings bear acknowledged names, may be recognized by distinctive characters, and distributed in divisions and subdivisions themselves named and characterized, in which they may be found."—*Cuvier's Animal Kingdom*, Intro. 15.

"And after all, what does it matter to science that thousands of species, more or less, should be described and entered in our systems, if we know nothing about them?"—*Agassiz's Nat. Hist. U. S.*, i. 57.

PREFACE.

The publication of Cuvier's Animal Kingdom established an epoch in the science of zoology. This eminent scholar brought to his subject the critical and reflective powers of a great intellect, and the varied and profound acquirements of a laborious life. Having possessed himself of the results of antecedent as well as contemporary investigations, and extended his researches with more or less exactness, over the entire animal kingdom, he was enabled to construct, upon the "System of Nature," that remarkable system for the classification of animals, which now forms the basis of zoological science.[1]

This system of classification is founded exclusively upon the anatomical structure of animals, whence comparative anatomy is the source of its materials. It not only rejects the habits and properties of animals as immaterial and transient, but it also leaves out of consideration their mental endowments, which, however important in other respects, were incapable of affording a basis of classification.

Under its clear and definite discriminations all the species of each of the four great branches of the animal kingdom are seen in intelligible and harmonious relations, notwithstanding their striking diversities of form. Unity of type runs through the structural organization of all the individuals comprised in each of these branches. The grandeur of this fourfold plan of creation is not more impressive than the wonderful adaptation of the surrounding elements to the condition and wants of the multitude of animal organisms which God has made.

It is not, however, the whole of the science of zoology to

---

[1] Agassiz dates the new period from 1812, "when Cuvier laid before the Academy of Sciences in Paris the results of his investigations * * * which had satisfied him that all animals were constructed upon four different plans."—*Natural History United States*, i. 193. The "Regne Animal" did not appear, however, until 1816.

furnish a systematic catalogue of animals, with its exposition limited to the frigid details of anatomical structure. This would restrict it to dead rather than to living forms. Each animal is endowed with a living, and, also, with a thinking principle, the manifestations of each of which are not less important and instructive than the mechanism of the material frames in which they reside. In a comparative sense the former are intrinsically of higher concernment.

A monograph upon each of the principal animals seems, therefore, to be desirable, if not absolutely necessary, to fill out, in some measure, this great programme; and to complete the superstructure of a science, the foundations of which have been so admirably established. These should contain a minute exposition of their artificial works, where such are constructed; of their habits, their mode of life, and their mutual relations. When the facts bearing upon these several subjects have been collected and systematized, the necessary materials will be furnished for the proper elucidation of the long neglected subject of Animal Psychology.

This volume upon "The American Beaver and his Works," although it falls much below the dignity and completeness of a monograph, is offered as an experiment in this special undertaking of collecting and systematizing our knowledge of the habits and mode of life of the inferior animals. Whether the zoologist will turn aside from the more intricate and fascinating subjects of his science to consider the personal acts and artificial erections of this humble, but most industrious mute; and whether the general reader will find either pleasure or profit in studying the manifestations of intelligence by a single animal, when spread out with so much detail, I cannot pretend to form an opinion. A treatise overdone is as distasteful to the reader as one imperfectly executed; and since this is liable to both objections, it is submitted, not without misgivings, to the public judgment.

As books of this description are more or less accidental productions, it is sometimes proper to state how they came to be written. Notwithstanding some reluctance to enter upon personal details, there is, in the present case, an urgent necessity for a brief explanation to bespeak the confidence of the reader in the results of this investigation. It furnishes an apology for introducing the following statement.

In the year 1852 a Railroad was projected and commenced by the late Honorable Heman B. Ely, to open the iron region on the south shore of Lake Superior, and introduce its rich and inexhaustible ores into the manufacturing industry of the country. In this enterprise his brothers, Samuel P. Ely, George H. Ely, and John F. Ely, and their uncle, the late Hervey Ely,[1] then residents, except one, of Rochester, New York, were associated. The magnitude of the undertaking will be appreciated when it is stated that this entire region was then an uninhabited wilderness, with the exception of a few hamlets at Marquette, the present port of the iron district on Lake Superior, and a few log cabins at the iron mines, which had shortly before been discovered, but were still undeveloped. At that time the St. Mary's Ship Canal, which three years later connected the lower lakes with Lake Superior, although projected, was not commenced; consequently navigation between these lakes was obstructed by the rapids in the St. Mary's River. Besides this obstacle, it was five hundred miles from Marquette to Detroit, the nearest point from which supplies could be obtained. Notwithstanding these formidable difficulties, the Messrs. Ely persevered in the enterprise until 1856, when they found it advisable, after a large expenditure, to accept the co-operation of other parties in the further prosecution of the work. Joseph S. Fay, Esq., of Boston, Edwin Parsons, Esq., of New York, and some other capitalists, were then admitted into the association. In 1858 the Railroad was completed to the three principal iron locations, and in 1865 to Lake Michigame, after an expenditure of about a million and a half of dollars.

Under the stimulus of commercial causes a Railroad was thus constructed through a rugged wilderness for a distance of forty

---

[1] I cannot mention the name of my venerable and noble friend, now deceased, without expressing my high appreciation of his great abilities, of his genial and unselfish nature, and of his liberal and enlightened sentiments. He will be favorably remembered as one of the great men of his day and generation. Born in West Springfield, Massachusetts, January 10th, 1791, he established himself in Rochester in 1813, where he engaged extensively in manufacturing and commercial enterprises, in which he continued until 1861, when he retired from business. He died in this city, November 23d, 1862. It was my privilege to know him intimately for nearly twenty years; and this passing tribute to his memory is founded upon personal knowledge of his worth.

miles, and opened a country which, but for its mineral deposits, would have been pronounced unfit for human habitation. With its unequaled summer climate, and its unlimited mineral wealth, it has now become one of the most attractive regions within our national limits.

It so happened that this Railroad passed through a beaver district, more remarkable, perhaps, than any other of equal extent to be found in any part of North America. By opening this wilderness in advance of all settlement, the beavers were surprised, so to speak, in the midst of their works, which, at the same time, were rendered accessible for minute and deliberate investigation, in a manner altogether unusual. A rare opportunity was thus offered to examine the works of the beaver, and to see him in his native wilds.

Having been associated in this enterprise from its commencement, as one of the directors of the Railroad Company, and as one of its stockholders, business called me to Marquette, first in 1855, and nearly every summer since to the present time. After the completion of the Railroad to the iron mines, it was impossible to withstand the temptation to brook-trout fishing, which the streams traversing the intermediate and adjacent districts offered in ample measure. My friend, Gilbert D. Johnson, Superintendent of the Lake Superior Mine, had established boat stations at convenient points upon the Carp and Esconauba Rivers, and to him I am specially indebted first, for a memorable experience in brook-trout fishing, and secondly, for an introduction to the works of the beaver within the areas traversed by these streams. Our course, in passing up and down, was obstructed by beaver dams at short intervals, from two to three feet high, over which we were compelled to draw our boat. Their numbers and magnitude could not fail to surprise as well as interest any observer. Although constructed in the solitude of the wilderness, where the forces of nature were still actively at work, it was evident that they had existed and been maintained for centuries by the permanent impression produced upon the rugged features of the country. The results of the persevering labors of the beaver were suggestive of human industry. The streams were bordered continuously with beaver meadows, formed by overflows by means of these dams, which had destroyed the timber upon the adjacent lands. Fallen trees, excavated canals, lodges, and burrows, filled up the measure of their works. These together seemed to me to afford a much greater promise of pleasure than could be gained with the fish-pole, and very soon, accordingly, the beaver was substituted for the trout. I took up the subject as I did fishing, for summer recreation. In the year 1861, I had occasion to visit the Red River Settlement in the Hudson's Bay Territory, and in 1862, to ascend the Missouri River to the Rocky Mountains, which enabled me to compare the works of the beaver in these localities with those on Lake Superior. At the outset I had no expectation of following up the subject year after year, but was led on, by the interest which it awakened, until the materials collected seemed to be worth arranging for publication. Whether this last surmise is well or ill founded, I am at least certain that no other animal will be allowed to entrap the unambitious author so completely as he confesses himself to have been by the beaver. My unrestrained curiosity has cost me a good deal of time and labor.

After measuring and attempting to sketch a number of these dams, I found it impossible to reproduce even a feeble copy. It was evident that the photographic art was alone capable of handling such a complicated subject; and of fixing, once for all, its remarkable features. It seemed, also, to be extremely desirable to secure an accurate representation of these structures while they were in a perfect state, as well as accessible; since it was certain that they would be abandoned by the beavers with the establishment of settlements in their vicinity, after which they would speedily fall into decay. While maturing a plan to take into the country for this purpose a party of photographers, the desire was gratified by the adventure of Mr. James A. Jenney, who came to Marquette in 1861, with an instrument and the necessary appliances for taking landscape views. With him I made an arrangement for a series of photographs. The following year, my friend, the Rev. Josiah Phelps, rector of St. Peter's Church at Marquette, who had taken up this beautiful art as an amateur, generously placed his instrument and his services at my disposal, and thus a large number of additional photographs were obtained from time to time. The engravings in this volume, with some exceptions, were made from selections from these photographs.

In addition to these, I made a general beaver collection, suffi-

ciently ample to illustrate other branches of the subject, consisting of mounted specimens of the beaver, and of his skeleton, skulls,
pelts, tree cuttings, and limb and pole cuttings, of all sizes and
kinds, engravings of specimens of which are given in the following
pages.

It has been my aim to speak in all cases, in which it was possible, from original specimens. In this manner, truth and certainty are both secured, and the amount of necessary description
is greatly abridged. It will be found, in the sequel, that this
account of the beaver rests essentially upon actual works reproduced by the photograph and copied by the engraver. Whatever
value it may possess is chiefly referable to this fact.

Marquette, which in 1853 consisted of a few scattering houses,
now contains twenty-eight hundred inhabitants. Situated upon
a bay of Lake Superior, and prosperous upon the large business
of the iron region, it is not too much to say that it is the most
beautiful village of the Northwest. The large investments made
for the development of the mineral wealth, and for the prosecution of the constantly increasing trade of the iron district, have
drawn to it a higher and more intelligent class of business men
than is usually found in villages of its size; and this, in turn, ha
given to Marquette, in a social sense, its superior and attractive
character. The climate also—a fact not suspected until the country was opened—is one of the finest, in the summer, to be found
within the limits of the United States; while in the winter,
from its steadiness and uniformity, it is less trying than that of
New England or New York. Marquette is destined to become a
city; and the principal centre of business on Lake Superior.[1]

Besides the persons previously named, I am under very great
obligations to many others for co-operation, information, and
assistance, in various ways, while engaged upon this investiga-

---

[1] This railroad, which was first known as the "Iron Mountain," then as
the "Bay de Noquet and Marquette," and now as the "Marquette and Ontonagon Railroad," has carried down from the mines to Marquette the following amounts of iron ore:

In 1858	31,000 Tons.	In 1863	200,000 Tons.
1859	65,000 "	1864	250,000 "
1860	116,000 "	1865	200,000 "
1861	45,000 "	1866	210,000 "
1862	115,000 "	1867	270,000 "

tion. First among them is my friend, Samuel P. Ely, Esq., now a resident of Marquette, and Vice-President and Managing Director of the Marquette and Ontonagon Railroad Company. He has taken a cordial interest in the subject, joined me in some expeditions, and seconded my efforts in every possible way. The inscription of this volume to him is but a slight recognition of the part he has taken in the collection of the materials. To Hon. Peter White, of Marquette; to Cornelius Donkersley, Esq., Superintendent; L. K. Dorrance, Esq., former Chief Engineer; and William H. Steele, Esq., Assistant Engineer of the same Railroad, I am also indebted for many personal favors; and to Charles H. Kavis, the present Chief Engineer, as well. I desire also to mention the friendly and faithful services of Wm. Badger, who has spent many nights with me encamped by beaver dams, and who, as a camp master and explorer, possesses high qualifications. To Capt. Daniel Wilson, an experienced trapper, as well as an accurate observer, I am indebted for valuable information. I am also indebted to William Cameron, William Bass, Paul Pine, and Jack La Pete, Ojibwa trappers, for an acquaintance with the "beaver lore" of the Indians, which is both curious and instructive. I desire also to mention my friend, George S. Riley, Esq., of Rochester, to whom I am indebted for valuable suggestions. There are still others whose names would be necessary to complete the list of those who have contributed in various ways to the materials contained in this volume, whose friendly offices are remembered with much pleasure.

It is perhaps superfluous to name my friend, Dr. W. W. Ely, of Rochester, since he is a direct contributor to these pages. Having articulated the skeleton represented in Plate III., he expressed a willingness to dissect a pair of beavers if they could be obtained, which was accordingly done. The carefully prepared and accurate presentation which he has made of this subject will furnish ample materials for the further comparison of the American and European beavers.

Rochester, *November*, 1867.

TABLE OF CONTENTS.

CHAPTER I.

CHARACTERISTICS AND HABITAT OF THE AMERICAN BEAVER; AND HIS
POSITION IN THE ANIMAL KINGDOM.

Order Rodentia—Characteristics of the Order—The Beaver a Rodent
—His Color—Black Beaver—Albinos—His Size—Movements—Functions of Tail—Vision short—Hearing and Smell acute—Social Propensities—Habitat of American Beaver—Their Numbers—Habitat
of European Beaver—Fossil European Beaver—*Trogontherium*—
Fossil American Beaver—*Castoroides*—Great Antiquity of the Beaver
Type—Systematic Position of *Castoridæ*—Brandt's Classification of
the Rodentia—Independence of this Family—American and European Beavers Varieties of the same Species............................ 17

CHAPTER II.

ANATOMY OF THE BEAVER.

Introduction—Description— Skeleton— Skull—Teeth — Muscles — Internal Organs: Mouth, Stomach, Intestines, Cæcum, Heart, Lungs,
Liver, Spleen—Respiration of Aquatic Animals—Brain 46

APPENDIX A. 1. Measurements of Skull. 2. Differences between
European and American Beavers considered. 3. Castoreum Organs,
and Generative Organs.. 287

CHAPTER III.

BEAVER DAM

Remarkable Beaver District—Number of Beaver Dams—Other Works
—Character of the Region—Beavers now abundant—Map of Area
—Object of Dams—Their Great Age—Of Two Kinds Interlaced
Stick-Dam—Solid-bank Dam—Great Beaver Dam at Grass Lake—
Its Dimensions—Surrounding Landscape—Mode of Construction—
Lower Face—Water Face—Great Curve—Mode of discharging Sur-

plus Water—Artistic Appearance of this Dam—Necessity for Continuous Repairs—Measurements—Cubic Contents—Photograph—Manner of taking same—Relation of Dam below—Same of one above—Manner of Repairing Dams.. 78

CHAPTER IV.

BEAVER DAMS.—(CONTINUED.)

Solid-bank Dams—Places where constructed—No Dams in deep Water—Where impossible, the Beavers inhabit River Banks—Description of Solid-bank Dam—Opening for Surplus Water—Pond confined to River Banks—Similar Dam with Hedge—Fallen-tree Dam—Use of Tree accidental—Spring Rill Dam—Series of Dams on the Carp—Dams in a Gorge—Lake Outlet Dams—High Dam—Long Dam—Description of same—Manner of Photographing same —Dams in other Districts of North America—Petrified Beaver Dams in Montana.. 104

CHAPTER V.

BEAVER LODGES AND BURROWS.

Habits of Beaver—Our Knowledge limited—Indians and Trappers as Observers—Source of Buffon's Extravagant Statements—Disposition of Beavers to pair—The Family—Outcast Beaver—Beaver Migrations—Adaptation to Aquatic Life—Suspension of Respiration—Length of Time—Artifice of Musk-Rat—Burrowing Propensities—Varieties of the Beaver Lodge—Island Lodge at Grass Lake—Size and Form—Chamber—Floor—Wood Entrance—Beaver Entrance—Their Artistic Character — Bank Lodge — Mode of Construction — Chamber—Entrances—Another Variety of Bank Lodge—Chamber and Entrances—Nature of Floor—Lake Lodge—Differences from other Varieties — False Lodge of Upper Missouri — Lodges Single Chambered—Burrows—Their Form, Size, and Uses—Examples, with Measurements—Number of Beavers to the Lodge—Number of Lodges to the Pond.. 132

CHAPTER VI.

SUBSISTENCE OF BEAVERS.

Subsistence exclusively Vegetable—Kinds of Bark preferred—Roots of Plants—Incisive Teeth Chisels—Their cutting Power—It diminishes with Age—Provisions for Winter—Season for collecting—Felling Trees—Their Size—Number of Beavers engaged—Manner of cutting—Chips—Short Cuttings—Moving them on Land—Floating

them in Water—Sinking them in Piles—Wood-eating—Evidence that
they eat Clear Wood—Brush-heap at Lodge—Restricted to Particular Places—Their Use—Ponds in Winter—Winter Life of Beavers... 166

CHAPTER VII.

BEAVER CANALS, MEADOWS, AND TRAILS.

Beaver Canals—Their Extraordinary Character—Originated by Neces-
sity—Their Uses—Evidences of their Artificial Character—Canals
at Natural Pond—Their Form and Appearance—Canal on Carp
River—Use of Dams in same—Canal Across Bend of Esconauba—
Same across Island in Pond—Beaver Meadows—How formed—Their
Extent—Beaver Slides on Upper Missouri—Scenery on this River—
Bluffs of Indurated Clay—Bad Lands—White Walls—Game—Con-
nection of River Systems with Spread of Beavers......................... 191

CHAPTER VIII.

MODE OF TRAPPING BEAVER.

Other Habits of the Beaver—Indications of Age—Tame Beavers—Nursed
by Indian Women—Building and Repairing Dams—Great Beaver
Districts—Hudson's Bay Company—American Fur Company—Private Adventurers—The Steel Trap—Trapping Season—Trapping at
the Dam—At the Lodge—Traps sprung—Whether the Beaver when
caught bites off his Fore Foot—Trapping under the Ice—Catching
in a Pen—Trapping Bank Beavers—Catching in Burrows—Trappers as a Class—Custom of hanging up Skulls—Statistics of Fur
Trade — Early and Recent Exportations — Immense Numbers of
Beavers.. 218

CHAPTER IX

ANIMAL PSYCHOLOGY.

Inquiries proposed—Whether the Mutes possess a Mental Principle—
Whether its Qualities are similar to those manifested by the Human
Mind—Whether the Differences are of Degree, or of Kind—Consider-
ations from Structural Organization—The Principle of Life—Memory
—Reason—Imagination—The Will—Appetites and Passions—Lu-
nacy of Animals—General Conclusions................................... 248

APPENDICES.

A.—Notes to Chapter II.. 287
B.—Samuel Hearne's Account of the Beaver........................... 306
C.—Bennett's Article on the Beaver...................................... 317

THE AMERICAN BEAVER.

CHAPTER I.

CHARACTERISTICS AND HABITAT OF THE AMERICAN BEAVER; AND HIS POSITION IN THE ANIMAL KINGDOM.

Order Rodentia—Characteristics of the Order—The Beaver a Rodent—His Color—Black Beaver—Albinos—His Size—Movements—Functions of Tail —Vision short—Hearing and Smell acute—Social Propensities—Habitat of American Beaver—Their Numbers—Habitat of European Beaver— Fossil European Beaver—*Trogontherium*—Fossil American Beaver—*Castoroides*—Great Antiquity of the Beaver Type—Systematic Position of *Castoridæ*—Brandt's Classification of the Rodentia—Independence of this Family—American and European Beavers varieties of the same Species.

In structural organization the beaver occupies a low position in the scale of mammalian forms. His low respiration and clumsy proportions render him slow of motion; and being a coarse vegetable feeder, and adapted both to water and to land, he is inferior to the carnivorous, and even the herbivorous animals, in those characteristics upon which the gradations of structure are established. In intelligence and sagacity he is undoubtedly below many of the carnivora which depend exclusively for subsistence upon their skill in entrapping and seizing prey; neither is it probable that he is possessed of higher endowments than other animals of a corresponding grade. And yet no other animal has attracted a larger share of attention, or acquired by his intelligence a more respectable position in public estimation. The reason is obvious. In a pre-eminent degree he requires artificial erections to promote his happiness, and to secure his safety; consequently, we are enabled to place our hands upon his works, and to trace step by step, through tangible forms, the evidences of his architectural skill. Around him are the dam, the lodge, the burrow, the tree-cutting, and the artificial canal; each testifying to his handiwork, and affording us an opportunity to see the application as well as the results of his mental and physical powers. There is no animal, below man, in the entire range of the mammalia, which offers to our investigation such a series of works, or presents such remarkable materials for the study and illustration of animal psychology.

The specific characteristics and habitat of the American beaver, and his position in the animal kingdom, require some notice before entering upon the subject of his artificial erections, habits, and mode of life. Our interest in this animal will be much increased by a preliminary consideration of these several topics.

Of the nine orders of mammals established by Cuvier in his systematic treatise upon the Animal Kingdom, the fifth is the order *Rodentia*, or the *gnawers*. To this order the beaver belongs. He is thus found in the same category with the squirrel, the rat, the marmot, the porcupine, and the rabbit, and with many other mammals, all of which agree in the possession of two large incisive teeth in each jaw, separated from the molars by an empty space. These incisors are the distinctive characteristic upon which the order is founded. With jaws thus mounted, the rodents are physically incapable of seizing a living prey, and consequently are formed to draw their nutriment from the vegetable kingdom. The general characteristics of this order are given by Cuvier as follows:

"Two large incisors in each jaw, separated from the molars by a wide interval, cannot well seize a living prey or devour flesh. They are unable even to cut the aliment; but they serve to file, and by continued labor to reduce it into small particles; in a word, to *gnaw* it; hence the word *rodentia* applied to animals of this order; it is thus that they successfully attack the hardest substances, frequently feeding on wood and the bark of trees. The better to accomplish this object, these incisors have enamel only in front, so that their posterior edges wearing away faster than the anterior, they are always naturally sloped [or chisel like]. Their prismatic form causes them to grow from the root as fast as they wear away from the tip [their formative pulp being persistent], and this tendency to increase in length is so powerful that if either of them be lost or broken, its antagonist in the other jaw, having nothing to oppose or comminute, becomes developed to a monstrous extent. The inferior jaw is articulated by a longitudinal condyle in such a way as to allow of no horizontal motion, except from back to front, and *vice versa*, as is requisite for the action of gnawing. The molars also have flat crowns, the enameled eminences of which are always transversely, so as to be in opposition to the horizontal movement of the jaw, and better to assist trituration."[1]   *   *   *   *

"Throughout the present group, the brain is almost smooth, and without furrows.   *   *   *   In a word, the inferiority of these animals is perceptible in most of the details of their organization."

Baird remarks upon the rodents: "They exist in all parts of the world, and are especially abundant in America, which contains nearly as many species as all the rest of the world put together. South America, however, counts more species than the northern half of the New World, the preponderance being caused principally by the large number belonging to the genus *Hesperomys*, of which our little deer-or white-footed wood-mouse, is a familiar example."[2]

Waterhouse introduces the order Rodentia in the following language : " The Rodentia, so called from their gnawing propensities, form one of the most clearly defined groups of the mammalia; a group which has representatives in all parts of the world, and the species of which are very numerous. They feed upon vegetable substances, and are of small size, few exceeding the common hare in bulk. The most striking characters of the rodents are those furnished by the teeth; the long, vacant space which separates the incisors in front, here adapted for gnawing, from the masticating teeth behind.   *   *   *   * Sometimes the width of the incisor is very great, and exceeds the depth; the rodents which burrow, and live almost entirely under ground, present this form

---

[1] Animal Kingdom.   Carpenter and Westwood edition, p. 107.
[2] Explorations for a Railroad Route, etc. to the Pacific, viii. 235.

of incisors, their powerful teeth being, no doubt, used to gnaw through the roots which would otherwise obstruct their subterranean course.   *   *   * Those of the upper jaw are always shorter than those of the lower, and usually describe about three parts of a circle. The larger incisors of the lower jaw form a smaller segment of a larger circle."[1]

Among living rodents the beaver is the largest with the exception of the capybara of South America, which is about one-third larger.[2] The form and general appearance of the American beaver are well known. His color is a reddish brown, but varying in some localities to a yellowish tinge upon brown, and in others to a glossy black. Reddish-brown, however, is the prevailing color. I have two pelts in my collection of a dark chestnut, this being the color of the coarse fur or hair which in all cases determines the general color of the skin. The fine or true fur is of a clear uniform brown from the root to the tip, and the staple is short. It varies in length from one-half to three-quarters of an inch, while the coarse hairs, which resemble bristles, are from one and three-quarters to two and a half inches in length, and sufficiently abundant to completely overspread the fur. Black beavers are scarce, and appear to be confined to higher northern latitudes. The fact that they are sometimes found of this color is attested by Hearne. "Black beaver," he remarks, "and that of a beautiful

---

[1] Nat. Hist. of the Mammalia. Lond. ed., 1848, ii. 1.

[2] One shot by Darwin at Montevideo weighed 90 pounds. In general appearance it resembles the hare much more than the beaver.

gloss, are not uncommon; perhaps they are more plentiful at Churchill than at any other factory in the bay; but it is rare to get more than twelve or fifteen of their skins in the course of one year's trade."[1] The skin of the foetal beaver, of which I have two specimens in my collection, is covered with a thick fur, which is soft and silky to the touch, and of a clear brown, with a slightly reddish tinge. In these skins the coarse hairs are undeveloped. Albinos are occasionally found, but they are rare. Upon this subject the same author remarks: "In the course of twenty years' experience in the countries about Hudson's Bay, though I have traveled six hundred miles to the west of the sea-coast, I never saw but one white beaver skin, and it had many reddish and brown hairs along the ridge of the back. The sides of the belly were of a glossy silvery white."[2] Prince Maximilian speaks of white beaver as occasionally found upon the Yellowstone River. He says: "I saw one beautifully spotted with white; yellowish-white and pure white are not unfrequently caught on the Yellowstone."[3] The skin of the beaver when tanned is thicker than the thickest calf skin, and coarse in texture.

When full grown, the weight of the American beaver varies from thirty to sixty pounds, the latter weight being rarely attained. The weight of the three largest Lake Superior beavers of which I have reliable knowledge, was fifty-eight pounds each to two

---

[1] Hearne's Journey to the Northern Ocean. Dublin ed., 1796, p. 241.

[2] Ibid., 240.

[3] Travels in North America. Lond. ed., 1843, p. 332.

of them, and sixty pounds for the third.[1] One mounted specimen in my collection was a full-grown three-year old beaver when taken, and weighed thirty-five pounds. He measured from the tip of the nose to the end of the tail, three feet and eight inches; around the centre of the abdomen two feet and one inch; and around the head, back of the ears, one foot and two inches. That part of the tail which is covered with scales measured nine inches in length, and four and a half in width at the centre, from which point it narrowed in both directions. A second mounted specimen, also in my collection, and a male, weighed, when taken. thirty-two pounds, and measured in his greatest length three feet six and a quarter inches; around the centre of the abdomen two feet two and a half inches; and around the neck, back of the ears, one foot two and a half inches. A third mounted specimen, the one represented in Plate I., and also in my collection, was a two-year old beaver, and a female, and weighed twenty-nine and a half pounds. She measured in her greatest length three feet six and a quarter inches; around the centre of the abdomen two feet; and around the neck, back of ears, one foot one inch. The skeleton represented in Plate III., now in my collection, is that of a female beaver, full grown, and three years old and upwards. She weighed forty-three and a half pounds, and measured in her greatest length three feet six inches; around the centre of the abdomen two feet and six inches; and around the neck, back of ears, one foot three inches. That part of the tail covered with scales measured ten inches in

---

[1] One caught by Capt. Daniel Wilson weighed 58 pounds, and two by John Armstrong weighed respectively 58 and 60 pounds.

length, and five and a half inches at its greatest
width.   Another beaver, whose pelt I have, weighed
thirty-three and a half pounds.   It was caught in
the year 1862, upon the same dam and at the same
time with the one whose skeleton is shown, and
was probably her mate, and if so, a male.   These
beavers, all of which were taken on the south shore
of Lake Superior, may be regarded as average specimens of the beaver of this locality.   From a comparison of their skulls with others in my collection from
the same district, sixty pounds is not an improbable
weight in occasional instances.   The skull belonging
to the skeleton referred to, and which is No. 4 in the
Table of Measurements prepared by Dr. Ely (Appendix
A, note 1), measures $4\frac{88}{100}$ inches from the end of the
nasal bones to the occipital ridge, while that marked
No. 40 in same table measures $5\frac{56}{100}$ inches.   As the former beaver weighed forty-three pounds, it is a reasonable inference that the latter must have weighed at
least sixty pounds.   The beavers of the Upper Missouri are about the same size, while those in Oregon
and California are said to attain a larger average size,
with how much of truth I cannot state.   Brandt, in
his elaborate work on the Rodents, and which is particularly full upon the beaver, concludes, after a comparison of a large number of specimens, that the
Asiatic, European, and American beavers are not dis-
tinguishable from each other in size.[1]

In form the beaver is short between the fore and
hind legs, broad, heavy, and clumsy, and his motions
are slow and awkward.   He walks with a waddling

---

[1] Mémoires de l'Académie Impériale des Sciences de St. Petersbourg Sixth Series. Sciences Naturelles, tome vii. p. 61.

gait, with his back slightly arched, with his body barely clearing the ground, and his tail dragging upon it. He runs slowly, with alternating steps, but when he makes his most rapid movement, it is by the regular quadruped gallop, the fore feet being raised together and followed in the same manner by the hind. An ordinary dog could overtake him in a short chase. In the water, however, his motions are free and graceful. Water is his natural element, and he cannot trust himself far from it with personal safety. The usual representations of the beaver show a gradual increase in the size of the body from the head to the thighs, with the posterior portion much the largest. While the hips are broader than the shoulders, he is the largest around the centre of the abdomen, from which the body tapers in both directions, but more forward than back.

Some of the details of the structural organization of the beaver are of a striking character. The muscles which regulate the movements of the inferior jaw are large and powerful, as may be inferred from the relative size of the head, and particularly from the measurements of the neck immediately behind the ears. This jaw has a free horizontal movement from side to side, as well as forward and back, the inferior incisors moving both to the right and to the left of the superior, thus enabling the beaver to masticate his food by a transverse and diagonal as well as forward and back movement of the molars on each other. Incapacity for this transverse movement of the inferior jaw is made one of the characteristics of the rodent order. Cuvier deduced its necessary movements from the nature of its articulation, and from the main direction of the enameled eminences of the molar teeth, and then limited its horizontal movement to a single direction, which was forward and back. The American beaver is an exception to the general rule.[1] The powerful muscles, before referred to, give to this animal the "horrid bite" (*horrendus morsus*), to use the language of Pliny, for which his tree-cuttings, if not his combative propensities, show him to be distinguished. Each condyle is movable upon its fulcrum, which is a plain surface, and must be held with immense strength to sustain the grasp of the incisors while in the act of cutting down trees.

In swimming, the propelling power is furnished by the hind legs. To adapt their feet for this purpose they are completely webbed to the roots of the claws, and are capable of a lateral spread of eight or nine inches on the exterior line of the membrane. The legs are thrown out behind, in the act of swimming, like those of a duck, and nearly in a horizontal line. While swimming, the fore feet are not used, but are pressed back against the abdomen,[2] their smallness rendering them nearly useless for this purpose. Dr. Ely, however, discovered a rudimentary membrane between the fore fingers of these paws which is particularly conspicuous between the second and third. The paws are very small relatively to the size of the animal, and very much smaller than the hind feet; but as they are capable of a very considerable rotary movement, he is able to hold sticks and limbs of trees,

---

[1] The squirrel, the rabbit, and the rat also appear to be exceptions.

[2] The otter is a more rapid swimmer than the beaver, but does not use his fore feet, which are placed in the same position.

Plate II.

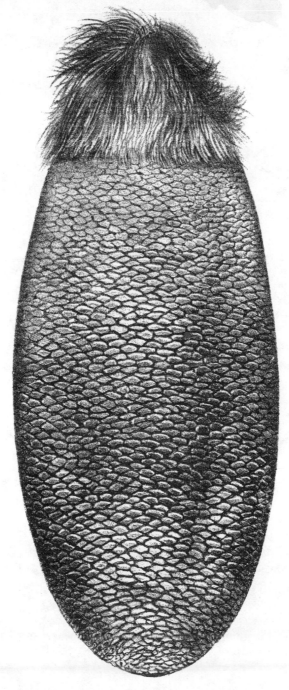

From a Photograph

P.S Duval, Son & Co Phila

TAIL of BEAVER, 5/9 nat. Size.

and to handle them with great dexterity while cutting them, and also to carry mud and stones. As he is capable of sitting up erect upon his hind legs, and of walking upon them, his paws are thus liberated, and by that means his architectural skill is rendered possible. Man's great superiority over the inferior animals is shown in nothing more conspicuously than in the freedom of his hands.

The beaver is a burrowing animal, his normal habitation being the burrow rather than the lodge. To enable him to excavate the large chambers under ground, hereafter described, his paws are armed with claws which are long, curving, and strong. In a full-grown beaver, the claw upon the third finger measures seven-eighths of an inch. Those upon the hind feet are still longer and broader, and equally well adapted to assist in excavating burrows. Upon the second toe of each hind foot there is an extra claw, set immediately under the true one and transversely. It is very thin, broad, and round edged, and projects nearly to the tip of the claw. It is peculiar to this animal.

In its form, structure, and uses, the tail, of which a representation will be found in Plate II., is the most conspicuous organ of the beaver. It is nearly flat, broad, and straight, and covered with horny scales of a lustrous black. These scales, which are such in appearance only, cover every portion of the surface both above and underneath. The tail is attached to a posterior projection of the body extending some inches beyond the pelvis, and is furnished with strong muscular attachments, by means of which its movements are determined. Its principal uses are to elevate or depress the head while swimming, to turn the body and vary its direction, and to assist the animal in diving. It is also used to give a signal of alarm to its mates. When alarmed in his pond, particularly at night, he immediately dives, in doing which the posterior part of his body is thrown out of water, and, as he descends head foremost, the tail is brought down upon the surface of the water with a heavy stroke, and deep below it with a plunge. The violence of the blow is shown by the spray which is thrown up two or three feet high. While watching upon their dams at night I have been startled by this tremendous stroke, which, in the stillness of the hour, seemed like a pistol shot. I have heard it distinctly for half a mile, and think it can be heard twice or three times that distance under favorable conditions. On the Upper Missouri, beavers are frequently seen in the river by day, or basking in the sun under its banks. I have seen them dive in this river in the daytime, and without giving the signal stroke. In such cases, their motions, in going under, are quick and graceful, the upper line of the body, from the head to the tail, coming into view in a curve, although but one-third of their length is above the surface at one time. While swimming in a direct course, with the head above the water, the tail is not used, but is extended motionless behind. It is capable of a diagonal movement from one side to the other, and *vice versa*, and also of assuming a nearly vertical position. This enables them to use it as a scull, which they do when entirely under water, and swimming at the most rapid rate. It is most flexible at the intersection of the tail proper with the posterior projection of the body to which it is attached. The muscles for its down motion are several times stronger than for either its upward or lateral movements. He is able to turn his tail under him and sit upon it, or to use it extended behind him as a prop while sitting up upon his hind feet. Young beavers, while feeding or resting, usually swing their tails around by their side in the same manner as a cat, but with the lower surface uppermost. It has often been asserted that the beaver uses his tail as a trowel in preparing mortar from mud. This mistake is sufficiently explained by stating that he uses mud and soft earth, sometimes intermixed with roots and grass, precisely as he finds them, and without any preparation whatever, for their conversion into mortar. But he uses his tail to pack and compress mud and earth while constructing a lodge or dam, which he effects by heavy and repeated down strokes. It performs in this respect a most important office, and one not unlike some of the uses of the trowel.

The eye of the beaver is disproportionately small, the optic nerve a mere thread, and its foramen one of the smallest in the skull. As his vision is of short range, he does not rely upon this sense except with reference to near objects. On the contrary, his hearing is very acute. The auditory tube, which is usually about half an inch in length, terminates in a tympanic cavity, or bulla, of nearly globular form, and large relatively to the size of the skull. It is considerably larger than in man, and its size is, to some extent, the measure of the strength of this sense. This provision to intensify the hearing is, however, equally conspicuous among the carnivora. Upon this sense the beaver relies to a much greater extent than upon his sight. He sits up on his hind legs to listen, which is his usual position when on the alert or suspicious of danger. He will often select a slightly elevated and exposed position, and, sitting up, listen for a considerable time and then retire, but to return at intervals and repeat the observation until satisfied whether or not danger is near. Since this attitude is one expressive of intelligence, as well as the one in which his form is seen at the best advantage, I have adopted it in the engraving (Plate I.) as the most suitable for his representation.

Scarcely inferior to this sense in power is that of smell, which is abundantly attested by the structure of the nasal organs. The cavity occupied by the ethmoid and turbinated bones is but little inferior in size to that in which the brain is enveloped. As these bones are laminated, the superficial surface of membrane exposed to the air is very large. It is evident from structural considerations that smell and hearing are the principal informing senses of the beaver.

Their social propensities furnish another characteristic. They pair, and with their offspring live in the family relations until the latter attain maturity, when they are forced to leave the parent lodge. It usually happens that two or more such families inhabit the same pond, and contribute their labor to the maintenance of the dam, whence the common and nearly universal opinion that they live and act in colonies, or associated in villages. This is altogether an overstatement. Each family has its own lodge and burrows, and its separate stock of winter provisions; and there is no authentic evidence of any concert of action among several families, either in building or repairing dams. If such instances have occurred they must be exceptional. This subject will be referred to again.

It is extremely difficult without dissection to determine the sex of beavers, as they are monotrematous, and there is nothing in their general appearance to indicate the difference. The female brings forth her young usually in May, and from two to five and sometimes six at a time. In some rare instances eight have been found in a fœtal state among the beavers of Lake Superior, and the same number born alive in the lodge. Upon this subject Hearne remarks: "The Indians, by killing them in all stages of gestation, have abundant opportunities of ascertaining the usual number of their offspring. I have seen some hundreds of them killed at the seasons favorable for these observations, and never could discover more than six young in one female, and that only in two instances; for the usual number, as I have before observed, is from two to five."[1] The female has but four nipples, two between the shoulders and two a few inches back of them. At six weeks, a young beaver, captured and domesticated, will wean itself and take to bark. The period of gestation is from three to four months, and the ordinary duration of their lives from twelve to fifteen years.

The habitat of the American beaver is unusually broad. It is not surpassed by that of any other animal upon the continent, the deer and the fox not excepted. He was found from the confines of the Arctic Sea on the north, to the Gulf of Mexico, the

---

[1] Hearne's Journey, p. 241.

Rio Grande, and the Gila rivers on the south, and southward of these ranges in Tamaulipas in Mexico, which is the southernmost point to which he has been definitely traced. Throughout all the intermediate areas, from Hudson's Bay and the Atlantic on the east, to the Pacific on the west, he was found distributed at the several epochs of European discovery. Climatically he may be said to belong to the temperate regions, from which his spread northward within the Arctic Circle and southward into Mexico is doubtless ascribable to the courses of the rivers and to his aquatic habits. Beavers were found in the greatest numbers in the thick wood country around Hudson's Bay, one-half of which, according to Sir George Simpson, is under water; around the shores of Lake Superior, upon the head waters of the Missouri and the Siskatchewun,[1] and upon the tributaries of the Columbia. The regions bordering on the Yukon, on the upper part of Mackenzie River, on Frazer's River, and on the Sacramento were also notable for beavers. New England, New York, Pennsylvania, and the Canadas were less abundantly but very well supplied at the period of colonization. Southward, toward the Gulf, they were less numerous, and in the vast prairie area in the interior of the continent they were confined, of course, to the margins of the rivers. With the commencement of colonization their habitat began to contract. They have now substantially disappeared from the United States east of the Rocky Mountains, except in the States of Michigan, Wisconsin, Minnesota, and Iowa; and in the Territories of Nebraska, Dakota, Idaho,

---

[1] Kis-sis-katch'-e-wun, " Swift Water." Cree Dialect.

Montana, and Colorado. They are still occasionally seen in Maine, New York, and Virginia. In the Hudson's Bay Territory, and in some portions of the Canadas, and west of the mountains in Oregon, Washington, California, and Nevada they are still numerous. They are also still abundant on the south shore of Lake Superior in Upper Michigan, where their works, in numbers and magnitude, are not surpassed by those of any other beaver district in North America.

Their immense numbers in former periods are sufficiently attested by the statistics of the fur trade, of which some notice will be given in a subsequent chapter. The earliest colonists found in their rich furs their first exportable merchandise; and thus this animal contributed, with his life, in no inconsiderable degree, to the colonization and permanent settlement of the Canadas and the United States.

The habitat of the European beaver was as widespread as that of the American. He was found in the British Islands, in all parts of the European Continent, in Siberia, and southward, in Asia Minor, to the Euphrates. He is now extinct in Europe, except upon some of the larger rivers of the Continent, and in some portions of Russia. In Scotland and Wales he was found as late as the twelfth century. He is still found in Siberia.

There are marked differences in the habits of the American and European beavers, although it is doubtful whether the species are distinct. The European beaver is said to lead a solitary life in burrows, rarely constructing lodges or dams; while the American beaver is pre-eminently a builder of both dams

and lodges. M. Myerink, of Berlin, described, in
1829, the operations of a small number of European
beavers established on the River Nuthe, an affluent
of the Elbe, which consisted in the construction of
burrows and lodges, and of a small dike or dam
about a foot high.[1] This last act was evidently regarded as noteworthy, if not exceptional. Instances
of this kind of work appear to be rare on the part
of the European beaver, while the American turns
the smaller streams, by means of dams, into a series
of ponds, one above the other, for miles together.
The region around the Black Sea was famous for
beavers in the classical period, whence he was called
by Pliny the "Pontic beaver." In his brief account
of this animal, he describes his practice of cutting
down trees, but is silent upon the far more remarkable performance of constructing dams for the purpose of forming artificial ponds. No other Roman,
and no Greek author, as far as I am aware, makes
mention of this practice. If the European beaver
had been a dam-builder to any considerable extent,
the fact would not, probably, have escaped the notice
of this indefatigable investigator.[2] It is surprising

---

[1] Bennett's Garden and Menagerie of the Zoological Society
Delineated. Quadrupeds, i. 158.

[2] Easdem partes sibi ipsi Pontici amputant fibri, periculo ur-
gente, ab hoc se peti gnari ; Castoreum id vocant medici ; alias
animal horrendi morsus, arbores juxta flumina, ut ferro, cædit ; ho-
mines parte comprehensa, non antequam fracta concrepuerint
ossa, morsus resolvit, Cauda piscium iis, cetera species lutræ,
Utramque aquaticum ; Utrique Mollior pluma pilus.—Plin. Nat.
Hist., Lib. viii. c. xlvii.

The ancients confounded the *testes* with the castor sacs, and
perpetuated as credible this conceit of self-amputation. Herodo-

how little can be gleaned from the Greek authors with reference to the beaver. Herodotus speaks of him (iv. 109) as a well-known animal, but without giving any particulars. Ælian describes him (Hist. Anim., Lib. vi. c. xxxiv.) as aquatic in his habits, spending the daytime concealed in the rivers, and roving by night upon the land. Strabo (Geograph., iii. 163) contents himself with pronouncing the castoreum of the Spanish inferior to that of the Pontic beaver; while Aristotle knew so little with reference to him that he describes the same animal under the names of castor (*κάστωρ*) and latax (*λάταξ*) as two different animals.[1]

---

tus is one of the oldest authorities for the mistake first mentioned. Book iv. c. 109.

Thus Ovid—

> Sic, ubi detracta est a te tibi caussa pericli,
> Quod superest, tutum, Pontice castor, habes.
>
> *Nux Elegia,* 165.

And Juvenal—

> —imitatus castora, que se
> Eunuchum ipse facit, cupiens evadere damno
> Testiculi, adeo medicatum intelligit unguen.
>
> *Sat.,* xii. 34.

Pliny, however, elsewhere states that Sextus, a Roman physician, questioned the truth of this statement. *Vide* Lib. xxxii. c. xiii.

[1] "Certain wild quadrupeds," he remarks, "also seek food around the lakes and rivers, but around no sea, the sea-calf (seal) excepted. Of this genus are the beaver (*κάστωρ*), and satherion (*σαθέριον*), and satyr (*σατύριον*), and otter (*ἐνυδροὶς*), and latax (*λάταξ*), which is broader than the otter, and provided with teeth very much more robust. Going forth commonly by night, it eats off the nearest bushes with its teeth. The otter also bites men, nor, as they say, does he loose his hold before he shall have

Another interesting fact with reference to the beaver is that of his great antiquity upon the earth. A presumption to this effect would arise from his coarse subsistence and his aquatic habits; but it is confirmed by decisive evidence. Both the European and American beavers are found in a fossil state, and under conditions which establish for each of them a very ancient epoch for their first existence among living animals. Upon the European fossil beaver, Owen observes: "That the present European beaver is not the degenerate descendant of the great *Trogontherium* is proved, not only by the differences in the dental structure pointed out in the preceding section, but likewise by the fact that beavers in no respect differing in size or anatomical characters from the *Castor Europæus* of the present day, coexisted with the *Trogontherium*. Remains of the beaver have been discovered by Mr. Green in the same fossilized condition, and under circumstances indicative of equal antiquity with the extinct mammoth, in the lacustrine formations at Bacton. * * * Remains of the beaver have been found associated with those of the mammoth, hippopotamus, rhinoceros, hyena, and other extinct mammals, in the pleistocene fresh-water or drift formations of the Val d'Arno; and remains of both *Trogontherium* and *Castor* were found fossil by Dr. Schmerling in the ossiferous caverns in the neighborhood of Liege. * *

---

heard the cracking from the bones. The hair of the latax, which is intermediate between that of the deer and seal, is rough." (*Περὶ ζώων θ. ζ.* Seun. vii. 5. Ed. Schneid. i. p. 362.) Pliny, by some misapprehension, speaks (*supra*) of the beaver as having the same pertinacious bite ascribed properly by Aristotle to the otter.

But the most common situation in which the remains of the beaver are found in this island, as on the Continent, is the turbary peat-bog, or moss-pit. * * * Remains of the *Castor Europæus* have been found at the depth of eight feet and a half beneath peat, resting upon a stratum of clay, with much decayed and seemingly charred wood, associated with remains of megaceros, or great Irish deer, at Higley, Norfolk."[1]

Beaver-gnawed wood was found in the same cavity with, and five feet above the skeleton of the mastodon discovered in 1867, at Cohoes, near Albany, New York. This wood, which was first noticed by Dr. S. B. Woolworth, is now in the State Cabinet of Natural History. It appears from the description of Prof. James Hall, who personally superintended the removal of the principal bones, that this mastodon was found in a pothole excavated in the shale rock (Hudson River group), and more than forty feet below the surface. The remains were imbedded in clay and river ooze, resting upon gravel, and covered with an accumulation of peat. In the presence of this beaver-gnawed wood so near the mastodon, some evidence is furnished that the beaver and the mastodon were contemporaneous.[2]

The fossil remains of the *Trogontherium* were first discovered by Fischer on the borders of the Sea of Azof, and afterward in various parts of England. Cuvier placed him in the genus *Castor*, and gave the name

---

[1] British Fossil Mammals and Birds. Lond. ed., 1846, p. 190.

[2] Prof. Hall, in describing the position and relations in which this skeleton was found, remarks : "In the peaty deposits where those bones have occurred, the remains of recent or existing vegetation are present; and the relations of these deposits show very clearly that the surface of the country has undergone no important

upon Fischer's description. Owen afterward, by means of additional specimens, detected variations in the forms of the jaws and teeth which led him to question this classification, and to assert a sub-generic position for this animal. He remarks: "The well-marked differences which the English fossils have demonstrated, not only in the proportions, but in the form and structure of the teeth of the *Trogontherium*, will, I trust, be allowed to yield the same grounds for its sub-generic distinction as has been proposed or accepted by the best modern zoologists for the subdivisions of the same value in the rest of the rodent order."[1] The *Trogontherium* was about one-fifth larger than the European beaver, the skull measuring seven inches and three lines from the occipital ridge to the most convex part of the incisors.

Since both the European beaver and the *Trogontherium* have been found in a fossilized state in the newer pliocene formations, and in deposits which have yielded remains not only of the mammoth and the rhinoceros, but also of the mastodon, and since there is evidence tending to show that the American beaver was cotemporaneous with the mastodon, the generic type of *Castor*, and also the family type of *Castoridæ* are thus carried far back into the tertiary period.

Upon the American Continent the American bea-

---

modification since the period of the mastodon. This animal, and the fossil elephant, *Elephas primigeneus*, were coeval with the existing flora and the present conditions of the surface of the continent; and there are no reasons, geologically, why they may not have coexisted with the human race."

[1] British Fossil Mammals and Birds, p. 188.

ver has likewise been found in a fossil state. On this subject, Baird remarks: "The bone caves at Carlisle yielded a large number of remains of beaver, both young and old. There are no satisfactory points of difference from the existing species, although in size some of the teeth are larger than any recent specimens I have seen, indicating a length of quite six inches for the skull."[1]

As the European beaver has its prototype in the *Trogontherium*, so the American species had its forerunner in *Castoroides*, a gigantic fossil beaver, surpassing in size all existing as well as extinct rodents. But few specimens have as yet been found. The first was described by Foster and named *Castoroides Ohioensis;* and the second by Hall and Wyman. The latter was found in a lacustrine formation subsequent to the drift in Wayne County, New York. From the geological relations in which these fossil remains were discovered, Hall pronounces *Castoroides* cotemporaneous with the mastodon. The skull, measured from a cast in my collection, is ten inches and fifteen hundredths in its greatest length, and seven inches and sixty hundredths in its greatest width. He must have been five or six times larger than the beaver of the present time. Baird observes that the genus *Castoroides* is nearer to the genus *Trogontherium* than to *Castor*, which is an interesting fact, showing that the fossil *genera* are nearer to each other than either is to the existing *genus*.

Although it thus appears that three distinct genera of the beaver family—if *Trogontherium* stands inde-

---

[1] Explorations for a Railroad Route, etc. to the Pacific, viii. 361.

pendent of *Castor*—have been ascertained, and that
the existence of its distinctive type extends backward
well toward the earliest epoch of mammalian life
upon the earth, yet it seems that the position of this
family in the animal kingdom is not as yet fully
determined. Whether the *Castoridæ* are entitled to
the full rank of an independent family, or should be
attached, as a sub-family, to some other group, is the
question.

Brandt, whose treatise upon the rodents is particularly elaborate with reference to the beaver, gives
prominence to this question, and also to that of
the specific differences between the European and
American beavers. He proposes to divide the rodent order into four sub-orders, and to arrange the
genera in twelve independent families. Under this
classification the *Castoridæ* become an independent
family of full rank. "The general structure," he observes, "and especially the character of the skull
being more accurately considered, the order of the
Gnawers manifests, as it seems to me, four quite distinct types, exhibiting the equivalent of the sub-orders
Sciuromorpha, Myomorpha, Hystrichomorpha, and *La-
gomorpha,* of each of which respectively the common
genera *Sciurus, Mus. Hystrix,* and *Lepus,* known to
all, may be declared the foundations. The four types
just indicated appear by no means to be constantly
separated by ascertained differences, but they rather
offer, by means of common marks and intermediate
forms, a series bound in unity with sufficient con-
cord."[1] The *Castoridæ* are placed in the second sub-

---

[1] " Structura generali et præsertim cranii ratione accuratius con-
sideratis Glirium Ordo typos quatuor admodum distinctos, ut mihi

order (*Myomorpha*), in which it constitutes the second family, and the third in the general series from the first. This arrangement appears merely to transfer without obviating the difficulty, and tends to complicate rather than simplify the question.

Baird introduces into the family *Castoridæ* the genus *Aplodontia*, consisting of a single species found in Oregon, and confined to the Northwest Coast. In some features of the teeth and skull it resembles *Castor*, and in other particulars affiliates equally well with other genera of rodents. He then, having placed the *Sciuridæ*, as other zoologists have done, in the front rank of the rodent order, attaches the genera *Aplodontia*, *Castor*, and *Castoroides* to this group as a sub-family, expressing, however, a doubt as to the propriety of the arrangement in the following language: "There has been of late a decided tendency to place them near or among the *Sciuridæ*. In this view I am disposed to concur, although there still remains the question, whether the two are not typical of as many different sub-families, themselves forming a family of full rank."[1]

Although unqualified to offer any solution of this problem, it appears to me plain that the greater rela-

---

videtur, subordinum valorem exhibentes manifestat: *Glires, Sciuromorphos, Myomorphos, Hystrichomorphos*, et *Lagomorphos*, quorum quidem singulorum fundamenta generalia genera *Sciurus, Mus. Hystrix*, et *Lepus* omnibus nota declarari possunt. Typi quatuor modo dici vero notis constanter diversis minime disjuncti apparent, sed notarum communium formarumque intermediarum ope series potius satis harmonice in unitatem conjunctas offerunt."
—Mémoires de Académie Imperiale des Sciences de St. Petersbourg. Sixth series. Sciences Naturelles, tome vii. 292.

[1] Explorations for a Railroad Route, etc., viii. 350.

tive antiquity of the three genera *Castor*, *Castoroides*, and *Trogontherium*, and the unique and distinctive type of animal life which they represent, should determine the question in favor of the independence of the *Castoridæ* as a family.

Another question remains, namely: whether the American and European beavers are the same or different species. Linnæus, who founded the genus *Castor* in 1735, made but one species—C. Fiber. The earlier naturalists, from Linnæus to Buffon and Cuvier, accepted, without investigation, the specific identity of the European and American species.

According to Brandt (Mémoires, etc., 44), Oken was the first in time (1816) who thought upon the question of a possible difference of species. In 1819, Frederick Cuvier (Hist. Nat. des Mamifers, No. 16) gave a pretty full description of the external characteristics of a Canada beaver in the Garden of Plants, but without discussing the question of its possible difference from the European. Again in 1825 (Ib., No. 51) he described a beaver of the Rhone, compared its skull with that of an American beaver, and then, for the first time, pointed out the differences in its skull which have since been recognized as establishing distinctness of species. He also named the American beaver *Castor Americanus*, and the European *Castor Gallicus*. Between these two periods (1820), Kuhl described a Canada beaver in the British Museum, and named it *Castor Canadensis:* but his description failed to show any grounds of specific difference.[1]

---

[1] " Castor Canadensis." " Supra rufus, infra rufescente cinereus. Extremitatum pallide brunescentium piles adpressis, brevibus,

Owen (1846), disregarding Fr. Cuvier's name of the European beaver, calls him *Castor Europæus*, in which he is followed by Brandt and other zoologists. With respect to the American beaver, if specifically different, it is doubtful whether there is such a priority of scientific determination in favor of Kuhl's name, *Castor Canadensis*, as to enforce its acceptance. *Castor Americanus*, from the great extent of his habitat, would be more appropriate.

The question, however, of a specific name for the American beaver is at least premature. It is necessary, first, to show that they are of different species, which cannot as yet be conclusively asserted. Brandt, who has investigated this subject more elaborately than any other zoologist, came to the same conclusion as Fr. Cuvier, that they were specifically different. Since the publication of his memoir upon the Rodents, this conclusion has been very generally acquiesced in by zoologists. It appears, however, that his observations and comparisons were limited to eight skulls of the European, and five of the American beaver. The differences revealed by these skulls undoubtedly justified the inference of difference of species. A comparison of a much larger number of skulls might show, nevertheless, that the variations relied upon were not constant; and such has proved to be the case. For the purpose of testing the constancy of these assumed variations, I increased my collection of

---

lucidis. Unguibus tegularibus obtusis, corneis. Cauda applanata, piles ad basin squamarum raris et brevibus. Dentibus surrufis. Longitudo corporis, 22½, poll, caudæ, 7″. Ejusque latitudo, 9½ pollicum. Ad Fretum Hudsoni. In Musco Britanico."—Beiträge zur zoologie und Verleichenden Anatomiæ. Frankf., 4, p. 64.

American beaver skulls to ninety-eight. Beside these, seven American skulls and one European were loaned from the Smithsonian Collection, and two American from the New York State Collection, which increased the whole number of American skulls examined to one hundred and seven. A comparison shows that the several variations between the skulls of the European and American beavers, claimed to exist by Brandt, are not constant; that the supposed differences shade off into each other and disappear, and that the tendency to diverge, which plainly exists, is no greater or stronger than would be unavoidably due to the long-continued separation of these stocks, and to climatic influences inseparable from their widely-extended habitat. If brought together, they would, without doubt, produce, *inter se*, a fertile offspring. The anatomical differences between them are probably less than between individuals of the most strongly contrasted families of mankind. It will not be necessary to present the comparative measurements in this connection, as they are fully given in Appendix "A," to which the reader is referred. The tendency to variation, however, is sufficiently marked to characterize the American and European beavers as varieties of the same species, which is the most that can, at present, be claimed. This would fix the nomenclature for the first as *Castor Fiber*, var. *Americanus*, and of the second, as *Castor Fiber*, var. *Europæus*.

The beaver, in the duration of his distinctive type, is one of the oldest of living mammals. He is also shown to have been the cotemporary of many species now extinct. His coarse subsistence, aquatic habits, rugged strength, and prolific nature, eminently fitted him for a long career of life upon the earth, transmitted through the species. It is not improbable that his first appearance antedates the present configuration of the continents. Of the mastodon but one species, I believe, has been found in America, while several have been discovered in Europe and Asia, neither of which is identical with the American species. How the beaver, adopting the conclusion of but a single species, propagated himself from one continent to the other, may be wholly unexplainable; but it does not affect the question whether the two beavers are of the same, or of different species. Of all the mammals without the Arctic Circle in Europe and America, with the exception of man, the beavers of the two continents are probably the only individuals whose specific identity can be established by anatomical comparisons.

The second chapter and Appendix A, as has elsewhere been stated, are from the pen of Dr. W. W. Ely, whose able and thorough exposition of the anatomical structure of the American beaver will command the attention of the comparative anatomist, and prove instructive to the general reader. The comparison of the skulls, referred to on the preceding page, was made by him.

CHAPTER II.

ANATOMY OF THE BEAVER.

Introduction—Description—Skeleton—Skull—Teeth — Muscles — Internal Organs: Mouth, Stomach, Intestines, Cæcum, Heart, Lungs, Liver, Spleen—Respiration of Aquatic Animals—Brain.

APPENDIX A. 1. Measurements of Skull. 2. Differences between European and American Beavers considered. 3. Castoreum Organs, and Generative Organs.

IN the study of animals for the purpose of determining their zoological relations, it has been found necessary not only to consider their external characteristics, but also to investigate their internal structure. The distinction of species is often impossible without the aid of anatomical research. In the case of the beaver, the closely-allied European and American animals could not be distinguished by anything in their external conformation. Anatomists resort, therefore, to a minute investigation of the cranial and other structures to discover essential points of difference.

For this reason, some account of the anatomy of the beaver seems appropriate to the present volume, which, although popular in its character, is sufficiently comprehensive in its design to admit of the introduction of the scientific element. A somewhat general resumé of beaver anatomy has been attempted in order to give greater completeness to the work. It would be impossible, in the limits of a chapter, to give all the details belonging to this subject, which would require a special treatise. The same objection applies to frequent references to comparative anatomy. If the scientific reader requires any other apology for omissions in the descriptive part, it must be found in the writer's desire to avoid compilation, and to give only the results of personal observation. In a few points he is at variance with authorities, but not without due consideration.

DESCRIPTION.

The beaver is the largest indigenous rodent in Europe, and the largest rodent now living except the capybara (Hydrochærus Capybara) of South America.

In the following description I shall refer to three adult animals, one male and two females, captured near Lake Superior, in February, March, and April, 1866. Two had lost an arm each from previous capture, the parts having entirely healed. The measurements here and elsewhere given, unless otherwise specified, are in inches and hundredths of an inch, U. S. standard measure. Weights in avoirdupois pounds and ounces. Sign for inches, ″; for hundredths of an inch, ‴.

	MALE. W't 32 lbs.	FEMALE. 29½ lbs.	FEMALE. 36 lbs.
	″ ‴	″ ‴	″ ‴
Length from tip of nose to end of tail..	42·25	42·25	42·
" of scaly portion of tail...........	9·75	10·	10·50
Circumference of head before ears......	14·	13·	
" behind ears.................	14·50	15·50	14·25
" behind shoulders.........	20·	19·	21·50
" middle of abdomen......	26·50	24·	27·25
" before hips..................	25·	22·50	24·50
" root of scaly tail.	7·	6·	8·
" middle of scaly tail......	8·50	8·75	10·50

The body of the beaver is largest at its centre, and diminishes in size toward each extremity. The animal has a ratlike appearance about the head and neck, and the smallness of the eyes and ears renders its physiognomy dull and uninteresting. The body is covered with reddish-brown hair of two kinds: the longer coarse hairs are about 2″ in length and $\frac{1}{140}$″ in diameter, and the shorter, which are of a lighter color, and partly concealed by the former, are about 1″ long, and $\frac{1}{1750}$′ in diameter. Both kinds present an imbricate epidermoid structure. The beaver has the peculiar odor of the castoreum, to be hereafter described. Its head is rounded, flattened above, and the muzzle is somewhat prominent. The upper lip is emarginate to the edge of the incisor gum, where it closely adheres. The lower lip is loose and pendant, so that the incisor teeth are prominent features. Both lips are somewhat drawn in behind the incisors, and are slightly hairy within. From the angle of the mouth a thin line of hairs extends backward one-fourth of an inch to a quadrangular patch of thickly set hairs on the inside of the cheek, 80‴ in length and 32‴ in breadth. From the emarginate upper lip (in one beaver) the hair extends 66‴ to the naked muffle, which is 90‴ long and 22‴ broad, covered with rough black epidermis. In two beavers the naked portion of the muffle includes the nostrils, and extends in a narrow line to the edge of the lip. The nostrils are lateral, hairy, round when expanded, and assume a sub-triangular or crescentic form, the convexity being in front. Width between nostrils in one, 75‴, in another, 66‴; diameter of nostrils, 20‴. There are five rows of bristles, the upper row having but few hairs.

The eyes are small, half an inch in diameter, and are midway between the nostrils and the ears; diameter of iris, 8′′′; length of closed eyelid, 50′′′. A few bristles over the eyes. The ears are short, very hairy on both sides, rounded and obtusely pointed. The posterior extremity of the beaver presents a singular formation. The body diminishes in size gradually from the hips, and terminates in a flat scaly tail, which, measured from the sacrum, is about 18″ in length; the first 8″ being covered with hair like the rest of the body. The scaly portion commences abruptly with a width of about four inches, and terminates with a rounded extremity. The scaly portion (Plate II) is slightly convex above and below, thin at the margin, and is covered with a black, tough, scaly epidermis. The scales are somewhat irregular in form and size, the most usual form being sub-hexagonal, about 32′′′ in length, and 12′′′ in width. They are arranged transversely in respect to length, in the so-called quincunx form, and they diminish in size toward the end of the tail; across the middle of the tail their number is 19 or 20 above, and 20 or 21 on the under surface. A few short, broken hairs pass out between the scales.

It may be observed here that although this structure is usually described as scaly, it is so only in appearance. M. Sarrasin[1] describes the "scales" as "couchées les unes sur les autres, jointes ensemble par une pellicule fort délicate, enchassés dans la peau dont

---

[1] Histoire do l'Académie Royale dos Sciences. Année 1704. Paris, 1745. Lettre de M. Sarrasin, médecin du Roy en Canada, touchant l'Anatomie du Castor, p. 61.

elles se séparent aisément après la mort de l'animal."
Thin longitudinal and transverse sections exhibit the
true character of this structure. The tail is composed largely of a dense fatty tissue; upon this lies
the derm or skin, 07′′′ in thickness, its outer surface being serrated, with the points of the serratures
toward the end of the tail. Over the serratures is ex-
tended the tough horny epiderm, $\frac{1}{63}$″ to $\frac{1}{90}$″ in thickness, which is inflected under the serratures, so as to
present the imbricate appearance. The longitudinal
divisions are merely dips or depressions, not imbricate.

FIG. 1.

Longitudinal section of scaly tail, twice the natural size.

The beaver, being an aquatic as well as a land animal, presents two types of structure. The arms and
hands are small, are adapted to burrowing, and, being
capable of partial supination, the hands may be used
for holding substances between them. The hind extremities are strongly developed, and are constructed
after the aquatic type. The feet have been compared
to those of the turtle. Each extremity has five digits.
The back of the hand is thickly covered with short
hairs; the palm is naked, with a tough black epidermis, and two tubercles, one opposite the fifth finger, the other under the metacarpals of the second,
third, and fourth. The fingers are furnished with
long claws, of which that of the third finger is the
longest, 92′′′ long, and 20′′′ broad. The first finger
(thumb) is shorter than its claw. Next in length is

Plate III

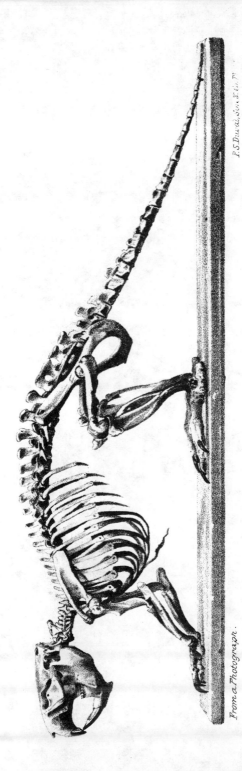

P.S.Duval Son & Co. P.

From a Photograph.

SKELETON OF BEAVER.

the fourth; then the second and the fifth. Between the third and fourth fingers is a rudimentary web, extending to the second phalanx, measuring on its edge 60‴. The foot is 6½ to 7″ long. The upper surface is covered with short silky hairs. Below it is naked. At the base of the first toe is a tubercle. The third toe is the longest; then in order of length the fourth, second, fifth, and first. The claws are larger than those of the hand, the third claw measuring from 87‴ to 1″10‴ in length, and 34‴ to 38‴ in width. There is an extra flattened claw lying under the regular claw of the second toe (Fig. 2). All the toes are connected, to their extremities, by a firm naked web or membrane, measuring on its margin, when the toes are spread, 7½ to 8½ inches. The beaver has four nipples, two between the shoulders, 3″ apart, and two, 3″ farther back, 4″ apart.

FIG. 2.

Inside view of double claws.

OSTEOLOGY.

The skeleton of the beaver, of which a representation is given Pl. III., affords 273 bones, including the aural ossicles and excluding the sesamoid bones. Of these there are 38 of the head, 20 teeth, and 215 bones of the trunk, tail, and extremities. The beaver has 55 vertebræ, viz., cervical, 7; dorsal, 14; lumbar, 5; sacral, confluent, 4; and caudal, 25.

The first and second cervical vertebræ are strong, the second and third are the smallest. Six have foramina for the vertebral artery. The head of the first rib is articulated between the bodies of the seventh cervical and the first dorsal. The last four lumbar vertebræ have large transverse processes. The sacrum is straight, the first bone being somewhat prominent anteriorly. The caudal vertebræ gradually diminish in size and lose their vertebral characters. In the sixth, the posterior lateral articulating surfaces disappear, and the spinal canal in the tenth becomes a mere groove. The spinous processes also disappear in the eighth or ninth. The transverse processes are long, broad, and toward the end of the tail are bifid or double. The lateral foramina, which begin in the sacrum at the posterior edge of the transverse processes, continue to the sixth caudal.

The ribs are slender, rounded, in 14 pairs. Seven are articulated by cartilage with the sternum. The cartilages of the 8th and 9th are connected with the costal cartilages. The remaining ribs are tipped with free cartilage.

The sternum is composed of five narrow slender bones; the first and fourth are the broadest. The ensiform cartilage expands into a broad flat disk. Length of sternum and ensiform cartilage, 6″. The clavicles are strong, 2″ 16‴ in length. The scapula is 3″ 25‴ long, and 1″ 50‴ broad. Its spine is prominent, and the acromion is 1″ 18‴ in length.

The humerus is 3″ long; its body is triangular and compressed; the tubercle at the head is large; about the middle of the bone anteriorly is a large tubercle for the insertion of the deltoid muscle; the lower end is broad, thin, not perforated; the external condyle spreads out to a thin convex edge which passes up the middle of the posterior surface of the bone.

The radius is slender, and lies close to the ulna in its whole length. The olecranon is 94‴ long, and the entire ulna 4″ 37‴. The hands are small compared with the feet. In the upper carpal row there are two bones instead of the usual number of four. In the second row a crescentic bone connects the thumb with the lateral part of the head of the adjoining (first) metacarpal. On the head of this metacarpal are two smaller bones (trapezoids) overlying each other, and articulating with the scaphoid of the first row. On the third metacarpal is a wedge-shaped bone with the apex toward the scaphoid. Next in the row is a large bone (os magnum) receiving the heads of the 4th and 5th metacarpals. The next bone, occupying the position of the unciform, is large, and is attached to the ulnar bone of the first row, and supports the annular ligament. A third plate bone, connected by ligament with the scaphoid, lies over the root of the thumb and forms the other attachment of the annular ligament. The phalanges are normal, the thumb being very small.

The pelvis is long; the lateral bones being 6″ 50‴ in length, and the ilia having but rudimentary alæ. The ischium and pubis are thin, and their expansion is effected by the large thyroid foramen, 2″ long and 1″ broad, which is destitute of ligament. Between the ischial tuberosities it is 3″; the transverse diameter of the pelvis is 2″. The greatest depth of the acetabulum is superiorly and anteriorly in the line of the ilium. There is the usual pit for the round ligament which is well developed and strong, although R. Wagner affirms that it does not exist in the mammalia, except in man[1] (i. p. 15).

---

[1] Elements of the Comparative Anatomy of the Vertebrate Animals. By Rudolph Wagner. Transl. New York, 1845.

The femur is broad and very strong, 4″ 10‴ in length. Besides the two trochanters, there is a prominent process on the outer margin, below the middle of the bone, from which a sharp edge extends above and below; a deep pit exists on the under side of the great trochanter.

The tibia is 5″ 25‴ long, triangular above. Its body is excavated on each side of the posterior angle; below it is rounded, with but small development of the malleolar process.

The fibula forms a strong outer malleolar process in close apposition to the astragalus. It is attached for 1″ 25‴ to the lower end of the tibia, and after the epiphyses become consolidated the union is by anchylosis. The upper end of the fibula lies behind the tibia, and has a hamular process pointing outwardly and downward, which gives attachment to a strong ligament that extends from the lower part of the bone and passes from the process in question to the femur, forming an outer lateral ligament to the knee-joint.

The patella is subtriangular in form with the base above.

The plane of the foot is oblique with respect to the leg, requiring the feet to approximate to rest on a level surface. The tarsal bones are 8 in number. The astragalus requires no particular description. The calcaneum is flattened obliquely on its upper and under surfaces, and projects backward 84‴ It articulates with the astragalus and the cuboid. The scaphoid has a neck and a rounded head which is seen in the bottom of the foot. A nameless bone, subconical in shape, which is properly an appendage to the scaphoid, articulates with the astragalus on the inside of the foot and receives the apex of the first cuneiform, which is flattened and notched at the distal end to receive the phalangeal bone of the first toe.

A small cuneiform is articulated with the 2d metatarsal, and a large one with the 3d metatarsal, receiving also the head of the 4th metatarsal, which is the largest of its class. A portion of this 4th metatarsal is articulated with the cuboid. The 5th metatarsal is joined to the side of the 4th, and has no connection with the tarsus. On the tarsal end of the first toe a movable flat bone is placed, answering by its connection with muscles, the purposes of a patella.

The peculiarities of the tarsal articulation are: the supplementary scaphoid bone, the form and position of the 1st cuneiform, and the connections of the 4th and 5th metatarsals.

The sesamoid bones are found as usual. The phalanges present nothing remarkable. The terminal ones, to which the claws are attached, are furnished with a bony process to support the claw. The first toe is smallest and shortest, then the 5th and the 2d; the 3d and 4th are about equal in length. The claws of the 1st and 2d are placed obliquely, being turned inward, so that their points are not worn; the others become blunt and rounded at their extremities. The second toe has an extra claw growing from the skin and partly covered by the regular claw; it is flattened laterally and has a sharp edge above and a point.

The claws of the fingers are about as long as those of the toes, but are much narrower and more pointed. The 1st finger is shorter than the 5th; then the 2d, the 4th, and the 3d.

The hyoid bone forms a semicircle and has an anterior projection.

THE SKULL.[1]

The skull of the beaver exceeds that of other rodents in solidity and strength. It is much elongated, its length being more than twice and a half its height. Its upper line is nearly plane; a parallel line below touches the condyle, the palatal bone, and the point of the incisive septum. The principal surface of the occipital bone is vertical to this line. The molars occupy the middle of the skull, being separated by an arched space from the incisors. Viewed from above, the skull presents quite a different outline, the width being about two-fifths of the length. These proportions are shown in the lateral and the top views of the skull (Plate IV.).

The nasal bones occupy one-third of the length of the skull; are broadest anteriorly, and at their junction in front form an obtuse point. Their outer margin is a convex curve, where they are joined to the intermaxillaries. Their posterior extremities and those of the intermaxillaries join the frontal on a line with the anterior orbital tubercles of that bone. The intermaxillaries are very strong. A nearly vertical suture connects them with the superior maxillary; a little more than half of the sheath of the incisors is formed by them. The lateral and lower part of the nasal opening in front, which has the form of the

---

[1] References to figures of the skull, Plates IV. and V.:

1. Nasal bone.	6. Occipital.	11. Lachrymal.
2. Intermaxillary.	7. Temporal.	12. Palatal.
3. Frontal.	8. Malar.	13. Pre-sphenoid.
4. Parietal.	9. Tympanic.	14. Post-sphenoid.
5. Interparietal.	10. Superior maxillary.	15. Ethmoid.

Plate IV

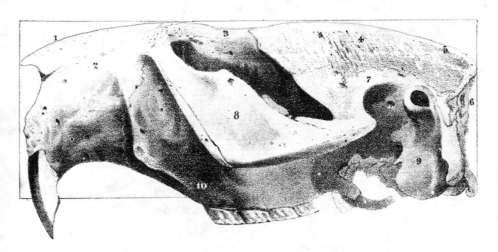

LATERAL VIEW OF SKULL, Nat.size.

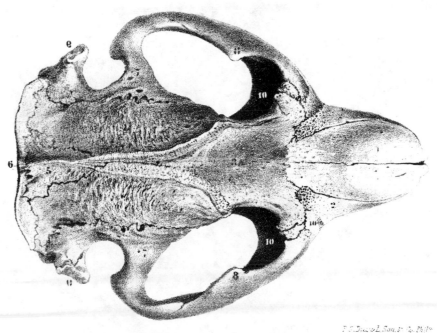

TOP VIEW OF SKULL. ⅚ nat.size

letter V, is formed by them. The frontal bone is flattened above. The two bones are early united, and in the adult present only the trace of a suture. The frontal is broadest anteriorly, spreading out to form the anterior orbital processes. From a rounded margin the orbital plate descends nearly vertically into the socket. This margin is a little prominent posteriorly, forming a smaller process. From this point the bone is wedge-form, passing backward between the parietals. In the orbital cavity the frontal joins the lachrymal, the superior maxillary and the ala of the pre-sphenoid. The lachrymal is triangular above, wedged in between the frontal and malar; it forms part of the inner anterior portion of the orbit. The parietal bones are about half the length of the skull. They are united in their middle third by suture, being separated anteriorly by the frontal bone, and behind by the interparietal; they extend back to the occipital and join the temporals by a longitudinal suture. Their anterior margin in the temporal fossæ is inflected, roughened, forming a crest which extends on the temporal to the zygomatic process; in the fossæ they join the alæ of both sphenoids; posteriorly and laterally their pointed extremities extend a short distance behind the temporals. The interparietal bone is triangular, but very variable in its form in different skulls. In young subjects it is in two portions, divided by the sagittal suture; in old skulls the place of the suture is occupied by a sharp crest. The base of this bone joins the occipital. The temporal bones are lateral. The zygomatic process extends downward and outward, in a flattened form, to constitute the roof of the glenoid cavity; then curves forward to unite with the malar—posteriorly a hooked process of the temporal winds around the back part of the auditory tube to the base of the mastoid process. Anteriorly and inferiorly it joins the ala of the post-sphenoid, and posteriorly it embraces the tympanic bone; the sutures of this bone are squamous. The glenoid cavity is a flattened groove of greater width than length, its outer margin formed by the abrupt termination of the malar, the inner boundary being the vertical portion of the temporal; the lower jaw moves freely, in a longitudinal direction, back into the space between the glenoid groove and the auditory tube.

The vertical portion of the occipital bone is much roughened for muscular attachment. Its upper margin is a sharp ridge, in front of which is the transverse suture. In young subjects the ridge is wanting. The occipital foramen is subtriangular or rounded—broader than its height. The condyles look downward, outward, and backward. The basilar portion lies between the tympanic bones, and is united in front by ligament to the post-sphenoid. An oblong, deep cavity in the basilar portion renders this bone very thin. The mastoid processes of the occipital are lateral to the condyles. In young subjects the bone consists of four portions, viz.: the upper squamous portion, the basilar portion, and the two lateral or condyloid portions.

The tympanic bone is very irregular in shape. It forms a small part of the vertical extremity of the skull, and its mastoid process joins that of the occipital. The bulla is thick and prominent. From the posterior part of the auditory tube, a sharp prominent crest extends downward to the bottom of the bulla— a long, rough process at the base connects it with the basilar process and the post-sphenoid—it is separated from the ala of the sphenoid by a large fissure—the foramen lacenum basis cranii. The auditory canal is prominent, extending upward, outward, and forward. The styloid bone lies in a groove of the bulla, attached by a ligament. The foramen for the Eustachian tube is a little above the junction of the long process of the sphenoid with this bone. The petrous portion has an uneven surface within. Above the internal auditory foramen is a pit which receives a process of the cerebellum, in the margin of which is a semicircular canal. The malar bones are long inferiorly. The ascending portion in front is firmly united with the transverse plate of the superior maxillary, the edge of which is seen in front of the malar. Above, the malar forms the outer third of the orbit—forming a process from which a ligament extends to the frontal to complete the orbital opening, separating the orbit from the temporal fossa—this large fossa is bounded laterally and posteriorly by the malar, temporal, and parietal bones.

The superior maxillary bone extends from the posterior line of the molars to the interparietal, and forms about half the arch between the incisors and the molars—and less than half the sheath of the incisors. The transverse malar plate commences at the back part of the first molar, extends outwardly to the anterior inferior angle of the malar, forming, as seen from in front, a broad arch. In front of the first molar, a ridge commences, becoming more prominent, and passing upward, parallel with the malar plate, crosses the suture, and is lost in the intermaxillary. The ante-orbital foramen is concealed from lateral view by the most prominent part of this ridge. The s. maxillary forms part of the orbit anteriorly. The alveolar part of this bone is more prominent on the outer surface—posteriorly it is supported by the pterygoid bone, and the triangular palatal bone enters as a wedge from behind as far as between the second and third molars. The outer alveolar surface has a sharp slope toward the middle portion of the skull, where it joins the perforated body of the pre-sphenoid. In young subjects, before dentition is complete, the upper alveolar part is bulbous and prominent In the orbit the maxillary touches the frontal. The palatal bone is somewhat cribriform—a ridge, commencing with a point of bone, extends from its base, and is continued along the maxillary, forming the posterior half of the septum of the incisive foramina. The posterior naris is nearly circular—the ascending portion of the palatal supports above the two sphenoid bodies.

The sphenoid bones are distinct, and about equal in length. The outer pterygoid process is short, strong, and divergent—the inner is long, and curves backward so as to touch a process of the tympanic bone, forming thus an oval lateral opening. Where the sphenoidal bodies join, by their side, is the large sphenoidal fissure, corresponding to the oval and round foramina—the small optic foramen is seen by the side of the pre-sphenoid.

Brandt[1] describes but one sphenoidal wing in the

---

[1] Mémoires de l'Académie Impériale des Sciences de Saint Pétersbourg. Sciences Naturelles, tome vii., 1855. Beiträge zur nähern kentniss der gattung Castor, etc. J. F. Brandt.

Plate V

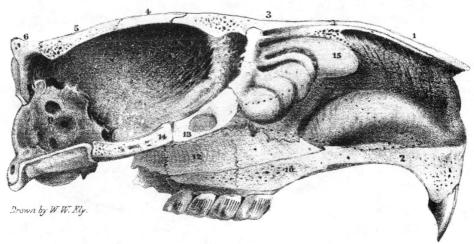

Drawn by W. W. Ely.

INTERIOR VIEW OF SKULL   Nat size

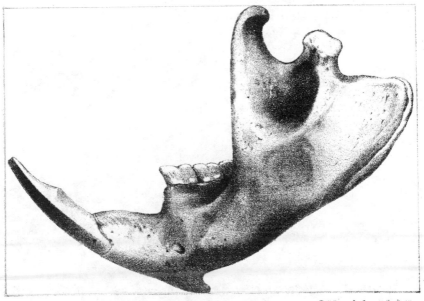

Drawn by W. W. Ely.   *P.S. Duval, Son, & Co. Phila.*

LOWER JAW   Nat size

temporal fossa. Although the sutures of the beaver's skull become consolidated early, and are sometimes made out with difficulty, the two sphenoidal wings can be traced in many skulls. In a young skull, after the temporal and parietal are removed, the broad squamous suture which connects the two wings can be opened. Cuvier says: "Le sphenoide postérieur touche un peu dans le tempe au frontal"[1] T. R. Jones, art. Rodentia in Cyc. of Anat. and Phys.,[2] adopts Cuvier's description of the sphenoids. In forming the suture, the wing of the post-sphenoid is anterior, but the other wing rises higher to join the frontal—the suture of the frontal passes back some distance under the parietal, but not far enough to touch the posterior wing, although they are closely approximated. In this instance, then, the statement of Cuvier is not confirmed.

The ethmoid bone has a cribriform body in the anterior part of the cavity that lodges the olfactory lobe. It has also a vertical plate and three sets of cells on each side, of which a representation is given (Plate V.); the vertical plate has been removed to show the cells entire. A turbinated bone in each nostril is attached by its base to the sheath of the incisor. It is formed of six or seven thin lamina of bone proceeding from its base and dichotomously subdividing and convoluting. This bone has been removed in Plate V. to show the sheath of the incisor. The vomer is represented in the same figure by the lower dotted lines. There

---

[1] Leçons d'Anatomie Comparée de Georges Cuvier, etc. Seconde edition Paris, 1835 to 1846.

[2] The Cyclopædia of Anatomy and Physiology, by R. B. Todd. London.

is also attached to the under surface of each nasal a long curved bone overlapping the turbinate, and serving to retain it in its position.

In addition to the ridges or crests which have been described, there are the parietal crests; these start from the interparietal crest, and, diverging, terminate at the junction of the temporals and frontal. Their usual form is represented in the top view of the skull, but it is subject to much variation. There is a straight glenoid crest at the junction of the temporal and sphenoid. The top of the hook process of the jugular bone forms a crest continuous with the sharp upper edge of the malar. Delicate ridges extend from the outer margins of the incisive foramina to the front edge of the alveolar processes, and from the temporal jugular process a crest extends backward toward the posterior point of the parietal.

The incisive foramina are in the intermaxillaries midway between the incisors and the molars. The spheno-palatine foramen[1] is just behind the orbital opening of the ante-orbital foramen, and opens into the nostril at the junction of the ethmoid and the s. maxillary. The small optic foramen is in the ala of the pre-sphenoid above the transverse opening in the body of the bone. The pterygo-palatine[1] is lower than the optic, and opens in the anterior part of the palatal bone. The external pterygoid plate is pierced with a large foramen which communicates with the sphenoidal fissure by what Cuvier calls the Vidian canal. The condyloid foramina are in front of the

---

[1] These foramina are named from analogy, the first is entirely in the maxillary, and the second in the maxillary and the palatal.

condyles opposite their middle. The lateral foramina in the vertical portion of the occipital are closed in the recent subject by membrane.

Wormian bones are occasionally but not commonly found in the sutures. Sometimes a rounded mass of bone is imbedded in the larger mastoid process.[1]

The lower jaw is very massive (Plate V.). The two parts are joined in front by a long and broad symphysis, forming below a pointed process. Its posterior angle is flattened into a broad process, hollowed within and tipped with a broad long crest—this part extends farther back than the condyle—at the root of the condyle on the outer side is a depression; above this the coronoid process arises and is pointed backward. The anterior line of the process passes downward and forward, the crest terminating at the extremity of the root of the first molar. The condyle is quadrangular, rounded, and is nearer the coronoid process than the posterior crest. The foramina for the nutrient vessels, etc. is behind the molars and higher than their crown surfaces; the mental foramen is below the anterior face of the first molar.

THE TEETH.

The character of the Rodentia as a natural order is made to depend upon a peculiar kind of cutting or incisive teeth, which are separated from the grinding or molar teeth by an empty space, the canine teeth being wanting. The teeth of animals bear a definite relation to their mode of subsistence, and from

---

[1] For measurements of the skull, and differences in the European and the American beaver, see Appendix A.

their correspondence with other structures of the body, the comparative anatomist is able to determine, by an inspection of these organs alone, the kind of animal to which they belong. The rodents generally derive their food from the vegetable kingdom.

Before describing the teeth of the beaver, we may premise for the general reader a few facts in relation to the dental organs. Mammalian teeth are composed of substances essentially resembling bone, of which three kinds are usually present, viz.: the external hard covering or enamel; dentine, which forms the body of the tooth; and cementum, or crusta petrosa, which is deposited on the surface, and usually on the dentine of the root. The divisions of a tooth are the crown, or portion above the gum; the root, or part inclosed in the socket; and the neck, or point of junction between the crown and the root. There are three kinds of teeth: the front, or incisive; the back, or molar; and the canine, or intermediate teeth, whose development is a striking feature in the jaws of the Carnivora. These are wanting in the Rodentia, and in the Edentata the incisive teeth are wanting. Some teeth are permanent, while others are deciduous, the so-called milk teeth, whose places are supplied by those of the permanent class. In some cases, teeth, when once formed, are unchangeable in their development or growth, and are therefore called "rooted" teeth. In other instances the teeth are so constituted that they grow continually as they are worn by use, and are called "rootless" teeth. Rootless teeth are generally cylindric or prismatic, with an expanded open cavity, containing a pulp organ capable of supplying an unlimited growth, while the rooted tooth, when once fully formed, is unchangeable, and the root serves merely as a support for the crown. The beaver has 20 teeth, viz., 2 incisors and 8 molars in each jaw. The anterior molars, 4 in all, are deciduous; the crowns of these teeth resemble the permanent ones; the upper have three divergent roots and the lower two. They are gradually protruded from their sockets by the permanent teeth rising beneath them.

Whether the cutting teeth of the beaver should be regarded as canine teeth rather than as incisors, has been questioned, inasmuch as they extend back into the superior maxillary bone. It is generally held that this relation is only to accommodate their great length, and that their uses and connection with the intermaxillaries are sufficient to sustain the ordinary view. The incisors of the beaver are nearly triangular, and extend far into the jaw, with a circular curve, the upper forming more, and the lower less than half the circumference of a circle, the radius of the curve in the upper being one inch, in the lower $1'' 75'''$. They are composed chiefly of dentine, having a thin layer of orange-colored enamel on their anterior surface and angles. The upper incisors are contained in a sheath which projects into the nasal cavity, the end of the tooth being separated by a thin vertical plate of bone from the first molar. The lower incisors pass under the roots of the molars to a point behind them and below the posterior foramina. The dentine of the incisors, being softer than the enamel, wears away and gives to the end of the tooth a beveled or chisel form, with a sharp anterior edge of enamel, so that they are called scalpriform teeth. The portion of the tooth inclosed in the socket has a conical cavity, filled with the pulp organ, which forms successive layers of dentine so that the tooth continues to grow as fast as it is worn away. As it sometimes happens that a tooth of this kind is broken off, the opposite tooth has been found to grow until its outward projection constituted nearly a circle. The incisors, it need hardly be said, are, according to the definition, "rootless" teeth. The molars are firmly and compactly set in the jaws. The upper set are supported on their outer edge by a firm alveolar ridge, but on the inside their sockets are shallow. The lower set are more deeply and strongly implanted in the jaw. The first molars are largest and longest, and the last are the smallest, and project but little from the jaw. The inner surface of the upper molars has one deep longitudinal groove extending to

Fig. 3.

Left upper molar, outside.   Left under molar, outside.

the end of the tooth, and the outer surface three grooves. These are similar, but reversed in the lower tooth. The surface of the crown is marked by a complicated folding of enamel, of which a diagram is given (Fig. 3).

The dentine between the layers of enamel is worn so as to leave the latter in ridges. Each molar is curved so as to present two concave surfaces. The upper set curve backward and outward; the lower set forward and inward. The surface line of the upper set is slightly convex, that of the lower is concave. Their surfaces are thus brought into apposition, and the bearing of the teeth in the sockets is effected without undue pressure on their extremities. The curves are rendered necessary also by the position of the teeth in the jaws; the distance between the upper molars, from side to side, being less than that of the lower. The lower set are also longer antero-posteriorly by half the length of the crown of a tooth than the upper set. The cementum is found on the outside of the teeth and in the spaces where there are inflections of enamel; but where dentine is opposed to dentine it is not deposited in layers; and, if at all, only in a granular form. The question arises whether the molars, like the incisors, belong to the rootless class of teeth. In Prof. Baird's elaborate Report on Mammals,[1] the sub-family Castorinæ, embracing the genera Castor, Aplodontia, and Castoroides, is defined as having "rootless molars." Brandt (*op. cit.*, p. 301) defines the family Castoroides—genus Castor—as having "molares radicati"—rooted molars. If we examine the molars of the beaver in the young skull, in their immature condition (Fig. 4), they are found to be prismatic; their extremities in the jaws are expanded, and present all the inflections of enamel seen on the crown surface. In this, their primitive condition, they grow as do other rootless teeth, until the jaws have attained their development. The tooth then becomes rooted (Fig. 5) and incapable of further growth—the pulp cavity contracts, the opening becomes lateral, and is sometimes entirely closed;

FIG. 4.

Section of "rootless" molar.

---

[1] General Report upon the Zoology of the several Pacific Railroad Routes, vol. viii. Mammals. By Spencer F. Baird. Washington, D. C., 1857.

the pulp organ is atrophied; the tooth is smaller within than without the socket. In a sec-

FIG. 5.

tion of the tooth the tips of the enamel inflections are seen of different lengths, as they have become gradually closed. Corresponding changes have taken place in the sockets; their bulbous projections in the upper jaw being no longer visible. While, therefore, the molars of the beaver are both rootless and rooted at different stages in the growth

Section of "rooted" molar.

of the animal, the latter is the characteristic of its mature condition.

MUSCLES.

It would exceed our limits to enumerate the muscles of the beaver. Their specification is the less necessary as the muscles of the mammalia present few important variations from the human standard. They may, however, be so modified in connection with particular functions as to merit notice, and for this reason we shall allude briefly to the muscles of mastication. The power required for cutting and grinding hard ligneous substances is supplied in the beaver by the development of the masseter muscle. This muscle arises from the whole length of the lower part of the malar bone, and is inserted into the crest of the lower jaw, and side of the jaw to the anterior end of the crest. It is strengthened by tendinous fibres passing from the root of the crest into the body of the muscle. At the junction of the superior maxillary and malar inferiorly a tendon runs forward to the process covering the ante-orbital foramen. The inner part of the masseter arises further forward by muscle, and still further by tendon, as far as between the 1st and 2d molar, and is inserted into the whole space of the maxillary before the transverse plate, into the anterior surface of this plate, and its lower arched edge. By means of its anterior tendon, the muscle of one side acting, turns the jaw laterally to the opposite side; while the double action of this part of the muscle brings the condyle forward and fixes it in the glenoid cavity for cutting operations. The cutting and grinding power of this muscle must be very great. The temporal muscle arises from the crest on the temporal bone as far back as the occipital crest, and from the parietal bone; also from a tendinous expansion extending from the malar to the top of the skull, and from the internal surface of the malar; and is inserted into the coronoid process of the lower jaw. The pterygoid muscles require no particular description. The digastric muscles are large, and fill the space anteriorly between the lateral parts of the jaw. Their tendon in front of the hyoid bone is connected with the mylo-hyoid. Posteriorly they are smaller and are inserted at the base of the mastoid process.

The tail has free motion laterally; also by extension and flexion, particularly the latter. An upper lateral muscle connected with the transverse processes of the bones joins the gluteal. Another lateral muscle extends from the side of the tail to the tuberosity and ramus of the ischium. The flexors and exten. sors arise from the corresponding surfaces of the sacrum, and are each in two layers. The flexors are the stronger muscles; they extend to the commencement of the scaly portion of the tail, and send great numbers of tendons to the different bones and their processes.

INTERNAL ORGANS.

The beaver presents many peculiarities of internal structure; indeed, as a whole, it is a unique animal; one that has hitherto baffled the skill of naturalists to classify it.

The cavity of the mouth is small, and destitute of cheek pouches; the tongue is long and fleshy, and has a pointed elevation between the molars. The palate has a longitudinal ridge extending back from the incisors to four transverse ridges. The epiglottis is leaf-like and pointed, and the larynx is short.

It is generally supposed that the rodent, in grinding its food, is confined to the longitudinal motion of the jaws. This is inferred from the form of the glenoid cavities, and the condyles; and the motion in question has been adopted as a distinctive mark of the rodent family. Waterhouse[1] affirms that the rodents possess "very little lateral motion to the jaw, which, however, moves freely in the longitudinal direction." At the same time he admits that the motion in the hares is chiefly lateral, inasmuch as the crowns of their molars are never worn flat.

That the articulation of the beaver jaw admits of free lateral motion is easily demonstrated in the recent subject. Neither the ligaments nor the bony structures afford any impediment, while the flattened crowns of the molars, and the muscular provisions

---

[1] A Natural History of the Mammalia, by G. R. Waterhouse, vol. ii. Rodentia. London, 1848.

would lead to the conclusion that both longitudinal and lateral motions were concerned in the grinding operations.

FIG. 6.

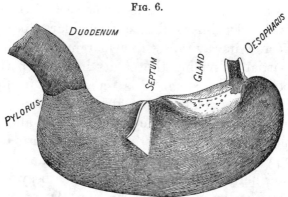

Stomach of beaver, inside view.   One-quarter natural size.

The insalivation of the dry food of the beaver is provided for by the extraordinary development of the salivary glands.   The parotid and submaxillary glands, united, are very large, and cover the front and sides of the neck.   The œsophageal membrane is white, thick, and loosely attached to the muscular coat.   Where it enters the stomach it has a free fringed margin.   The stomach is one of the most peculiar organs of the beaver; it is 10″ in length and 4″ in width, and when filled appears constricted in its middle portion.   This is not unusual in the rodents, but in the beaver the structure is peculiar.   At the cardiac orifice is a gland, or aggregation of follicles, through the margin of which the œsophagus passes.   This gland is half an inch in thickness and 3 inches in diameter.   It is composed of compound follicles, which open by 15 or 20 orifices in parallel rows.   When the stomach is distended with air, the gland is also inflated, and shows large cells and numerous septa. The constricted appearance of the stomach is due to a triangular valve or septum projecting into its cavity. The upper part of the stomach is doubled in, so that a triangular muscle extends across its cavity, its free margin measuring 2″, thus partially dividing the cavity into two portions. A section of the stomach is represented in Fig. 6, showing the triangular muscle and the gland. The pylorus is muscular, and the orifice much smaller than the duodenum. The intestine is twice the diameter of the pylorus, and is doubled back upon the stomach.

In northern regions, and in winter, the beaver must subsist either on wood or bark. The latter is comparatively innutritious. Besides, it would involve a vast amount of labor on the part of the animal to provide a winter stock of bark, which must be transported, together with its wood, to be submerged for future use. The proportion of bark to wood, of the kinds used by the beaver, is from $\frac{1}{10}$ to $\frac{1}{8}$. This question is settled by examining the aliment actually consumed by the animal. The stomach has been found distended with finely comminuted woody fibre, and the same material was found in the colon. In another case the contents of the stomach, partly filled, were the same, weighing 1 lb. 3 oz. The masses in the colon were of the same character. If bark were ingested with the wood it must have been in small quantity. The conclusion, therefore, is that the beaver derives its nutriment from the vegetable gum, sugar, and albumen contained in the alburnum or sap-wood, when it cannot obtain succulent roots and vegetables.

The length and size of the intestines in animals are proportionate to the nature and nutritious qualities of their food. In the carnivora, the intestinal canal is shorter and less complicated than in the herbivora. In the beaver, the length of the small intestines averages 25 feet. They are destitute of valvulæ conniventes, which are confined to man,[1] but the villous coat is well developed. Sixteen patches of Peyer's glands were counted in one subject. The pancreas is long and delicate. Its duct enters the intestine 25″ from the pyloric orifice, while that of the gall-bladder enters but 4″ from the pylorus.

The extremity of the small intestine projects a little into the colon, and the orifice is circular.

Between the colon and cæcum is a circular band of muscular fibres acting both as a constrictor and a valve. The cæcum is larger than the stomach. Its capacity when filled with water is 5 pints and 3 gills, and that of the stomach is 3 pints and 1 gill. The cæcum is on a line with the colon for 7″ or 8″, it then forms an angle, and gradually diminishes in size to its extremity. In shape it resembles a

[1] "It is remarkable that these folds (valvulæ conniventes) are peculiar to the human subject. No other animal, so far as we know, exhibits any arrangement of transverse folds of the intestinal mucous membrane resembling them."—"The Physiological Anatomy and Physiology of Man. By Todd and Bowman." Phila. ed., p. 574.

NOTE.—In the stomach of the beaver I have found a very fine filamentous worm, 40‴ in length, species unknown. Large numbers of a long, slender white worm, 3″ to 5″ in length, were found in the peritoneal cavity (Filaria, species not known), also in the colon, and especially in the cæcum, sclerostema, male and female, species not known, and the amphistoma subtriquetrum.

sickle. The follicular cavities in the cæcum and colon, surrounded by columnar epithelium, give to the surface a warty appearance. The reticulated or cellular appearance of the colon is similar to what is usually seen in this portion of the intestine.

FIG. 7.

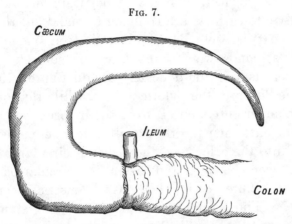

Cæcum of beaver. One-sixth natural size.

The greatest width of the cæcum is 4″, and its length, measured on its outer surface, is 2 feet 6″. The colon, measured from the circular band to the rectum, is 7 feet 6″. At its commencement there are two longitudinal bands, forming numerous folds and sacculi; after continuing 7″, a third band starts at an acute angle and continues 25″, terminating as it began. The colon then diminishes in size, and in place of cells is alternately expanded and contracted to adapt itself to its contents.

The liver is long, flattened, with two principal lobes, two smaller ones, and several fissures. It is hardly necessary to say that glucose is obtained from it. The spleen is small, long and linear in form. In

one animal it was $3\frac{1}{4}''$ in length, in another, $4\frac{3}{4}''$, with
an average width of $40'''$. Weight of the largest spleen,
110 grains.

The right lung has two lobes, one of them bifid.
The left lung has four lobes. The supra-renal capsules in the rodents are relatively large. The kidneys present nothing remarkable. Weight of one
kidney 640 grains. The heart weighs 714 grains,
and resembles the human in its cavities, valves, vessels, etc. In one beaver a large calcareous deposit existed above the aortic valves. In another there was
incipient atheroma in patches in the same situation.

M. Sarrasin, in his account of the beaver, describing
the heart, says the right auricle being smaller than the
left, the right ventricle is filled by the conjoint action
of the auricle and the vena cava inferior; the latter
being at this point considerably expanded. The venous
sac, he adds, is narrower by the side of the liver where
it is closed by three valves, like the sigmoidal, which
prevent the reflux of the blood during the act in
question. M. Sarrasin's account of the beaver is so
generally correct that his misconception on this point
is the more remarkable. It is well known that in
diving animals, whether birds or mammals, a provision exists in the venous system against the evils of
suspended respiration. R. Knox, Esq., claims to have
first noticed it in the case of the beaver. His account
is contained in the Memoirs of the Wernerian Society, vol. iv., part ii., 1823. This provision consists
in an enlargement of the inferior vena cava as it
passes through the fissure of the liver, constituting a
sinus in which a considerable quantity of blood may
be temporarily arrested.

In the beaver the inferior cava begins to enlarge opposite the kidney. The largest part of the sinus is where it receives the hepatic veins. After passing through the diaphragm it contracts to its original size. The four hepatic veins are also capable of containing a large quantity of blood, the largest readily admitting the adult fore finger. On opening the vena cava in its length, its linear width, opposite the kidney, is two inches; in the hepatic fissure it is three inches; and before reaching the right auricle it is two inches. The capacity of the venous sinus is not fully indicated by these measurements, as the vein probably yields to distention. The "sigmoid valves," described by M. Sarrasin, are merely the openings of the three hepatic veins seen from above. The blood corpuscles of the beaver measure $\frac{1}{3500}''$ in diameter. The mean of 24 rodents, as given in Gerber's Anatomy, is $\frac{1}{3757}''$. The eye of the beaver is small. The optic nerve is but $5'''$ in diameter. In decussating within the skull the nerve of the right side passes under the left. The reputed sagacity of the beaver is not accounted for by the size or development of the brain. The implacental mammals (marsupials and monotremes) are the lowest of the mammiferous class, according to Prof. R. Owen; their brains resembling those of birds, in the absence of the great commissure, or corpus callosum. The brains of rodents are a step in advance. The beaver brain is entirely smooth on the surface, and, although the cerebellum is uncovered, the posterior development is greater than in the marsupials. The olfactory lobe is large. The optic lobes are covered. Width of cerebral hemisphere, $83'''$; of corpus callosum, $60'''$; length of brain before removal,

1″ 80‴. Weight of cerebrum, 336 grs.; of cerebellum, 68 grs.; of medulla and peduncles, 69 grs.; total of encephalon, 473 grs. The proportion of the marsupial brain to the body in three animals, as stated by Prof. Owen, is 1 to 520, 1 to 600, and 1 to 614. In the beaver it is 1 to 532. The average of the mammalia, according to Leuret, is 1 to 186; of birds, 1 to 212. In man it is 1 to 36.

NOTE.—For description of the castoreum and generative organs of the beaver, see Appendix A, Note 3.

CHAPTER III.

BEAVER DAMS.

Remarkable Beaver District—Number of Beaver Dams—Other Works—
Character of the Region—Beavers now Abundant—Map of Area—Object
of Dams—Their Great Age—Of Two Kinds—Interlaced Stick-Dam—
Solid Bank Dam—Great Beaver Dam at Grass Lake—Its Dimensions—
Surrounding Landscape—Mode of Construction—Lower Face—Water
Face—Great Curve—Mode of discharging Surplus Water—Artistic Ap-
pearance of this Dam—Necessity for Continuous Repairs—Measurements
—Cubic Contents—Photograph—Manner of taking same—Relation of
Dam below—Same of one above—Manner of Repairing Dams.

THE particular beaver district which I have selected
for presentation is situated upon the summit level of
the coast range of hills that skirt the southwest shore
of Lake Superior, immediately west of Marquette.
It is the district shown upon the map. In length,
from east to west, it is eight miles, and six miles
broad, from north to south. This area is traversed by
a small stream, known as Carp River, which empties
into Lake Superior, and also by the Ely Branch of
the Esconauba[1] River, which rises in this area and
flows southward into Lake Michigan. It is, therefore,
seen to embrace a portion of the dividing ridge that
separates the drainage of the two great lakes, with
slopes in both directions. Within this district are
situated the three remarkable hills of rock iron ore,
now so well known throughout the country as the
Jackson, Cleveland, and Lake Superior Iron Mines,

---

[1] *Ish-ko-nau-ba.*

besides several other iron locations of great value. These are but the commencement of those vast ferruginous deposits which distinguish this portion of Upper Michigan over all other parts of the United States.[1] Lake Angeline, situated upon the summit level of the coast range, is 850 feet above the level of Lake Superior, from which it is distant about sixteen miles. From the number of small lakes in this inconsiderable area, from the hills and lowlands into which it is broken up, and from the number of small streams to which they give rise, it is well watered, and therefore extremely well adapted to beaver occupation. There are other districts of the same extent, in its immediate vicinity, particularly around Lake Michigame,[2] and upon the main branch of the Esconauba, scarcely inferior to it in the number of beaver dams and other erections which they contain; but the one selected is sufficiently furnished in these respects to yield ample materials for the illustration of the works of the beaver. Since it is a material part of

---

[1] The great richness of this ore is shown by the following analysis :

Iron	70·22	Or Peroxide of Iron	90·58
Oxygen	29·53	" Magnetic Oxide	9·17
Insoluble	20	" Silica	20
	99·55		99·55

Foster and Whitney's Report, Geology Lake Superior Land District. Executive Doc., No. 4 (Senate), 1851, p. 74.

[2] *Mä-she-gä'-me*, large lake. The Ojibwas classify lakes into three kinds : *Sä-qä-é'-qä*, small lake ; *Mä-she-qä'-me*, large lake; and *Git-chē-gä'-me*, great lake. The last is applied to the "great lakes" indiscriminately, and to the ocean.

my plan to show how completely they occupy a given
district, as their numbers increase, as well as the relations of their dams and other erections to each other,
I have explored the area covered by the map with
more thoroughness than any other, in order, as far as
possible, to exhibit all of their works within its limits.
Undoubtedly many of the lesser have escaped observation, but the principal and most important have been
found.   There are within this area sixty-three beaver
dams, without reckoning the smallest, from those
which are fifty feet in length, and forming ponds cov-
ing a quarter of an acre of land, to those which are
three hundred and five hundred feet in length, with
ponds covering from twenty to sixty acres of land.
It also contains many acres of beaver meadows, many
lodges, burrows, and artificial canals.

A dense forest overspreads the land, with the exception of the beaver meadows and the clearings
made near the mines.   Upon the margins of the
principal streams the prevailing trees are the tamarack and the spruce; upon the first rising ground,
back of these, we find the white and yellow birch,
the soft and bird's-eye maple, the poplar and the ash;
and upon the hills the sugar maple, the oak, and several species of pine.   Among the bushes are the willow, the alder, and the cranberry.   In this area,
therefore, are assembled all the elements tending to
form an inviting beaver district; namely, numerous
small rivulets flowing through hard wood lands, upon
the bark of the trees of which they depend chiefly
for subsistence; and shallow, sluggish rivers, sufficiently narrow between their banks to be traversed
by dams, and having deciduous trees adjacent, and

reachable by means of artificial canals cut through the lowlands and filled with water from the ponds.

With the exception of Marquette, and a small settlement at the mouth of the Chocolate River, and with the further exception of several settlements upon the lines of the Marquette and Ontonagon, and the Peninsular Railroads, the entire region from Keweenaw Bay of Lake Superior to Green Bay of Lake Michigan, is still an unbroken and an uninhabited wilderness. Prior to the discovery of the iron deposits in this district, about the year 1846, it had scarcely been traversed except by the trapper, the surveyor, and the Ojibwa Indians, the latter of whom possessed the country as a part of their hereditary domain. From the dense undergrowth of the forest, from the swampy character of a large portion of the lands, and from the numerous windfalls, extending in some places for miles, it is even now extremely difficult to traverse this region in any direction except upon Indian trails; and no one but an experienced woodman can safely undertake an expedition into this wilderness for any considerable distance. Throughout this entire area beavers are now abundant, and for the most part undisturbed in their habitations. Their works meet the eye at almost every point on the numerous streams with which it is covered as with a net-work; and they afford to the observer the additional advantage of being in a perfect condition as well as in actual use. Each dam is not only complete in itself, but there is a series of these dams, one above the other, on the same stream, so located as not to interfere with each other, and constructed so near together that the lower one of two usually sets back its pond quite near to

that immediately above.   In this manner every portion of a stream is appropriated by them for the purposes of habitation.

The accompanying map,* which embraces but a fragment of the area described, was drawn by Mr. L. K. Dorrance, chief engineer, and afterwards revised by William H. Steele, Esq., assistant engineer of the Marquette and Ontonagon Railroad, from materials furnished by the author.   Each section delineated is a mile square, the sections corresponding with those upon the official United States Township maps.   With this integer of measurement, the distances between the several dams and the size of the several ponds can be readily ascertained as well as the actual location of each.   The size of some of the ponds may be somewhat exaggerated, but the map is substantially accurate.   For convenience of reference the dams are numbered consecutively.   The sites of a large number of lodges, the location of the principal beaver meadows, and of several beaver canals are also indicated on the map.

The dam[1] is the principal structure of the beaver. It is also the most important of his erections as it is the most extensive, and because its production and preservation could only be accomplished by patient and long-continued labor.   In point of time, also, it precedes the lodge, since the floor of the latter and the entrances to its chamber are constructed with reference to the level of the water in the pond.   The object of the dam is the formation of an artificial pond, the principal use of which is the refuge it affords

---

[1] O-ko'-min, beaver dam.
*[Following p. 83 in the Dover Edition.]

to them when assailed, and the water connection it gives to their lodges, and to their burrows in the banks. Hence, as the level of the pond must, in all cases, rise from one to two feet above these entrances for the protection of the animal from pursuit and capture, the surface level of the pond must, to a greater or less extent, be subject to their immediate control. As the dam is not an absolute necessity to the beaver for the maintenance of his life, his normal habitation being rather natural ponds and rivers, and burrows in their banks, it is, in itself considered, a remarkable fact that he should have voluntarily transferred himself, by means of dams and ponds of his own construction, from a natural to an artificial mode of life.

Some of these dams are so extensive as to forbid the supposition that they were the exclusive work of a single pair, or of a single family of beavers: but it does not follow, as has very generally been supposed, that several families, or a colony, unite for the joint construction of a dam. After a careful examination of some hundreds of these structures, and of the lodges and burrows attached to many of them, I am altogether satisfied that the larger dams were not the joint product of the labor of large numbers of beavers working together, and brought thus to immediate completion; but, on the contrary, that they arose from small beginnings, and were built upon year after year until they finally reached that size which exhausted the capabilities of the location; after which they were maintained for centuries, at the ascertained standard, by constant repairs. So far as my observations have enabled me to form an opinion, I think they were

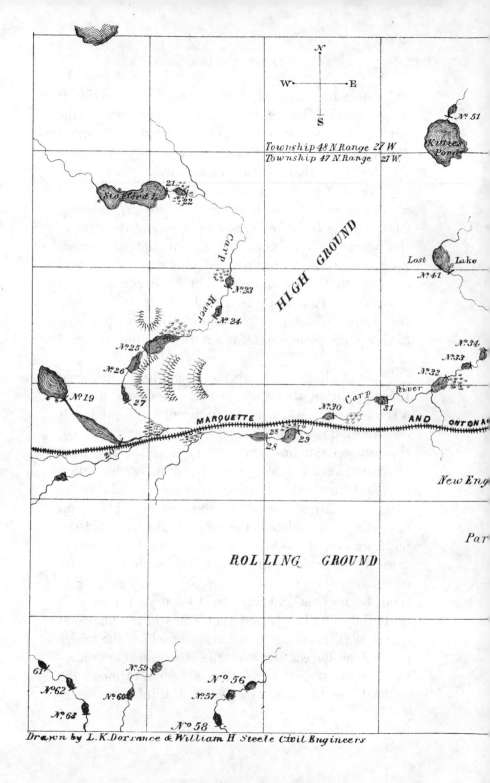

N
W · E
S

Township 48 N. Range 27 W
Township 47 N. Range 27 W.

L. N°. 51

Kittle Ponds

HIGH GROUND

Staford

21
22

Carp River

N°. 23

N°. 24

N°. 25

N°. 26

27

N°. 19

26

Lost Lake
N°. 41

N°. 34
N°. 33
N°. 32

Carp River

31

AND ONTONA

N°. 30

MARQUETTE

28
28
29

New Eng

Par

ROLLING GROUND

61
N°. 59
N°. 62
N°. 60
N°. 63

N°. 56
N°. 57
N°. 58

Drawn by L. K. Dorrance & William H. Steele Civil Engineers

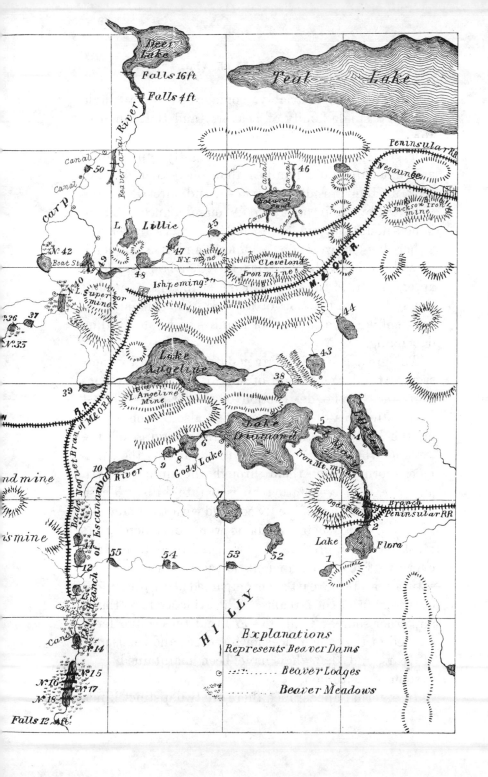

Deer Lake

Teal Lake

Falls 16 ft.
Falls 4 ft.

Beaver Canal River

Canal
Canal
Canal

Peninsular RR

50

46

Negaunee

Canal
Canal

Carp

Jackson Iron mine

L. Lillie

45

N.Y. mine

M.L.O.R.R.

Nº 42
Boat St.

49

47

Cleveland Iron mine

44

48

Ishpeming

L. Superior mine

Nº 40

Nº 36   37

Nº 35

Lake Angeline

43

39

L. Angeline Mine

38

nd mine

Lake Diamond

5

Iron Mt. mine

R.R.

Back Noquet Bran. of M.L.O.R.R.

10

Goose Lake

6

9   8

Cody Lake

4

Branch of Escanaba River

7

Ogden Dam

Branch Peninsular RR

2

s mine

11

55

54

53

52

Lake Flora

1

12

HILLY

14

Canal West Branch of Escanaba

15

Nº 16   Nº 17

Nº 18

Falls 12 ft.

Explanations

Represents Beaver Dams
Beaver Lodges
Beaver Meadows

usually, if not invariably, commenced by a single pair, or a single family of beavers; and that when in the course of time, by the gradual increase of the dam, the pond had become sufficiently enlarged to accommodate more families than one, other families took up their residence upon it, and afterward contributed, by their labor, to its maintenance. There is no satisfactory evidence that the American beavers either live or work in colonies; and if some such cases have been observed, it will either be found to be an exception to the general rule, or in consequence of the sudden destruction of a work upon the maintenance of which a number of families were at the time depending.

The great age of the larger dams is shown by their size, by the large amount of solid materials they contain, and by the destruction of the primitive forest within the area of the ponds; and also by the extent of the beaver meadows along the margins of the streams where dams are maintained, and by the hummocks formed upon them through the annual growth and decay of vegetation in separate hills. These meadows were undoubtedly covered with trees adapted to a wet soil when the dams were constructed. It must have required long periods of time to destroy every vestige of the ancient forest by the increased saturaiton of the earth, accompanied with occasional overflows from the streams. The evidence from these, and other sources, tends to show that these dams have existed in the same places for hundreds and thousands of years, and that they have been maintained by a system of continuous repairs.

In external appearance there are two distinct kinds

of beaver dams, although they are all constructed on the same principle. One, the stick-dam, consists of interlaced stick and pole work upon the lower face, with an embankment of earth, intermixed with the same materials on the upper, or water face of the dam. This species is usually found on brooks, and upon the larger streams without defined banks. The greater proportion of beaver dams are of this description. The other is the solid-bank dam, which is usually found lower down on the same stream, where its banks have become defined, and it has a channel of some depth, and a uniform current. In such places the large amount of earth and mud, used to strengthen the work, buries and conceals the greater part of the brush and poles used to bind the embankment together; thus giving to it, in the course of time, the appearance, on both slopes, of a solid dike, or bank of earth. In the first species the surplus water percolates through the dam along its entire length, while, in the second, it is discharged through a single opening in the crest formed for that purpose.

At the place selected for the construction of a dam, the ground is usually firm and often stony; and when across the channel of a flowing stream, a hard rather than a soft bottom is preferred. Such places are necessarily unfavorable for the insertion of stakes in the ground, if such were, in fact, their practice in building dams. The theory upon which beaver dams are constructed is perfectly simple, and involves no such necessity. Soft earth intermixed with vegetable fibre is used to form an embankment, with sticks, brush, and poles imbedded within these materials to bind them together, and to impart to them the requisite solidity to resist the effects both of pressure and of saturation. Small sticks and brush are used, in the first instance, with mud, earth, and stones for down weight. Consequently these dams are extremely rude at their commencement, and they do not attain their remarkably artistic appearance until after they have been raised to a considerable height, and have been maintained, by a system of annual repairs, for a number of years.

The open stick-work dams are the most interesting as well as the most common, and they will be first presented.

This dam, which is represented in the engraving (Plate VI.), and which is marked No. 8 upon the map, is the most remarkable of all the structures of this description of which I have gained a knowledge. I have seen others that were longer, and still others that were higher for short distances, but none that united, to the same extent, the two features of great length and continuous elevation, or that contained so large an amount of solid material. It is two hundred and sixty feet and ten inches in length, measured with a tape line along the crest of the dam, and six feet and two inches in vertical height at the centre of the great curve, with a slope, at the latter point, on the lower side or face of the dam, of thirteen feet in length.

The site was well selected for a structure of this magnitude. Lake Diamond is situated about half a mile to the eastward, in the midst of high hills, and maintains its level about fifteen feet higher than the level of the pond formed by the dam. Its outlet forms a small brook a few feet over and a few inches deep, and is the commencement of the

Plate VI

From a Photograph.

P.S.Duval, Son & Co.Phil.

GREAT BEAVER DAM.—GRASS LAKE
260. feet long.

Ely Branch of the Esconauba River. Across this brook, and about half a mile below the point where it emerges from the lake, the dam was constructed. It was undoubtedly small at first, but was raised and extended in course of time, until it reached the base of the hills on either side. At this point the hills approach each other within three hundred feet, while immediately above it they recede both to the right and to the left, and back, near the outlet of the lake, close in again, thus forming an amphitheatre of hills, with a slight depression at the outlet, and another depression to the right, and inclosing a level area of about one hundred acres of land. The large pond created by the dam, and which is known as Grass Lake, overspreads about sixty acres of this level area. A forest of heavy timber covers the whole tract with the exception of the pond, and of a narrow fringe of beaver meadow here and there. Along the skirts of the pond, in its shallowest parts, trees, though dead, are still standing, from which it is evident that the dam now maintains the pond at a higher level than in former years, or, in other words, that it has been raised to a higher level within the lifetime of these trees. These several features of the landscape are distinctly seen in the engraving. For a large dam, and the formation of a large pond, which were to result from the labor of many years bestowed by many successive generations of industrious beavers, this site was not only well selected, but it afforded greater advantages than any other within the area indicated on the map.

At the place where it is constructed the ground is neither soft nor alluvial, but composed of firm earth, intermixed with loose stones, large and small. The crest line of the dam is, of course, horizontal, although sinuous, while its base line conforms to the irregularities of the original surface. At the point where it crossed the thread of the stream it would necessarily be the highest. Here the difference in level between the water in the pond and the water below the dam was ascertained to be five feet; the crest of the dam rising but two inches above the level of the pond, and the water below it being twelve inches deep. The vertical height of the structure at the great curve, therefore, was six feet and two inches. This difference of level decreases as either end is approached, until it diminishes to one foot. At the ends, consequently, the precise condition of the structure, at its lowest stages, could be seen; not as at first constructed, but as it would appear after it had settled down and had been repaired and strengthened from time to time. Here it was built with small sticks, from half an inch to an inch in diameter, and from one to two and three feet in length. On the lower side, which we shall call the face of the dam, the sticks are arranged promiscuously, but usually with their lower ends against the ground, and their upper ends elevated and pointing up stream, against the water slope of the dam, thus forming an inclined bank of interlaced stick-work. Earth and mud, intermixed with sticks and brush, form the water face or upper slope of the dam, giving to it the nature and appearance of a solid embankment. Thus the lower face of the dam presents a mass of interlaced sticks closely banked together, but still open and loose, and free from earth, while the upper or water face is a

Plate VII.

From a Photograph.

SECTION of GREAT BEAVER DAM. GRASS LAKE.

solid bank of earth bound together by a mass of sticks imbedded and concealed from view. A transverse section, therefore, is a triangle with the base longer than either side. We thus have a section of a dam about a foot high, constructed with the least amount of materials, but holding the water securely, and yet so fragile that the weight of a man would sink it below the surface of the water.

At the great curve, near the centre of the dam, the minute as well as general structure of a large beaver dam can be seen to the highest advantage. The engraving (Plate VII.) represents a section, upwards of one hundred feet wide, through the centre of the dam, including the great curve. It is engraved three-fourths the size of the photograph. Small sticks are no longer used, but billets of wood and poles trimmed of their branches and stripped of their bark, and varying in size from one to three inches in diameter, and from three to seven and ten feet in length. These short cuttings and poles, which are interlaced and arranged in every conceivable way, form a sloping bank at an angle of from 35° to 40°. Their main direction is from the ground upward toward the water face of the dam. They are neither parallel with each other, nor in courses, but are banked together in an irregular but compact mass, and are so adjusted as to form an innumerable series of props or braces, with their lower ends against the ground, and their upper ends incorporated in the embankment which forms the water face of the dam. These poles, however, formed no part of the original structure, but were added from year to year to repair the waste of the dam from settlement and decay, and to increase its height. We may therefore conceive that the dam at this point was commenced, as near the ends, with brush and poles laid horizontally, but lengthwise with the current, and filled in with earth and mud intermixed with roots and grass, and that as the work advanced, the upper ends became imbedded and concealed from view, while the lower projected beyond the embankment.   In course of time, by the process of enlargement and repair, it would assume its present form as shown in the engraving.   With its increase in height, the crest of the dam would tend to draw down stream from a line perpendicular with the original centre of its base.   In consequence of this, the open stick and pole work, which forms the face of the dam, advances upward and under the water of the pond as you descend vertically from its crest to the bottom of the structure. None of the poles on the face of the dam at the great curve were as long as the slope itself.   They appeared to be loosely thrown together, but on attempting to raise a number of them they were found to be fast at one end or the other, or so interlaced that it was difficult to remove them.

It will be observed that the dam, at the place where the greatest strength was required, is in the form of a curve, with its curvature up stream, and that the line of this curve is more than a hundred feet in length.   The use of the curve in beaver dams is of very common occurrence, and it has always been regarded as a striking evidence of the intelligence of its builders.   In the engraving its form does not distinctly appear, from the reduced scale upon which the work is shown, but when the original photograph is placed in a camera of large magnifying power, the

Plate VIII.

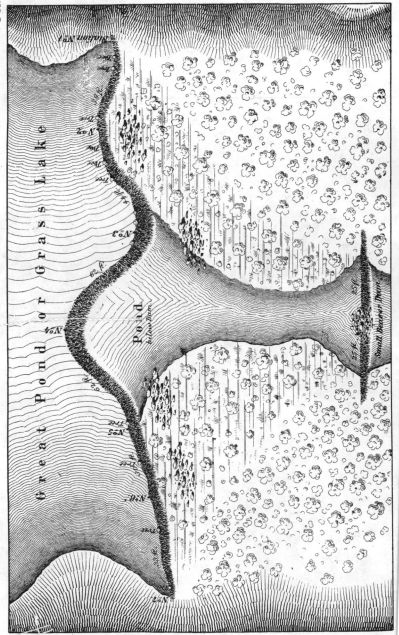

Great Pond or Grass Lake

Pond
below dam

LAKE DAM Ground Plan

outline of the curve is fully revealed. In order to indicate still more completely the crest line of the dam, a ground plan of the entire structure, drawn from actual measurements, is given in the engraving, Plate VIII.

It is designed to show the crest line and the lower face of the dam. With the engravings, and the measurements in detail, hereafter given, the general appearance, form, and structure of the dam will be fully understood.

The curve is one of the striking features of a beaver dam. They are almost invariably found where the thread of the stream originally ran, and are restricted to the class of dams now under consideration. In the largest structures, the convexity of the curve is usually up stream, but this is not always the case. Several of those represented on the map curved down stream at the point where the dam was the highest. This one shows a reverse curve down stream nearly as large and well defined as the principal one in the opposite direction. It is generally asserted that the introduction of a curve, with its convexity up stream, was the result of intelligence and design on the part of the architects; and that its use at the precise point where the pressure of the water is the greatest, affords conclusive evidence that the beavers understood its mechanical advantages. Whether these curves were the result of accident or of design is a question. We must suppose that this dam was commenced at the thread of the stream where the great curve is found, and it seems not improbable that its curvature may be due to the flow of the water on either side when the original channel was first obstructed by their

rising work. After a quantity of materials had become firmly anchored in the bed of the stream, the
tendency would be to a downward movement of its
margins by the force of the water, which would give
to it at its commencement a curvilinear form. With
the obstruction of the channel a pond would begin to
rise, but the surplus water would pass by on either
side at a higher level; consequently, as the work pro-
gressed, the contest with the water would be renewed,
with similar results at other points, and when the
dam was raised sufficiently high, and extended sufficiently far to arrest the flow of the water in open
channels, and to discharge it through the dam, it
would be very sinuous throughout its entire extent.
Such, in fact, is the general character of all the dams
constructed upon the smaller brooks.   In larger
streams, with their channels deepest in the centre,
we may conceive of a downward movement of their
materials by the force of the current, or the pressure
of the water at the point where the stream is the
deepest, and that this movement may have occurred
while the work of construction was in progress.   A
downward curve is much more common than the
reverse in the larger streams.   It is not a little singular that the dams across the streams that discharge
the largest volume of water are shorter and lower
than those upon the smaller brooks, and that in the
former the prevailing direction of the curve at the
highest point in the structure is down stream, while
in the latter it is in the opposite direction.   The
mode of construction undoubtedly varied with the
character of the stream, and with the volume and
rapidity of the current.   A comparison of a large

number of these dams, constructed in very dissimilar situations, tends to show that their curvature is purely accidental.

The remainder of this dam is nearly as remarkable as the central portion, and much longer as well as larger than the engraving represents (Plate VI.), unless due allowance is made for perspective. The focal point occupied by the instrument was so near the struc-ture as to depreciate quite rapidly its extreme parts. Throughout its entire extent of two hundred and sixty feet the face of the dam is composed, as at the centre, of interlaced sticks and poles, and presents the same general appearance, with a gradual abate-ment in height.

On the water face of the dam neither a stick nor a pole is seen, but a regular sloping embankment of earth, from the crest downward, under the waters of the pond. This face of the dam is precisely in the form of the shelving bank of a stream.

There is no opening in the top of the dam, in any part of it, for the discharge of the surplus water; neither does it pass over its crest; but it percolates through the thin bank of earth near its crest in nu-merous places along its entire length. The dams of this class all agree in this respect. In the most of these dams the rapidity or slowness with which this surplus is discharged, is undoubtedly regulated by the beavers, otherwise the level of the pond would con-tinually vary. There must be a constant tendency to enlarge the orifices through which the water passes, which, if left to itself, would in due time draw down the pond, and expose the entrances to their lodges and burrows; on the other hand, if the embankment was made impenetrable, the water would rise and flow over its crest, to its waste and injury. At ordinary stages of the water the pond is maintained at a uniform level; but after a sudden rise, or in time of freshet, it flows over the summit. The structure is better able to bear an overflow than rents through its embankment. This dam was rarely if ever overflowed, for a special reason, which will be stated hereafter. Those upon the Carp, however, are submerged with every considerable rise of the stream, which, having a wide drainage, is subject to sudden freshets. I have seen the water run over the tops of these dams a foot deep. After the flow subsided, the rents were speedily repaired. At ordinary stages the surplus water passed through the dams by percolation, straining through them near the crest as though they were fine basket-work. I have visited the Grass Lake dam six different years, and at high and low stages of the water in the neighboring streams, and always found the pond at the same level, and full to the crest of the dam, until the year 1865, when it was lower than usual, and the dam itself exhibited signs of neglect. From this fact it seemed probable that after centuries of use and maintenance by unnumbered generations of beavers, this interesting and remarkable structure was about to be abandoned by its natural proprietors.

At the time the photograph was taken, the water of the pond stood quite near the summit of the dam along its entire length. In some places it came within one or two inches, while in others it stood upon it and trickled over. The crest is very narrow along its whole extent, diminishing from a few inches at its widest expanse to a mere line. It is a conspicuous feature of beaver dams of this class that they are so perfectly constructed as to hold and retain water until it rises to their very summit. A fine sod, composed of roots of grass intermixed with loam, is used to finish the water line of the dam. On taking up a handful of this sod, freeing it from earth and rinsing it clean, it yielded one-half of its original bulk of vegetable fibre, mostly fine roots and tendrils, still green and undecayed. It was thus made evident that it had been quite recently laid.

In constructing dams, loose stones are incorporated, here and there, for down weight, and to give solidity to the structure. We found stones upon this dam which would weigh from one to six pounds. They are most frequently discovered where the dam is the lowest, although found in all parts of the work.

No one standing upon this dam, and observing its fragile character, could fail to perceive that its maintenance would require constant supervision and perpetual labor. The tendency to increased leakage from the effects of percolation, and to a settling down of the dam, as its materials decayed underneath upon its stick-work half, would demand unceasing vigilance and care to avert the consequences. In the fall of the year a new supply of materials is placed upon the lower face of these dams to compensate this waste from decay. They use for this purpose the cuttings of the previous fall, which during the winter have been stripped of their bark for food, and laid aside apparently for this object. It is from this practice, and the manner of repairing their dams, that they assume, in course of time, the highly artistic appearance upon the lower slope which the engraving displays. The sticks, poles, and billets of wood, when laid upon the face of the dam, impart to this slope its regular and symmetrical form. When first constructed, as before remarked, and when at their lowest stages, they are extremely rude, and only take on the appearance in which they are usually seen after they have been maintained for a long series of years. Fresh beaver tracks are usually seen imprinted upon the soft earth on the crest of these dams, and fresh beaver cuttings are often found upon their lower faces, thus showing that they are in the constant habit of traversing and repairing the works. There is generally no difficulty in walking over the larger dams with dry feet, by keeping on the lower slope, except near the ends, where the structure is not usually strong enough to bear up the weight of a man. Upon the sloping face of the great curve of Grass Lake Dam twenty men could stand together without making any impression upon the structure. The series of dams on the Carp, shown upon the map, are similar to this, and would average about three feet in height. While fishing in this stream for brook trout, three of us found no difficulty in landing from our boat upon their lower slopes, and drawing the boat over without injuring them in any respect.

The following measurements will indicate, in another manner, the size and proportion of parts of this great structure, as well as convey some impression of the amount of solid materials employed in its erection:

Length of Dam measured on the Crest Line.

From Station No. 1 to Station No. 2 (See Plate VIII.)..... 39 feet.
"   "   " 2   "   " 3............................ 44 "
"   "   " 3   "   " 1.......................... 02 " 10 ln.
"   "   " 4   "   " 5........................... 52 "
"   "   " 5   "   " 6............................ 30 "
"   "   " 6   "   " 7............................ 33 "

Total Length... 260 feet 10 in.

Other Measurements.

	No. 4.	No. 4½.	No. 3.	No. 2.
Height of structure from ground, or base line......................	6 ft. 2''	5 ft. 3''	3 ft. 6''	2 ft. 1''
Depth of water in small pond below dam..............................	1 ft.	1 ft.		
Difference of level of water above and below dam......................	5 ft.	4 ft.		
Height of water above base line..	6 ft.	5 ft.	3 ft. 2''	2 ft.
Approximate width of base, transverse sections	18 ft.	15 ft.	12 ft.	6 ft.
Length of slope of poles, lower face of dam.........................	13 ft.	11 ft. 9''	9 ft.	6 ft.
Length of slope of water face of dam................................	7 ft. 6''	8 ft.	7 ft.	4 ft.
Depth of water in pond at the end of slope............................	4 ft.	3 ft. 6''	3 ft.	2 ft.

The following figure represents a transverse section of the dam at the head of the great curve, Station No. 4, and distinguishes the part which is a solid embankment from that which consists of sticks and poles free from earth.

FIG. 8.

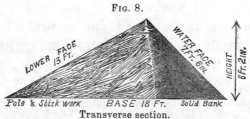

Transverse section.

A computation made from the preceding, and some additional measurements, shows that this dam contains upwards of seven thousand cubic feet of solid materials, all of which were transported and wrought into this structure by its industrious and ingenious architects.

The photograph of this dam, from which the engraving was made, was taken by Mr. James A. Jenney in August, 1861, upon four plates, each eight by ten inches in dimensions; and from one position, in order to show the dam, the pond, and the background in one symmetrical picture. As a preparatory measure, the trees, for fifty feet immediately below the dam, were cut down and removed, the under-brush was cleared, and the weeds and grass, which were growing through the dam, were pulled out, that the work might be shown free from all obstructions. A scaffold for the instrument was then erected in front of the great curve, about sixty feet distant from it, and twelve feet high. It was my first intention to have the dam photographed in four sections, with the instrument placed immediately in front of each, thereby sacrificing the background in order to show the relative size of all the parts of the dam. The first two plates were taken on this plan. But the other method was finally substituted for the reason that it would show the central portion of the dam perfectly, while the imperfect and reduced appearance of the remainder would, it was believed, be more than compensated by the completeness of the representation as a whole. These photographs, when adjusted together, make a picture thirty-six inches in length by seven in width, and, in all respects, faithfully and strikingly reproduce the original in miniature form. I esteemed it, at the time, peculiarly fortunate that I was able to secure an exact representation of this great structure while it was in a perfect state, although not then as well assured, as at present, that it is not surpassed in magnitude by any other beaver dam in North America.

Two adjuncts of this dam remain to be noticed. Of these, the first is a remarkable effort of engineering skill, if from the end it subserves we are at liberty to infer an intention on the part of the beaver to produce that end. It is a second dam, in two sections, each twenty-five feet long and two feet high, constructed across the thread of the stream, and about one hundred feet below the great curve. It is shown in Plate VIII. At this point, the waters that flowed through the dam above have again become collected into a small running stream. This low dam forms a shallow pond, in itself of no apparent use for beaver occupation, but yet subserving the important purpose of setting back water to the depth of twelve or fifteen inches in the great curve. At this point the pressure of the water in the pond against the dam is the greatest, because here the bed of the channel is the lowest, and the structure the highest; and the small dam, by maintaining the water a foot deep below the great dam, diminishes, to this extent, the difference in level above and below; and neutralizes, to the same extent, the pressure of the water in the pond above against the main structure. Whether the lower dam was constructed with this motive, and for this object, or is explainable on some other hypothesis, I shall not venture an opinion. I have found the same precise work repeated below other large dams.

The second is also a dam which is constructed across the outlet of Lake Diamond at the place where it issues from the lake. It performs the important office of protecting the great dam below from the effects of a sudden rise of the waters of the lake. In construction, it is in all respects like the Grass Lake dam. It is ninety-three feet long, and two and a half feet high at the centre, from which it diminishes gradually to the ends. I first saw it in 1860, and last in 1866, when it was still in good condition. A dam at this point is apparently of no conceivable use to improve the lake for beaver occupation. It has one feature, also, in which it differs from other dams except those upon lake outlets: and that consists in its elevation, at all points, of about two feet above the level of the lake at ordinary stages of the water. In all other dams except those upon lake outlets, and in most of the latter, the water stands quite near their crests, while in the one under consideration it stood about two feet below it. This fact suggests, at least, the inference, although it may have but little of probability to sustain it, that it was constructed with special reference to sudden rises of the lake in times of freshet, and that it was designed to hold this surplus water until it could be gradually discharged through the dam into the great pond below. It would, at least, subserve this purpose very efficiently, and thus protect the dam below it from the effects of freshets. To ascribe the origin of this dam to such motives of intelligence is to invest this animal with a higher degree of sagacity than we have probable reason to concede to him; and yet it is proper to mention the relation in which these dams stand to each other, whether that relation is regarded as accidental or intentional.

I have now given a full as well as somewhat detailed description of a beaver dam of the ordinary kind constructed by this architectural mute. This explanation, and the engravings together, will render unnecessary a special description of other dams of the same class. In the remaining dams noticed, I shall limit the description to the special features or differences by which they are distinguished, giving, at the same time, ground plans and measurements for the purpose of comparison.

New dams are occasionally commenced, and old ones, previously abandoned for some cause, are repaired and reoccupied, in beaver districts which are undisturbed except by trappers. The increase or decrease of beavers in numbers, influences, to some extent, their movements in these respects. The season preferred for this work is during the months of September and October, after the strong currents have run out of the streams, and they have subsided to their lowest levels. It is also the period during which they cut and store their winter wood, with the immersion and safety of which their ponds are intimately connected. Hence we find that the active season for beaver work is late in the fall; and that it is performed with reference to the approaching winter, of which they are not unmindful. These several subjects will be elsewhere considered.

For the purpose of ascertaining how beaver dams are commenced, and especially to find whether an attempt is made to insert any portion of the materials in the ground, as a means of holding them in their places, I have taken up to the bottom both old and new beaver dams, and examined, with some care, the disposition and arrangement of the materials. The result demonstrated that neither stakes, brush, nor poles were inserted or imbedded in the ground, but on the contrary that they were laid flatwise upon the bed of the channel, and held down with mud and earth carried in and deposited upon them. A new dam was commenced a year ago on the main branch of the Carp, close beside the track of the Marquette and Ontonagon Railroad, about twenty-three miles out from Marquette. At the point selected for the dam the Carp is a mere brook, and the railroad embankment, which passes parallel with, and a few feet from it, seemed to the observant eye of the beaver to afford some advantages as a barrier, upon one side, to their proposed pond; and notwithstanding the daily passage of trains over the road, they commenced the dam, and raised it about a foot high across the channel of the stream. A conflict of interests thus arose between the beavers, on the one hand, and one of the chief commercial enterprises of the country, on the other. The track-master, fearing the effects of an accumulation of water against the railroad embankment, cut the dam through the centre, and thus lowered the water to its original level. As this was no new experience to the beavers, who were accustomed to such rents, they immediately repaired the breach. For ten or fifteen times it was cut through, and as often repaired before the beavers finally desisted from their proposed work. On taking up the remains of this dam the present season (1866), I found that it was commenced with brush and poles, with the bark on, from ten to twelve feet in length, and that they were arranged horizontally upon the bed of the channel,

Esconauba after it has passed dam No. 13, and on
Carp River after passing dam No. 39. The channel
of the first-named stream will then average seventy
feet in width, with vertical banks from three to four
feet high, and with a depth of water of about twenty
inches at its lowest stages, and in its shallowest parts.
Through the level areas it moves also with a sluggish
current. It will be seen, therefore, that in building
a dam across such a channel, it must be done in deep
water as compared with brooks; and further than this,
that the difficulty of construction increases with the
increase of the depth of the water, until it finally
becomes insurmountable. For this reason there are
no dams on the Carp below No. 50, and none on the
Esconauba below the junction of the Ely Branch
with the main stream. There is no instance within
the area represented by the map where a dam has
been constructed across a stream having a greater
depth than two feet at the site of the structure when
the water is at its lowest level. It thus becomes
apparent that beaver dams are necessarily confined
to the sources of the principal rivers and to the small
tributaries which flow into them along their courses;
and that some change in the character of the dams
would be rendered necessary by the transformations
which occur with their increase in size or depth.
Where beavers inhabit rivers too large for dams,
they burrow in their banks, for which reason they
are distinguished by the trappers under the name of
bank beavers. These general considerations will serve
to explain the manner in which given districts are
occupied by beavers; the circumstances which render
some localities more favorable than others; and the

influence of topographical features upon the character
of their dams.

The first solid-bank dam to be described (Plate IX.)
is in the Ely Branch of the Esconauba River, and is
marked as No. 14 on the map. When photographed it
was not in a perfect condition. It had been cut through
in two places by the miners, some three years before,
to draw off the water from the beaver meadows preparatory to cutting the grass from these meadows for
hay, and had thus been exposed to waste.   The
water in the pond then stood but a few inches above
its natural level, leaving the dam mostly uncovered
on both slopes, and its lower face littered with loose
materials from these breaches.   It exhibited the remains only of what originally was one of the most
perfect structures of its kind.   Upon the right bank
of the stream (left side of the engraving) was the
lodge, with its heap of brush, for the lodgment of cuttings, sunk in the pond immediately in front, and rising
above the surface; and on the opposite side was a
beaver meadow of considerable extent, back of which
was the forest.

The dam is constructed at a bend in the stream,
where the channel is about seventy feet wide and of
uniform depth, and where the bottom is smooth and
hard.   It is substantially a solid embankment, and is
thrown across the stream diagonally, but in a straight
line, from bank to bank.   Between these banks it is
seventy-five feet long.   On the right side it is built
into the bank, and, rising above it, is extended, as a
low dam, for thirty feet beyond, and on the left for
fifteen feet, thus giving to the structure a total length
of one hundred and twenty feet.   Between the banks,

CHAPTER IV.

BEAVER DAMS—(CONTINUED).

Solid-bank Dams—Places where constructed—No Dams in deep Water—
Where impossible, the Beavers inhabit River Banks—Description of Solid-
bank Dam—Opening for Surplus Water—Pond confined to River Banks—
Similar Dam with Hedge—Fallen-tree Dam—Use of Tree accidental—
Spring Rill Dam—Series of Dams on the Carp—Dams in a Gorge—Lake
Outlet Dams—High Dam—Long Dam—Description of same—Manner of
Photographing same—Dams in other Districts of North America—Petri-
fied Beaver Dams in Montana.

THE solid-bank dam, which we are next to consider,
although constructed upon the same principles as the
kind previously described, presents a very different
appearance. This difference of external form is the
result of the altered conditions under which it is
erected, occasioned by a gradual transformation in the
character of each particular stream in its descending
course. In the capacity thereby displayed of adapt-
ing their works to the ever-varying circumstances in
which they find themselves placed, instead of following blindly an invariable type, some evidence of the
possession, on their part, of a *free intelligence*, is undoubtedly furnished.

After a stream has emerged from its sources in the
hills, and acquired volume with its onward flow, it
soon begins to develop banks as well as a broader
channel, and these banks assume a vertical form in
the level areas where the soil is alluvial. Such are
the changes which occur on the Ely Branch of the

and lengthwise with the flow of the stream instead or transversely. In general the large ends of the poles, and of the limbs with their branches attached, were up stream, which of itself would tend to strengthen their hold upon the bottom. Upon these materials, which were compactly arranged, earth and mud, in small quantities only, were accumulated for down weight, and to fill up the intervening spaces; but it was confined to the central and upper portions. On the upper margin, which was to form the water face of the dam, small sticks were used, together with loam, intermixed with fine roots, for the purpose of arresting the flow of the water through the rudely-arranged materials of the dam. At this stage it was extremely rude, and devoid of those striking characteristics which these dams assume with age.

The manner in which they repair their dams is both curious and interesting. It will be sufficient here to state that ordinary repairs are made, whenever they seem to be required, by each beaver acting independently, and without any concert with his mates. In case of a breach in the structure, several of them have been seen working together for its restoration. They usually go down to the dam nightly, one after the other, and as they pass along its margin, each, upon his own motion, does such work upon it as he chooses to perform. In another connection some facts will be stated upon this subject.

Plate IX.

From a Photograph.

P S Duval Son & Co Phila.

BEAVER DAM SOLID BANK.

the dam was of uniform width and height, as the bed of the channel was level. At the base of the structure its average width transversely was sixteen feet, diminishing to twelve feet at the original surface level of the stream, which here was twenty inches deep, and to four feet in width at the height of three feet from the bottom. Above this last level the crest was rounded up about sixteen inches higher, where it was still two feet wide, the embankment having a total height of four feet and four inches.

In constructing dams where the water is of such depth, larger quantities of brush and poles are used than in dams of the other class, and it is also necessary to use larger amounts of earth. The brush is required to hold the earth where it is placed, which otherwise would be dissolved and flow away with the current: and the earth in turn anchors the brush, and when packed around it, the two together form a firm and solid embankment. The principle on which brush and sticks are used for their binding properties is the same which led to the use of straw in mud brick. Neither, separately, would answer the end designed. So much earth was used upon this dam that the brush and poles upon the lower face, as well as on the water slope, were buried and concealed from view, except the ends which projected in different places. So firm and solid had the embankment become, and such was its breadth near the summit, that a horse and wagon might have been driven across the river upon it in safety, but for the opening on the left side for the passage of the surplus water. The only differences, therefore, in the two species of dams, consist in the filling in of the interstices on the lower face with mud and earth, which turns it into a solid embankment on both slopes, and throughout its whole extent, and in the special method resorted to for discharging the surplus water, which remains to be noticed.

From the solidity of these dams the water is not able to percolate through them as before stated, neither was it allowed at ordinary stages to pass over their summits. A regular opening is left in the crest of the dam, usually in the line of the thread of the current, several inches lower than its summit. On the water face above the opening is found the ordinary embankment, while on the lower face it is constructed of interlaced stick-work precisely in the form of the dam first described. This opening is usually from three to six feet long, so that the water passes over its top, and also through this narrow portion of the structure by percolation. It is evident, from the existence and peculiar character of these openings, that the beavers understood the injurious effects of allowing the surplus water to flow over the crests of their solid-bank dams, and also the importance of regulating the amount of the discharge, which could be effected by the enlargement or contraction of the openings. The dam was cut through at this point, which nearly obliterated this feature of the structure. This species of dam, when completed, might possess some advantages over the other in the matter of requiring less frequent repairs, and yet with each freshet it would suffer more or less of waste.

The pond above is narrow, it being confined within the natural banks of the stream, with the exception of shallow water upon portions of the beaver

Plate X

BEAVER DAM   SOLID BANK

F.S. Durell, Son & Co Pints.

meadows; but it was, nevertheless, spacious from its length and from the depth of the water, since the dam set back the pond more than a quarter of a mile, and was in places where depressions existed in the bed of the river, ten or twelve feet deep. A short distance above the lodge there is a beaver canal of considerable size running back to the hard wood lands. The beaver lodge belonging to this dam is seen upon the bank on the left side of the engraving, with a brush pile in the water immediately in front, the uses of which will be hereafter explained.

There are four dams below this shown on the map of the same general character and size, except that they were shorter. They were so near each other that each dam set back the water to the one immediately above. When I first saw them in 1860, they had been cut through by the miners, and were deserted, and when I last saw them, two years later, they were wasting away.

Upon small brooks, having defined banks and some depth of water, dams of this description are occasionally found. The one represented in the engraving (Plate X.), and which is No. 49 on the map, is situated upon an affluent of the Carp, a short distance above the boat station. It is fifty-five feet long, extending upon the bank on either side, and nearly three feet high. The embankment was several feet wide and composed of earth, the brush and poles having decayed and disappeared externally. Upon its top and lower face alder bushes had germinated and produced a hedge so dense that it was extremely difficult to penetrate it sufficiently for the inspection and measurement of the work. Near the north end was the usual opening, about six feet wide, where the lower face was constructed of interlaced sticks, while the water face was banked in with earth. In the engraving, which was made from a drawing, the hedge is removed for the purpose of showing the embankment. The fall of water which passed over the crest of the dam at the opening, was about a foot and a half. I was first drawn to the place by the sound of the falling water while passing by on the trail at some distance.

This dam realizes the earliest current descriptions of these works by Buffon and other writers, particularly its opening for the surplus water, and the hedge growing upon its summit. In the Lake Superior region, and upon the head waters of the Yellowstone and the Missouri, they are comparatively rare. All the large dams are of the other kind. In some instances both forms are found in the same dam, as will hereafter be shown.

It was another conspicuous feature of beaver dams, according to the early descriptions, that the trunk of a tree, cut down for the purpose, often served as the foundation of the structure. After selecting a proper site, their first act, as a general rule, was said to be the felling of a tree across the channel upon which the work was to be constructed. There is one dam, and but one, within the area of the map (No. 9), which has incorporated within it the trunk of a fallen tree. Except for this circumstance it would not deserve a special notice.

The tree in question (Plate XI.), which was a pine, three and a half feet in diameter, had fallen from its own decay. For aught that appeared, it might have fallen upon a dam previously constructed, and become

Plate XI

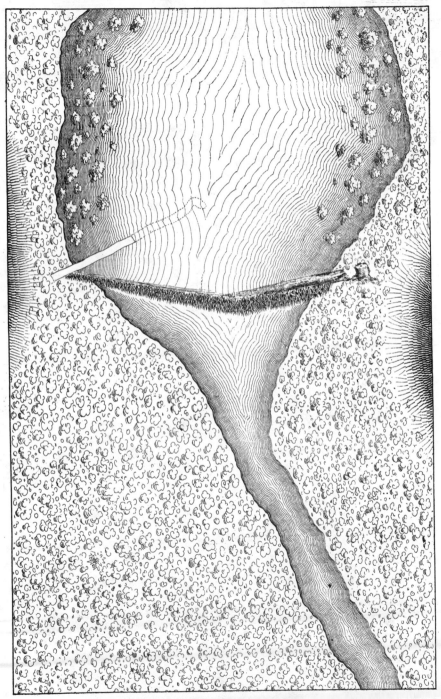

FALLEN TREE DAM.

subsequently incorporated within it; or it may have been seized upon after its fall as a convenient part of a new structure. At all events, the most singular fact connected with it is, that the dam was constructed below the log, so far as sticks and poles are used, while it was banked in above the trunk with earth. The log part of the dam was twenty-five feet long, and the remainder sixty-one feet, with a vertical height at the centre of four feet eight inches, and a slope of pole and stick work on the lower face of nine feet. From the nature of the positions in which beaver dams are usually constructed, fallen trees, if cut down on purpose, could be of but little advantage; and it is therefore probable that the use of trunks of trees in building dams was purely accidental, as in the present case.

In addition to the two species of beaver dams which have been described, there are varieties of each that possess special characteristics resulting from the nature of the localities in which they are erected. Some notice of these dams is necessary to complete the exposition of these structures.

The beavers do not restrict themselves to the principal streams, nor yet to the small brooks, but wherever they find flowing water, however small in quantity, they avail themselves of it if the place affords the other requisite advantages. There is one dam, not shown upon the map, situated at a short distance from a spring in the midst of a dense forest, and upon low and swampy ground, which may be called a spring rill dam. As live trees were standing in the pond, it was evidently of recent construction. A depression in the ground formed a basin for the water on all sides, except where the dam brought up the deficiency; and a small spring supplied the water in quantities barely sufficient to change the waters of the pond.   To prevent the escape of the water, the dam was extended until it reached the length of one hundred and thirty-three feet; after which the surplus was discharged through it by percolation. The lower face of the dam was constructed of sticks and twigs interlaced, and the water slope was an embankment of earth.   Its height varied from one foot to two feet and a half, with a difference of level in the water above and below the dam of twenty inches at the highest part of the structure.   The pond was too small to afford much protection to its occupants; but this deficiency was in some measure compensated by the abundance of hard wood upon its margin, and by the seclusion afforded by the density of the surrounding forest.   It seemed surprising, nevertheless, that a beaver family should take up their residence within an eighth of a mile of the line of the railroad, on which nine trains per day each way were then (1860) running.   With their reputed shyness and caution they were evidently waiting for some overt act of hostile interference before they surrendered their habitation.   The snare was already prepared for them, for on the day I measured the dam I saw two traps, set in the usual manner, in the pond.   Upon the impulse of the moment, I was in the act of springing them, to save the inoffensive mutes from their peril, when it occurred to me that I had no indefeasible right thus to interfere with the vocation of the trapper; whereupon, with some misgivings that I had failed to perform my duty, I left them to the chances of the trapper's art. That night the beaver, whose skull is number one in the table of measurements in the Appendix, was caught, and this, together with the tail and feet, were sent to me the following day, by the successful trapper, who proved to be my friend, Captain Bridges, the trackmaster of the railroad.

On Carp River there is a series of thirteen dams, one above the other, commencing with dam No. 50 on the map, which are much alike in size and external appearance, and may therefore be referred to in one group. They are constructed with interlaced stick-work and poles on their lower faces, and banked in with earth on their water slopes above, and discharge the surplus water, at ordinary stages, by percolation. While they are more or less sinuous in their crest lines across the channel, the principal curve, at the highest part of each structure, is usually down stream. These dams are all situated within a distance of six miles, measured along the winding channel of the stream, the borders of which are fringed, here and there, with beaver meadows, and these in turn are bordered with a forest of tamarack and spruce. I have passed over them in a fishing boat three successive seasons; the first time in 1860, and when they were in a good state of preservation, with their ponds full, and still occupied by beavers. They have since then been deserted, and the greater part of them have been carried away; thus showing the necessity for constant watchfulness and repairs which their preservation entails upon their builders. These dams were from forty to one hundred feet in length, and from three to five feet in vertical height at the thread of the stream. As each dam, in nearly every instance, sets back its pond to the one immediately above, in some cases two and even three feet in depth, the fall of water at each dam ranged from one to three feet. In times of freshet this river, although but a small stream, passes a considerable volume of water. I have seen it flow over the crests of these dams a foot deep, which, as it must occur, more or less, with every copious rain, subjects these structures to a severe test. Having seen them both before and after such occurrences, there was no injury observable that could not be speedily repaired. A detailed description of these dams, with their respective measurements, is scarcely necessary. Those higher up, on the same stream, are much larger, although the stream itself diminishes to a mere brook. One of these in particular, on account of its great length, will be hereafter described.

Dams are often found upon small mountain streams, and in the narrow gorges through which they flow. They are construcťed in the same manner as the ordinary stick-dam, but are deserving of notice from the nature of the localities in which they are erected. It seems to be no hinderance to such a use of these rapidly descending streams that the ponds thus formed must be extremely short and narrow, and consequently incapable of affording much protection. Many of the dams in the declivities of the Rocky Mountain chain, and in other mountain districts, are constructed in situations precisely similar to that of the series about to be described, and for this reason the latter are especially interesting.

To find an illustration of dams of this kind it is necessary to go without the area embraced in the

Plate XII

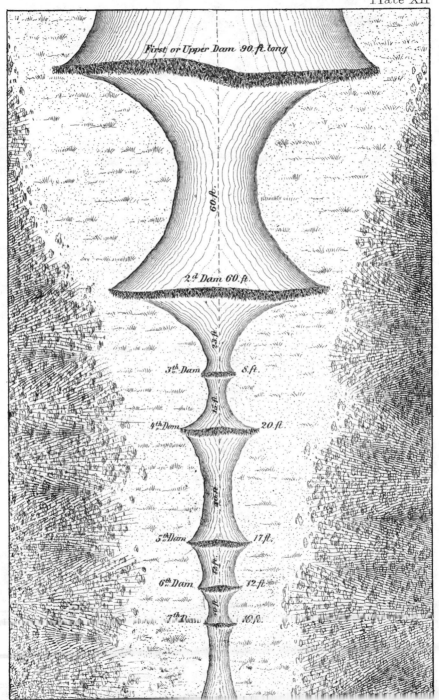

First or Upper Dam 90.ft. long

60.ft.

2.ᵈ Dam 60.ft.

23.ft.

3.ᵗʰ Dam   8.ft.

15.ft.

4.ᵗʰ Dam   20 ft.

30.ft.

5.ᵗʰ Dam   11.ft.

6.ᵗʰ Dam   12.ft.

7.ᵗʰ Dam   10.ft.

SERIES of DAMS in a GORGE

map. About six miles southeast of Lake Michigame, and two miles south of the Washington Mine, this series of structures, seven in number, is found, of which a representation is given in Plate XII. They commence at the entrance of a narrow gorge between hills of considerable elevation, and are distributed on a gradually descending line of one hundred and sixty feet, the lowest being constructed upon the verge of a nearly precipitous fall of about one hundred feet. Their size and height are sufficiently indicated by the following measurements, which were made when I first visited them in 1866, and for the opportunity of doing which I am indebted to Mr. John Armstrong, one of the officers of the Washington Mine:

	1st Dam.	2d Dam.	3d Dam.	4th Dam.	5th Dam.	6th Dam.	7th Dam.
	Ft. In.	Ft. In.	Ft. In.	Ft.	Ft. In.	Ft.	Ft.
Length of dam	90	60	8	20	17	12	9
Slope of lower face	13	6 9	4	8	5	3	3
Vertical height	5 6	3 9	2 6	4	2 10	1	2
Distance between it and next	60	23	15	30	12	10	10 to falls.

The second and third measurements given were from the highest part of each structure respectively. Taken together, these dams are quite remarkable. The upper one, which is large throughout its entire extent, forms a pond covering about ten acres of land. A dense forest of hard wood overspreads the surrounding hills, on the slopes of which a beaver-slide down into the pond is occasionally seen. At the upper end of the valley there is a beaver canal cut through the low ground two hundred and fifty feet in length, upon the margin of which the tree cuttings were numerous. Each of the lower dams has a small and narrow pond, but too inconsiderable in size to afford much protection, since the banks, from their rocky character, were unfavorable for burrows. The volume of the stream was below that of the smallest brooks, but, after rains, it sends down, undoubtedly, an abundance of water. In each case the dam was extended from one side of the gorge to the other, and constructed of stick-work on the lower face, and earth embankment on the upper, in the ordinary form. It is difficult to understand the uses of any of these dams, except the upper one, which sustains the main pond; but we are not at liberty to suppose that all this labor would have been performed without some adequate object. A tame beaver shows an irresistible propensity to dam up flowing water,—a propensity which seizes him even when he sees water running in rills in a yard, after a copious shower. Whether these apparently unnecessary dams owe their origin to some such unregulated fancy, I leave as a problem to such as adopt the theory of the fettered intelligence of the mutes. These dams show an aggregate descent in the bed of the stream of about twenty-two feet in one hundred and sixty; and are found to stand in definite relations to each other.

In the mountain districts, and in the high lands which are broken up into ranges of hills, small lakes are usually numerous. They are also favorite resorts of beavers, who inhabit them not less readily than the flowing streams. There are several such lakes within the area embraced by the map, and they form the most attractive features in the landscape. Embosomed in the midst of hills still mantled with the primitive forest, and reflecting, in the pure atmosphere of this elevated region, the brilliant sunshine from their glittering faces, they enliven the solitude of this wilderness with their cheerful aspect, as well as break up by their presence its otherwise boundless spread.

The outlets of nearly all of these lakes are obstructed with dams, the most of which are without any apparent necessity, unless by means of them they are enabled to hold the lakes at a higher and more uniform level. The first of these which will be noticed is upon the outlet of Lake Mary. It is represented as No. 5 upon the map. While it is of moderate dimensions, being seventy feet long, with an average height of two and a half feet, it was peculiar in this, that for a considerable portion of its length on either end it is a solid-bank dam, and a stick-dam in the centre across the original channel of the outlet. On the southwest end the embankment was fifteen feet long, extending for a short distance upon the bank; on the other twenty-five feet long, overlapping the bank in the same manner; and in the interval or central portion it was constructed, for thirty-one feet, of interlaced sticks and poles.

Upon the outlet of Lake Helen there is another dam (No. 4), which is one hundred and twenty feet long, and two feet six inches high at its greatest elevation. It was situated so far down the outlet that the water of the pond did not set back as far as the lake. At an early day this lake was known among the trappers as Beaver Lake, from the number of beavers found inhabiting its banks.

There are two dams on the outlet connecting Lake Flora with Lake Mary, which are numbered 2 and 3 on the map. Of these the lower one is an ordinary dam, apparently constructed to strengthen the one above. The upper one is situated about six rods down the outlet from Lake Flora, and is a large and remarkable structure. It is two hundred and three feet in length, with a nearly uniform height of three feet from one end to the other, and with a lower face of stick and pole work, ranging from six to nine feet in length, measured on its slope. The difference in level in the waters above and below the dam, at the thread of the outlet, is three feet; but, as the dam below sets back the water about two feet deep at this point, the vertical height of the structure here is five feet and over. From these measurements an impression is afforded of the large amount of solid materials this dam contains. Although inferior to the Grass Lake dam, it compares with it not unfavorably. The size of Lake Flora is materially enlarged by this barrier across its outlet, since it raised the water permanently from two and a half to three feet. This dam, with its appurtenances, was the possession, among other proprietors, of the beaver whose skeleton is represented in the plate. She was caught upon it in the year 1862, while in the act of repairing a breach made by the trapper, a few days before I visited and measured the work. The great amount of materials contained in this structure is shown by the unusual width of its crest or summit, which presupposes a corresponding transverse width at its base.

	At 70 feet from southwest end.	At 95 feet from same end.	At 140 feet from same end.
Width of dam at crest.............	4 ft.	4 ft.	4 ft.
Slope of lower face................	7 ft.	8 ft.	9 ft.
Vertical height....................	3 ft.	3 ft.	5 ft.

About a quarter of a mile above Lake Flora there is another small lake, or more properly a pond, formed by two beaver dams, about one hundred and fifty feet apart, but with no pond between them. They have the appearance of one dam in two lifts, although entirely distinct; and are shown on the map as No. 1. The lower one is one hundred and twenty feet long, and high enough to set back water three feet deep to the dam above. Its only apparent object, as in a previous case, is to strengthen the upper dam, by diminishing the pressure upon it of its pond. The latter is fifty feet long and three feet in height above the water below it at the centre, which, as it is three feet deep, gives a total height of six feet to the structure at this point.

The highest dam, of which I have gained a knowledge, is situated on a tributary of the Pishikeeme River, in township 49, range 30, and section 34, about ten miles north of the east end of Michigame Lake. It is constructed in a gorge between high hills. As described to me by William Bass and Paul Pine, two native Ojibwa trappers, who have seen it many times, it is the highest of all the dams known in the Lake Superior region. It is about thirty-five feet long, twelve feet in vertical height, and with a slope of interlaced poles on its lower face upwards of twenty feet in length. I have not been able to visit this re-

markable structure and ascertain its dimensions by
actual measurement; but, judging from the character
and extent of the other erections of the beavers
within this area, I see no reason for disbelieving the
statement.   It was named and described by them as
the highest beaver structure within their knowledge.

Some of the dams in this region are not less remarkable for their prodigious length, a statement of
which, in feet, would scarcely be credited unless verified by actual measurement.   The longest one yet
mentioned measured two hundred and sixty feet, but
there are dams four hundred, and even five hundred
feet long.

There is a dam, in two sections, situated upon a
tributary of the main branch of the Esconauba River,
about a mile and a half northwest of the Washington
Mine.   One section measures one hundred and ten,
and the other four hundred and twenty feet, with an
interval of natural bank, worked here and there, of
one thousand feet.   A solid-bank dam, twenty feet in
length, was first constructed across the channel of the
stream, from bank to bank, with the usual opening,
for the surplus water, five feet wide.   As the water
rose and overflowed the bank on the left side, the dam
was extended for ninety feet until it reached ground
high enough to confine the pond.   This natural bank
extended up the stream, and nearly parallel with it,
for one thousand feet, where the ground again subsided,
and allowed the water in the upper part of the pond
to flow out and around into the channel of the stream
below the dam.   To meet this emergency, a second
dam, four hundred and twenty feet long, was constructed.   For the greater part of its length it is low,

but in some places it is two and a half and three feet high, and constructed of stick-work on the lower, and with an earth embankment on its water face. In effect, therefore, it is one structure fifteen hundred and thirty feet in length, of which five hundred and thirty feet, in two sections, is artificial, and the remainder natural bank, but worked here and there, where depressions in the ground required raising by artificial means. As this dam had been cut through, and the water drawn out of the pond about two years before I visited and measured the work in 1866, it was then falling into decay.

Three miles north of Clarksburg, in the southeast quarter of section 25, there are three large beaver dams, constructed on the same stream, and from a quarter to a third of a mile apart. They are situated upon an affluent of the main branch of the Esconauba River. The first or lower dam measured three hundred and eighty-five feet in length, and is a large structure throughout its entire extent. It was four feet high where it crossed the channel of the stream, and three feet high for two-thirds of the remainder of its length. Along this stream the prevailing trees are spruce, tamarack, and cedar, interspersed with poplar, with the latter of which the dam was constructed. As the poplar is a soft wood, larger, and often shorter billets were used, than in the dams previously described. This dam, in external appearance, was much inferior to those made of hard wood. The upper dam measured five hundred and fifty-one feet in continuous length along its crest. Divided into sections it gave the following vertical elevations:

First section of 84 feet................................. 3 feet high.
Second   "   100 "   2   "
Third   "   100 "   .... 1 foot 6 inches.
Fourth   "   100 "   .... 1 foot.
Fifth   "   100 "   .... 9 inches.
Sixth   "   67 "   6   "
                         _____
Total length,   551 feet.

For two hundred feet on the east end of the dam, which was its lowest part, it was carried up the stream parallel with its course, and a few rods in front of the rising ground which formed its bank. Here it was constructed almost entirely of mud and sod. This left a narrow channel of water along the crest of the dam, which answered the purposes of a canal, the ground being a swamp on either side. In places it was simply a ditch, excavated in the soft wet earth, the materials being thrown up in the form of a continuous embankment on the lower side, thus forming a low dam with a narrow water channel on the upper side. The excavation was from two to three feet deep, and the embankment rose about six inches high. This seems scarcely credible, especially as it resembled so closely the work of the spade, but nevertheless it was the handiwork of beavers.

A mile and a half southwest of the mine last named, there is another very fine beaver dam three hundred and eighty feet long, and unusually high and broad throughout its entire extent. It will average three feet high for two hundred feet, and at the centre it is four feet high, and quite massive. The amount of solid materials in this structure is not less than in that at Grass Lake. Mr. John Armstrong, before mentioned, with whom I spent a part of a night upon this dam, captured thirteen beavers upon it in the fall and winter of 1865. There are three lodges upon the borders of the pond, which would give to them, before they were disturbed, twenty-one beaver occupants, by the usual rule of computation. There were also two beaver canals connected with the pond.

In the year 1862, I heard, through Capt. Daniel Wilson, of a long dam, constructed upon a small brook which falls into Carp River high up on this stream; and went with him to ascertain its length by measurement. This dam is marked No. 19 on the map. It proved to be a fine structure, and of extraordinary length. On careful measurement with a tape-line, following the crest of the dam, we found its total length on a continuous line to be four hundred and eighty-eight feet. For two hundred feet, from its commencement on the left bank of the stream, it is one of the most perfect and artistically formed structures in the Lake Superior region, although not so high, and, for this reason, not equal to that at Grass Lake. The pond was full to the crest of the dam, thus showing that it was occupied by beavers, which fact was afterward further confirmed by opening the lodges upon its borders. It seemed to me to be very desirable to perpetuate this dam in a photograph while in its present perfect condition; not so much to show the best part of the work, as to verify, in a manner that would admit of no future question, the fact of its extraordinary length when considered in connection with the limited physical powers of its architects. This desire was strengthened by the further consideration that these dams begin to decay as soon as they are deserted by the beavers, and quickly thereafter disappear; and that in no case do the latter remain in any district long after the establishment of the first settlements in their vicinity. If anything was done, therefore, it was imperative that it should be done immediately. Having ascertained that my friend, Rev. Josiah Phelps, Rector of St. Peter's Church at Marquette, had an excellent instrument, and the necessary chemicals, which, with his skill, he was willing to place at my disposal, and that Mr. Walter Kidder, who, like Mr. Phelps, was an amateur photographer, was willing to assist in the work, a programme was arranged among us to secure a photographic representation of this interesting structure. As a conclusion to the subject of beaver dams, I propose to give some account of the manner in which this enterprise was accomplished.

At the time the photograph was taken, the Marquette and Ontonagon Railroad, which now passes within a mile of this dam, was not completed beyond the Lake Superior Mine; but a very good trail had recently been cut out which, passing within half a mile of its site, made it comparatively easy of access. It was necessary, as a preparatory measure, to cut away the forest for some distance below the dam, and to clear the latter of grass and weeds. The area immediately below was heavily wooded with tamarack, cedar, and spruce, interspersed with thickets of alder and willow upon the lowest ground. To prepare the dam for being photographed, and to arrange the stations for the instrument, I went in with a party of men in advance, and commenced the work. Having previously ascertained that the instrument would take, upon a ten-inch plate, fifty feet of the dam measured in a straight line, when stationed at a distance of sixty-two feet, and show its structure with sufficient minuteness, we adopted a plan to photograph it upon seven such plates. In the first place, eight stations were established, and flag-staffs erected, defining the space assigned to each plate. Of these, the first six were in a straight line, and each was in, or near the crest line of the dam. At the sixth station the general direction of the dam inclined down stream, with which divergence the last two were made to correspond. We then cut a line ten feet wide through the thickets of willow and alder, removing the forest trees as well, running it parallel with the flag-staffs, and sixty-two feet below them. This line was for the movement as well as to afford a position for the scaffold for the instrument. After this, it was necessary to determine the position for the scaffold in front of each section of fifty feet of the dam, and then to cut out a triangular opening between the two, having its apex at the scaffold station. It was further found advisable to make the first section of the dam, commencing at the end on the right, seventy feet long; the second, third, fourth, fifth, and sixth, each fifty feet; and the seventh and last, seventy feet. The first plate taken was to be of the second section, with the scaffold immediately in front of its centre, and the second of the first section, by turning the instrument to the right, and not otherwise changing its position. At this angle it would embrace the whole seventy feet, as well as make the background harmonious as to these two plates. After that the scaffold was to be removed successively to the centre of each remaining section on to the sixth, from which point the last section of seventy feet was to be taken by turning the instrument to the left, without changing its focal position, as done in the previous case. This would give to the seven plates a lineal length of three hundred and ninety feet, and an actual length of dam, measured upon its sinuous crest, of four hundred and twenty-six feet. The dam, for the last-named length, is shown in the plates, with the background of the pond and surrounding forest three times repeated in the three central plates. Besides this, however, a portion of the dam sixty-two feet long is not shown. When the dam had approached within six feet of the bank on the left side, it turned directly down stream parallel with it, and was extended for the distance last named, when it finally terminated in the bank; thus forming a narrow canal which followed the dam down to its extreme end. The point where it turns is concealed from view by a clump of cedar-trees which are seen in the left end of the plate. Two days were expended by this advance party in cutting out the several lines, establishing the stations, and in making a commencement of the work.

On Tuesday, the 30th day of September, 1862, with the instrument and chemicals packed in boxes, we went up the railroad from Marquette to the Superior Mine, where we organized and provisioned our party for an encampment of several days at the dam, some six miles distant. The next day proved unfavorable, with mist and rain, but we reached our destination without accident to the materials, erected two brush-camps, framed and put together a movable scaffold twelve feet high, with a ladder to mount it, and finished clearing away the area in front of the first two sections. The work of chopping was also continued, as we found it necessary to cut down and remove all the trees for twenty-five feet in width along the entire front of the dam, as well as from the triangular space in front of each scaffold station. Besides this, the dark tent for preparing the plates was also erected. When, at a late hour, we sat down to our dinner, in this secluded place, our party of nine men, with their camps under the shade of the tall tamaracks, and the great dam stretching across from hill to hill, presented quite a novel spectacle.

The next day, Thursday, came out clear and bright, and we commenced early. Section two was first taken, and the attempt proved successful; then section one, and after that section three, with equal success. After this, the fourth plate was tried and failed; three other plates of the same section were also successively tried and failed; whereupon, at four o'clock, we gave up for the day, except the work of chopping and clearing, which were continued to the last hour of our stay.

About ten o'clock that night it clouded up, and soon thereafter we had wind and rain. Friday morning came in with fog and mist, which lasted throughout the day, with a breaking up toward evening, but no sun. We took two other plates of section four, and decided to keep the last. On the afternoon of this day I made a new and careful measurement of the dam, with the result given below, and also opened and measured the two lodges appurtenant to the structure. The next day would be Saturday, and our last chance, and we had three plates yet to take. As we were six miles from the nearest habitation

and twenty-three from Marquette, we would be compelled to break up our encampment at noon to reach
town that night, where my friend, the rector, was
needed to officiate in another capacity on the ensuing
Sabbath. I began to fear for the residue of my picture,
as the night set in rainy, with thunder and lightning.
Morning came, bringing with it no sun, but a gale of
wind, which set the tall tamaracks crashing down
around us. Those, against which our camps were
constructed, were twisted off; but as the wind came
down the pond, we were safe in the open space below
the dam, and besides this, it soon lifted the clouds.
Having moved the scaffold the day previous to the
front of the fifth section, with the first appearance of
sunlight this section was taken successfully on the
first trial, after which it was removed to the fifth and
last position, from which the sixth and seventh plates
were taken with equal success. As the last three
plates, like the first three, were taken in sunshine
more or less strong, while the fourth was taken under
heavy clouds, we moved back the scaffold in front of
the latter section, tried again and succeeded, and our
work was done. We then packed up our materials,
broke up our camp, and returned to the railroad station in time for the last train to Marquette; having
accomplished, whether important or otherwise, the
undertaking of preserving a permanent memorial of
this remarkable beaver structure.[1]

The pond covers about twenty-five acres of land,

---

[1] The photographs put together make a picture six feet and
eight inches long. It was expected, when the text was written,
that this dam would be engraved.

and continues across the entire length of the dam, although quite narrow upon its left half.

Measurements.

	Straight line.	Crest line of dam.
First section	70 feet.	83 feet 6 inches.
Second section	50 "	58 " 6 "
Third section	50 "	65 " 6 "
Fourth section	50 "	60 " 6 "
Fifth section	50 "	57 " 6 "
Sixth section	50 "	57 " 6 "
Seventh section	70 "	54 " 6 "

Here the dam turns down stream 10 ft. from bank, and runs 62 "

Total length of dam measured on crest line,   488 feet.

Other Measurements.

	At 50 ft. from end.	At 85 ft. from end.	At 144 ft. from end.	At 200 ft. from end.	At 260 ft. from end.	At 317 ft. from end.	At 375 ft. from end.
	Ft. In.	*Ft. In.*	*Ft. In.*	*Ft. In.*	*Ft. In.*	*Ft. In.*	*Ft. In.*
Slope of lower face	3 6	8 6	10 8	8	8	6	5
Slope of water face	8	10	12	9	8	7	6
Depth of water at end of slope	7	8	9	7	5	5	4
Vertical height of dam	2 2	3 2	4 9	2 8	1 8	1 8	1 8

This dam is a continuous work from one end to the other. In two or three places there is a natural rise of the ground as high as the top of the dam for a few feet in length, but the inner slope is banked with earth, and the summit worked. There are other places where the embankment is solid, showing very little wood intermixed, but it is artificial. The depth of the pond a few feet back, or at the end of the water slope, does not necessarily show the original ground surface, as earth may have been brought up from the bottom to place upon the dam; and yet the removal of the earth from a point so near would seem to endanger the work, and to be for this reason improbable. Taken as a whole, and as a beaver structure, it is an extraordinary piece of animal mechanism, whether considered with reference to its great length, the amount of materials it contains, or its artistic appearance. It has undoubtedly been built upon and repaired year after year until it reached its present dimensions; and it is not in the least improbable that it has existed and been continued for centuries.

There are other districts in North America where beaver dams are not less numerous than in the regions bordering upon Lake Superior. Along the Rocky Mountain chain, for a distance of more than two thousand miles, there are particular localities, on both sides of the range, where these erections are found in considerable numbers. They are also numerous in the streams which flow from the Wind River, the Big Horn, and the Laramie Mountains, and from the Black Hills, but they are usually small, ranging from fifty to one hundred feet in length, and from two to three feet high. On Eagle River and other tributaries of the Colorado, and upon the affluents of the Rio Grande, near its sources, beaver dams of considerable magnitude have been noticed by explorers. In the thick wood country along Hudson's Bay, and for a circuit of three hundred miles around and back of its shores, they are especially numerous. From general descriptions of these dams, obtained from various sources, and particularly from trappers, with whom these several regions are familiar, it is evident that they are all constructed on the same general plan, and in the same manner as the varieties herein described. Dams constructed of cotton-wood and willow, of which I have seen a number of specimens on the tributaries of the Upper Missouri, between the Yellowstone and the Rocky Mountains, are inferior in appearance to those in which hard wood is used, as in the Lake Superior region; but the differences do not affect the stability or efficiency of the structures.

Before concluding the subject of beaver dams, one other variety remains to be noticed, which in novelty surpasses all others. In Montana Territory three beaver dams have been discovered in a petrified state. They were found upon a small stream that runs through the Point Neuf Cañon, and empties into the Snake River, one of the tributaries of the Columbia. This cañon is about three hundred miles north of Salt Lake City. In length these dams are from fifty to sixty feet, with a fall of water over two of them, at the centre, of from three to four feet, and over the third of about one foot. They were not in that complete and final state of petrifaction which involves the change of every particle of the original woody materials, and the substitution of solid substances; but rather incrusted with lime, which, penetrating and solidifying the entire structures, had given to them a permanently durable form. It seems not a little singular that Nature should thus wrap up with her kindly and preserving hand these memorials of the skill and labor of the beaver, and hold them as a part of her vast record of the past. My friend, Prof. Henry A. Ward, of the University of Rochester, discovered these dams while engaged in a geological exploration in Montana, in the year 1865, and from him I received the above account.

CHAPTER V.

BEAVER LODGES AND BURROWS.

Habits of Beaver—Our Knowledge limited—Indians and Trappers as Observers—Source of Buffon's Extravagant Statements—Disposition of Beavers to pair—The Family—Outcast Beaver—Beaver Migrations—Adaptation to Aquatic Life—Suspension of Respiration—Length of Time—Artifice of Musk-Rat—Burrowing Propensities—Varieties of the Beaver Lodge—Island Lodge at Grass Lake—Size and Form—Chamber—Floor—Wood Entrance—Beaver Entrance—Their Artistic Character—Bank Lodge—Mode of Construction—Chamber—Entrances—Another Variety of Bank Lodge—Chamber and Entrances—Nature of Floor—Lake Lodge—Differences from other Varieties—False Lodge of Upper Missouri—Lodges Single Chambered—Burrows, their Form, Size, and Uses—Examples, with Measurements—Number of Beavers to the Lodge—Number of Lodges to the Pond.

NOTWITHSTANDING our familiarity with the beaver, through the persevering efforts made for his capture by both American and Indian trappers, the amount of our minute information concerning him is not as large as might have been expected. Any attempt to pronounce definitely upon his habits and mode of life will lead us into errors, if we pass beyond such facts as are susceptible of verification. These facts, from the nature of the case, are difficult of ascertainment. Although not exclusively nocturnal in his habits, the beaver performs the principal part of his work at night. He is both shy and timorous of disposition, and, when seen, it is usually by accident, for a brief space of time, and when engaged in one particular act. No single observer, however favorable his opportunities, could cover the field, for which reason it is necessary to collect and compare the observations of a large number of persons to ascertain even the principal facts. While, therefore, their artificial erections speak for themselves, their habits, in other respects, can only be determined by a series of authenticated acts, in the ascertainment of which the greatest caution should be used. There is enough, within the limits of the veritable, which is sufficiently remarkable, without entering the domain of fancy to produce a picture.

The Indian is a close, and, in the main, an accurate observer of the habits of animals. Without hesitation he places the beaver in the highest rank among them for intelligence and sagacity. It is also a part of the vocation of the white trapper to be versed in their characteristics and manner of life to prosecute efficiently his calling. From these sources of information, and particularly from the last, the extravagant statements concerning the domestic economy of beaver communities were derived, which Buffon was among the first to adopt and promulgate under the sanction of his distinguished name. The reaction which followed the disproval of these fictions tended rather to arrest further investigation than to turn it in the right direction; so that from Buffon's time to the present but little progress has been made in our knowledge of this animal. After considerable intercourse with Indian and white trappers on the south shore of Lake Superior, in the Hudson's Bay territory, and upon the Upper Missouri, I have been able, through them, to verify but a small number of facts tending to establish, as well as to illustrate, the habits and mode of life of this long-observed rodent. At the same time the amount of speculative opinion with reference to his ways, which is cherished and believed among them, is very great. To reject all their conclusions, for want of complete verification, would be not less unwise than to adopt them unconditionally. It will, therefore, be my plan to state, as facts, such only as I can assert upon personal observation, or have verified upon reliable testimony; and to introduce, from time to time, in addition thereto, such statements and conclusions of other persons, and upon their authority, as have a probable basis of truth; leaving their verification or disproval to future investigators.

Beavers are social animals in an eminent degree. This disposition is manifested in their strongly developed propensity to pair and live in the family relation. It is still further exemplified by the construction of dams, lodges, burrows, and canals for objects which are common to them as a family; and by providing a store of subsistence for winter use. A beaver family consists of a male and female, and their offspring of the first and second years, or, more properly, under two years old. The females bring forth their young, from two to five at a time, in the month of May,[1] and nurse them for a few weeks, after which the latter take to bark. I have seen upon the Upper Missouri a domesticated beaver of three weeks old sustain himself upon twigs of cotton-wood. They attain their full growth at two years and six months, and live from twelve to fifteen years. This last statement is upon Indian authority. The cry of a young beaver re-

---

[1] The rutting season is in the month of February.

sembles very closely that of a child a few days old. A trapper illustrated to the author the completeness of his deception by this cry, when he first commenced his vocation in the Rocky Mountains, by relating the following incident: he was once going to his traps when he heard a cry which he was sure was that of a child; and, fearing the presence of an Indian camp, he crept in cautiously through the cotton-wood to the bank of the stream, where he discovered two young beavers upon a low bank of earth near the water, crying for their mother, whom he afterward found in one of his traps. On one occasion I was similarly deceived in an Indian lodge at the mouth of the Yellowstone River, where a young beaver was lapping milk from a saucer while an Indian baby was pulling its fur. It was not until after several repetitions that I noticed that it was the cry of the beaver instead of the child. When the first litter attain the age of two years, and in the third summer after their birth, they are sent out from the parent lodge to seek mates and establish families for themselves, in which movement they are followed by each successive litter upon the attainment of the same age. Such at least is the uniform testimony of both Indian and white trappers, in support of which they assign the following reasons: first, that when they capture an entire family in one lodge or burrow, which is not unfrequent, they rarely, if ever, find more than two old beavers, the remainder being under two years old; and that the usual number found in one lodge ranges from four to eight, and rarely exceeds twelve: secondly, that these numbers exhaust the accommodations of the lodge: thirdly, that old beavers are jealous of, and hostile to their young after they attain maturity: and, lastly, their well-known propensity to pair. A fanciful notion prevails among the Indians, that if young beavers, thus sent out, fail to pair, they are allowed to return to the parent lodge and remain until the ensuing summer; but as a mark of parental disapprobation, for their ill matrimonial success, they are required to do the work of repairing the dam. There is another ramification of the same conceit, to the effect that if they fail again to mate in the ensuing summer, they are not allowed to return a second time, but that they become from thenceforth "outcast beavers." The existence of such a class is believed in, to some extent, both by the Indians and trappers, and the two notions together furnish the only foundation for the fiction at one time believed that there was a class of slave beavers.[1] These "outcasts," so called,

---

[1] This belief in the existence of a class of slave beavers appears to have been of Arabian origin. In the "Wonders of Creation," by Kazwini, an Arabian author who wrote in A.D. 1288, is the following account: "The beaver (kundur) is a land and water animal that is found in the smaller rivers of the country Isa [north of the present government of Novgorod]. He builds on the bank of the river a house, and makes for himself in this an elevated place in the form of a bench; then, on the right hand, about a step lower, one for his wife, and on the left, one for his young ones, and on the lower part of the house, one for his servants. His dwelling possesses in the lower part an egress toward the water, and another higher one toward the land. If, therefore, an enemy comes on the water side, or the water rises, he escapes by the egress leading to the land; but if the enemy comes on the land side, by that which leads to the water. He nourishes himself on the flesh of fishes and the wood of the *Chelendech* (? willow). The merchants of that country are able to distinguish the skins of the servants from that of the masters; the former hew the *Chelendech* wood for their masters, drag it with their maw, and break it

are probably such beavers as, having lost their mates, refused afterward to pair, and led thenceforth solitary lives in burrows.

Beavers migrate from place to place more or less every season, and particularly when a district becomes overstocked. There is an annual migration down the Missouri River, usually in the month of June, which becomes the more marked from the inability of the migrants ever to find their way back against its powerful current.[1] The Indians affirm that in their local migrations the old beavers go up stream, and the young go down, assigning as a reason that, in the struggle for existence, greater advantages are afforded near the source than lower down upon any stream, wherefore the old beavers wisely appropriate the former.

For his aquatic life, he needs, as well as possesses, special organic adaptations. He is not only capable of suspending respiration for an interval of several minutes while swimming under water, but also of putting forth, at the same time, his full physical strength. With a relatively small heart and lungs, his respiration is necessarily moderate in amount; but

---

in pieces with their forehead, so that in consequence of this office the hair of the head falls out on the right and left side. The merchants, who are aware of this fact, recognize in the hair of the forehead thus rubbed off the skin of the servant. In the skin of the master this mark of recognition is wanting, as he employs himself with catching fish."—(Brandt, Mémoires de l'Académie de S. Petersbourg, tome vii. 349.)

[1] A trapper whom I met on the Missouri River, in 1862, below Fort Piere, in Nebraska, informed me that the beavers were then (May 27) coming down the river; that he saw them daily, and had taken over fifty.

as the blood must circulate while respiration is suspended, other and independent vessels are provided near the heart for its reception, where it accumulates until respiration is resumed. If this blood were thrown upon the lungs while their functions were suspended, it would produce suffocation. It is said that he will swim a quarter of a mile under water without coming to the surface. Trappers differ as to the time he will remain under water, but agree in placing it between five and ten minutes. Mr. Atchinson, a Lake Superior trapper, informed me that he once held a beaver, caught in a trap, under water for the full space of ten minutes, as he believed, without extinguishing life. In the winter they are often compelled to swim fifty and a hundred rods under the ice to find open water; and they have been seen to take in a fresh cutting, through a hole in the ice, and swim with it for thirty rods to their lodge.

The musk-rat, whose aquatic habits, and use of the pond, the burrow, and the lodge, affiliate him with the beaver, resorts to a singular but well-attested expedient to lengthen the period of suspended respiration, which may be mentioned in this connection. When swimming under ice he comes up to its lower surface, and, having expelled the air from his lungs, waits for a moment, and then, after drawing in again the bubbles of air, proceeds on his way. This fact has been confirmed to me by so many different observers, that I see no reason to disbelieve its truth. Whether the air, by its contact with the ice, recovered some property of which it had become exhausted, I leave as a question to those capable of its determination. It is claimed that the beaver resorts to the same expedient, but I have not been able to verify the fact.

The body of the beaver is nearly, if not perfectly, balanced upon his hip joints. From these points as fulcrums, and by means of his hind legs, feet, and tail, he has the full command of his bodily motions, particularly in the water, without depending upon his fore feet. In swimming, the propelling power is in the hind feet and legs, which are so furnished and articulated as to make him a rapid and powerful swimmer. For the same reason, when on land, his paws become liberated, and he is thus enabled to take up earth and stones, and, holding them under his throat, to carry them short distances, walking upon his hind feet; and also to handle sticks and limbs of trees. It is thus in his structural organization that we discover the possibility of his architectural skill.[1]

It is another characteristic of the beaver that he is a burrowing animal. Indulging this propensity, he excavates chambers under ground, and constructs artificial lodges upon its surface, both of which are indispensable to his security and happiness. The lodge is but a burrow above ground, covered with an artificial roof, and possesses some advantages over the latter as a place for rearing their young. There are

---

[1] The otter is balanced much in the same manner, but he is smaller, more slender, and more agile in his movements. As a swimmer he is superior to the beaver. He will pursue and capture a fish with ease and certainty. In swimming, his fore feet are not used, but are pressed back against his body, as in the case of the beaver. His bite sustains the statement of Aristotle with reference to the European otter, *minus* the fancy for hearing the cracking of the bones. (Supra, p. 36.)

reasons for believing that the burrow is the normal residence of the beaver; and that the lodge grew out of it, in the progress of their experience, by natural suggestion. This subject will be referred to again. We have before seen that one of the principal objects of the dam was the formation of a pond; thus showing a desire, on the part of its architects, to maintain a large body of water at a permanent level for some special use. We come now to inquire its uses, so far as they relate to the lodge and the burrow. There are several varieties of the beaver lodge, each of which is adapted to the peculiarities of its situation; but they collectively represent different applications of the same general principle of construction. Thus we find an island, a river bank, and a lake lodge, each of which has special characteristics. The same is true, in a less degree, of their burrows. Each will be considered in its order.

Where large ponds are formed by means of dams, it is not unusual to find small grass islands rising a few inches above the level of the water. These islands were probably produced by fallen trees which had been flooded and destroyed by the pond, and upon the decayed remains of which vegetation had sprung. In other cases there are islands of firm earth which chanced to rise naturally above the surface of the water. These, whether unsubstantial or firm, are generally selected as the sites for their lodges because of the additional protection which insulation affords.

The lodge represented in the engraving (Plate XIII.) is situated upon one of the low grass islands described, and is one of the two found in Grass Lake above the great dam. As it was engraved from a photograph, it

Plate XIII

From a Photograph.

P.S.Duval Son & Co.Phil^a

BEAVER LODGE   GRASS LAKE

is an accurate representation of a beaver lodge, and of its surrounding landscape. This lodge[1] is considerably above the ordinary size, and a good specimen. In the year 1860 I opened it, and measured its inner chamber. It was not accessible from the land without a boat, and we were compelled to fell a tree from the main land across to the island as a means of transit. When we reached it, we found it very unsubstantial; the turf, which was saturated with water, yielding under our feet with a rocking motion. The lodge was situated upon the edge of the island, and was girded around with a moat or trench about three feet wide, and from three to four feet deep, which opened out into the pond at the outer edge of the lodge. Externally it was a rounded and dome-shaped mass of poles and sticks, which were trimmed of their branches and stripped of their bark, and interlaced much in the same manner as those upon the lower faces of their dams. It was oblong in form rather than round, as will appear by the following measurements:

From the water level, on the right in the engraving, to the
  water level on the left, measured over apex of lodge..... 22 ft. 6 inches.
Width of lodge at base or water line............................ 16 "   4   "
From water level in front, to same on back side, measured
  over apex of lodge... 26 " 10   "
Width of lodge at base or water line, from front to back... 19 "   9   "
Vertical height of lodge above water level.................... 4 "   6   "

We commenced opening it at the top. A few of the poles on the surface were loose and easily removed, but at a few inches below the apex we found them so

---

[1] The Ojibwas call a beaver lodge *wig-e-wam'*, which is the same word they employ to designate their own bark house. When they make the distinction, they prefix the word for beaver, *ah-mick'*.

interwoven and imbedded in earth and loam, that it
was impossible to loosen them with our hands. About
a foot below the surface the walls were substantially
solid. With the aid of an axe, however, and after an
hour's hard labor, we succeeded in making an opening
through the roof about three feet in diameter, which
uncovered and disclosed the chamber very perfectly.

FIG. 9.

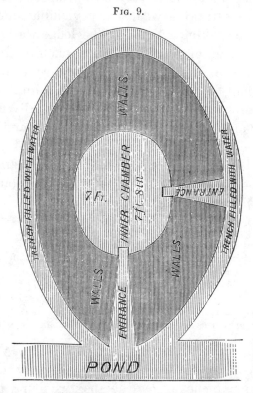

Ground Plan.   Island Lodge.

It is shown in the annexed figure (Fig. 9). The roof
had settled down in the centre from the superincum-
bent weight, but not so far as to interfere with the

accommodations of the chamber. It had no support under it of any kind whatever. After removing the materials which had fallen in from the roof upon the floor, we found the latter hard, smooth, and clean, with fresh-cut grass around the outer border for their nests; thus showing that it was an occupied lodge. In standing upon the floor of the chamber, the heel of a boot did not indent the surface, although it was but two inches above the level of the pond. This last fact was shown by the level at which the water stood in the entrances, two in number, which came through the floor in the outer edge of the chamber, as shown in the figure.

Measurements.

Longitudinal diameter of chamber .... 7 ft. 8 in.
Transverse... 7 "
Vertical height.. 1 ft. to 1 ft. 4 in.
Size of entrances through floor......................... 15 in. square.
Length of each entrance respectively .... 10 and 7 feet.

The roof was about three feet, and the side walls from four and a half to five and a half feet thick, which rendered it, as a structure, both strong and durable. Among the characteristics of the beaver is that of cleanliness in his lodges and burrows. Nothing appeared in this chamber to detract from his reputation in this respect. There was no opening for light or ventilation; but yet, from the porous nature of the materials, as put together, sufficient air would penetrate the lodge from without to satisfy the requirements of its occupants, whose low respiration enables them to endure the confined atmosphere of the lodge and the burrow. In the winter season, their breath, rising through the top of the lodge, dissolves the snow and forms a chimney opening over it, which not only continues their supply of air, but also reveals their habitation to the trapper.

The entrances to a beaver lodge, of which there are usually two, and sometimes more, are the most remarkable parts of the structure. They are made with great skill, and in the most artistic manner. In new lodges there is generally but one, but others are added with their increase in size under the process of repairing, until, in large lodges, there are sometimes three and four. These entrances are of two kinds. One is straight, or as nearly so as possible, with its floor, which is of course under water, an inclined plane, rising gradually from the bottom of the pond into the chamber; while the other is abrupt in its descent, and often sinuous in its course. The first we shall call the "wood entrance," from its evident design to facilitate the admission into the chamber of their "wood cuttings," upon which they subsist during the season of winter. These cuttings, as will elsewhere be shown, are of such size and length that such an entrance is absolutely necessary for their free admission into the lodge. The other, which we shall call the "beaver entrance," was the ordinary run-way for their exit and return. It is usually abrupt, and often winding. In the lodge under consideration, the wood entrance descended from the outer rim of the chamber outward about ten feet to the bottom of the pond in a straight line, and upon an inclined plane; while the other, emerging from the rim of the chamber at the side, descended quite abruptly to the bottom of the moat or trench, through which the beavers must pass, in open water, out into the pond. Both entrances were rudely arched over with a roof of interlaced sticks filled in with mud intermixed with vegetable fibre, and were extended to the bottom of the pond and trench, with the exception of the openings at their ends. At the places where they were constructed through the floor they were finished with neatness and precision; the upper parts and sides forming an arch more or less regular, while the bottom and floor edges were formed with firm and compacted earth, in which small sticks were imbedded. It is difficult to realize the artistic appearance of some of these entrances without actual inspection.

These lodges, at first small, and with contracted chambers, are enlarged, both in external size and in internal accommodation, by the process of repairing. After their winter cuttings are peeled of their bark for food, they are put out of the lodge, and, in due time, a portion of them are placed upon its roof to supply the waste by settlement and decay. Late in the fall, each season, the sides of their lodges, nearly to the summits, are, in some cases, plastered over with mud, which, soon freezing, materially increases their strength. The decayed portion of the walls and roof which form the chamber within are, from time to time, removed, which gradually increases its size. By the two processes of external addition and internal enlargement, continued through a series of years, a lodge is finally produced of the size represented in the engraving. The quantity of sticks, poles, and billets of wood used in its construction was about a cord.

It has elsewhere been stated that the entrances of these lodges were from two to three feet below the surface of the water in all cases, and that in this lodge the level of the water in the pond stood within

two inches of the floor of the chamber. In every
lodge opened I have found the floor but a few inches,
usually from two to six, above the level of the water.
The nearer the two to the same level, the easier the
introduction of their cuttings, which must be dragged
in with their teeth at no small exertion of strength.
From the uniform relation found to subsist between the
level of the floor and of the pond, it is evident that the
beavers regulate the discharge of the surplus water
through their dams with a view to the maintenance,
as near as possible, of a uniform level of the pond.
Any great variation, in this respect, would either
flood their habitations or expose their entrances; and
therefore the maintenance of their dams becomes a
matter of constant supervision and perpetual labor.
We discover also a reason why their principal repairs,
both of their dams and lodges, are deferred to the last
moment before going into winter quarters; since their
comfort and security are involved particularly in the
stability of their dams, which for months together,
during the winter, are beyond their control. In
choosing the sites of their lodges, so as to be assured
of water in their entrances and at their places ot
exit, too deep to be frozen to the bottom; in the adjustment of the floors of their chambers to the level
of the ponds; and in their appreciation of the causes
of a change of level in these ponds, as well as of the
remedy, decisive evidence seems to be furnished of
their possession of a *free intelligence,* as well as of
constructive skill.

One other circumstance remains to be mentioned
with reference to this lodge. It was opened and
measured, as before stated, in 1860. The following

year, while going again to Grass Lake dam for the purpose of obtaining a photograph of the same, I regretted the destruction of the lodge, of which a representation was not less desirable than of the dam. On reaching the lake, I was both surprised and gratified to find that the lodge had been completely restored by the beavers; and the engraving (Plate XIII.) shows the lodge as it appeared after it had once been partially destroyed, and again repaired, in the manner stated.

FIG. 10.

Island Lodge.   Side view.

In this figure of the lodge (Fig. 10), which was taken from the island, its long side is shown, together with the moat by which it is surrounded. The two engravings together represent a beaver lodge so faithfully and completely as to render unnecessary any further description of their external appearance. Both engravings were made from photographs of the original.

The number of lodges upon the largest ponds rarely exceeds four. In some instances six and eight have been found. Upon Grass Lake, as before stated, there

are but two, both of which are upon grass islands
within the pond.   There are none upon its banks.

Another, and equally common variety may be called,
by way of distinction, the bank lodge.   They are of
two kinds.   One is situated upon the bank of the
stream or pond, a few feet back from its edge, and entered by an underground passage from the bed of the
stream, excavated through the natural earth up into
the chamber.   The other is situated upon the edge of
the bank, a portion of it projecting over, and resting
upon the bed of the channel, so as to have the floor
of the chamber rest upon the bank or on solid ground,
while the external wall, on the pond side, projects
beyond it, and is built up from the bottom of the pond.
There is a lodge of this description near dam No. 14
represented in Plate IX.   Originally it was a fine
lodge; but when I opened and measured it, in 1860,
it had been deserted for two or three years, and
had fallen into decay.   A ground plan is given in
Figure 11.   One-fourth part of it, which represents
the thickness of the external wall, projects beyond the
bank into the river, while the remainder, which in-
cluded the whole of the chamber, was upon the land.
It was constructed in the same manner, and presented
the same general appearance, as the one last described.

Measurements.

Height of lodge, on river side, from bed of channel.   6 ft. 6 inches.
Height on land side..   3 ft. 6   "
Diameter on base line, on level of bank...............   12 ft.
Transverse diameter..   14 ft.
Diameter of chamber..   6 ft.
Height of chamber from floor of lodge...................   2 ft. 6 inches.
Height of floor above level of pond when full.........   3   "
Size of entrances through floor............................   15   "   square.
Thickness of walls and roof..................................   3 ft. to 3 ft. 6 inches.

The floor of the chamber was hard, level, and clean, with small quantities of dried grass scattered here and there, but much decayed; showing that the lodge had been for some time deserted. At the two points where the walls of the lodge intersect the banks were the entrances. As the dam had been cut

FIG. 11.

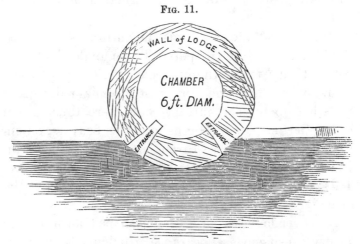

Bank Lodge. Ground Plan.

through and the river drawn down nearly to its original level, an excellent opportunity was afforded to examine these entrances where they came through into the chamber, and also the arched way which led down to the bed of the stream. The upper one was the wood entrance, or, at least, the most convenient for that purpose; although both were nearly straight, with a gradual descent, and surprisingly well constructed. The edges or rims of these passages, where they entered the chamber, were as hard, smooth, and regular as if finished with a mason's trowel; the covered way over each was constructed with a mass

of interlaced sticks, filled in with loam, and forming
a perfect roof; and the bed of each passage-way was
composed of earth, made solid by imbedded sticks,
and graded with a regular descent. There is nothing
—I repeat the statement—connected with the lodge
which excites so much astonishment as the mechanical skill displayed in the construction of these entrances.[1]

In lodges situated like this the entrances are called
the "angles" by the trappers. These angles had been
"staked out," to use the phrase of the trappers, some
years before, and the stakes still remained. Two
rows led up to each entrance, and were thus driven
in for the purpose of compelling the beavers, on entering the lodge, to pass through a narrow way, within
which the traps were to be set for their capture.
This is the usual method of trapping beavers at the
lodge.

A beaver lodge, from its dome-shaped form, makes
a very conspicuous appearance, particularly when it
is symmetrically formed and in perfect repair. But
they are neither as high nor as narrow at the base as
they have been usually represented; and the greater
proportion of them are much inferior to those described.

Lodges are more frequently situated a few feet
back from the edge of the bank than in any other
position. They are erected and maintained with less
labor, but they are usually smaller, and not as conveniently connected with the water as the varieties

---

[1] They are called *Ah-me-ko-ish'* by the Ojibwas, which signifies
" beaver door-way."

Plate XIV.

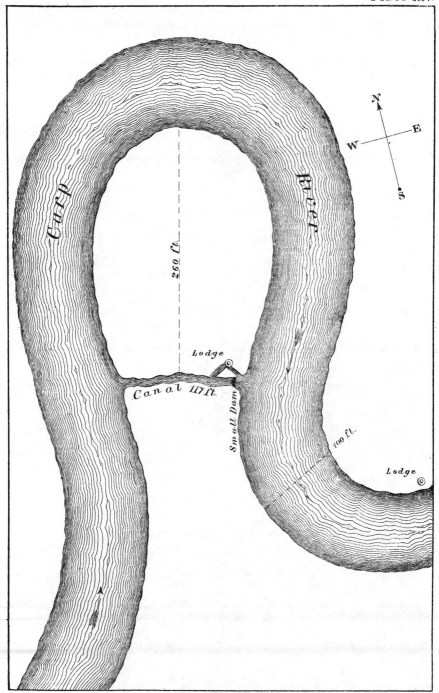

N
W — E
S

Carp
River
260 ft.
Lodge
Canal 117ft.
Small Dam
100 ft.
Lodge

BANK LODGE and BEAVER CANAL.

previously considered.   One other bank lodge only will be described, and it will differ from the last in being situated wholly upon land.   It is located on a neck of land formed by a bend in Carp River below dam No. 50, and is shown in Plate XIV.

Across the neck a beaver canal had been cut, about five feet wide on an average, and three feet deep, at one of the junctions of which with the river the lodge is situated.   The river here passes through low and swampy ground, and is broad and sluggish.   At high water there would be a current through the canal but for a small dam thrown across in front of the lodge, by which it is prevented.   The difference of level in the river at the two ends of the canal cannot exceed an inch.   In a subsequent chapter the nature and uses of the canals, which have occasionally been referred to, will be considered.

To reach this lodge we descended the river in a boat.[1]   It was opened and measured in September, 1862; it was of ordinary size and appearance, and gave the following external measurements:

From base, measured over apex, and parallel with canal. 16 feet 2 inches.
Diameter at base line 10   "
From base over apex at right angles with canal.............. 14   "   9 inches.
Diameter at base line................. 10   "
Vertical height of lodge above level of ground.......... 3   "
Height of ground above level of river ....   10 inches.

On the top of the lodge we found about three armfuls of the cuttings, of the previous fall, which had been denuded of bark and distributed irregularly over its roof.   Having removed the loose sticks and poles,

---

[1] My estimable friend, Rev. Henry Fowler, of Auburn, N. Y., was my companion on this occasion.

we came, at the depth of a few inches, to a mass of

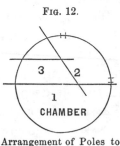

FIG. 12.

Arrangement of Poles to
form Roof of Lodge.

sticks and cuttings of various sizes imbedded in dry earth or muck, of which the roof was composed. When these materials had been removed and the chamber uncovered, we found the roof very cleverly supported by three poles, as shown in the diagram (Fig. 12). No. 1 was 6 feet 11 inches long, about 2 inches thick, and extended entirely across the chamber into the walls on either side. No. 2 was 4 feet 3 inches long, about $2\frac{1}{2}$ inches thick, and rested upon the wall and also upon pole No 1. And No. 2 was 4 feet long, of the same thickness, and rested the one end upon the wall and the other upon No. 2. Upon these was a network of smaller poles and sticks filled in with muck. The three principal poles formed a perfect and well-contrived support for the roof. Whether this was a new or an old lodge we had no means of ascertaining; and, therefore, it did not necessarily follow that they were so arranged by design. If an old lodge, these poles were probably once upon the top, and had come into their present position by the gradual progress of the settlement and decay of the materials underneath, which was followed by their removal from the roof of the chamber within as it was built upon above. The magnitude of the canal is an evidence of its great age, but this again is no evidence of the age of the lodge, which may have been erected after the latter was excavated. An examination of beaver lodges shows quite clearly that they can be continued for centuries by the simple process of repairing. Such is doubtless their history. New lodges would be demanded with an increase in numbers up to a certain limit, but otherwise they would not, in all probability, be constructed.

Around the outer rim of the chamber (Fig. 13) there was fresh dry grass for beds, which had evidently been recently cut from the meadows. In the centre of the floor there was a large quantity of old and decayed grass, damp and wet, on the removal of which a considerable depression of the floor was observable.

FIG. 13.

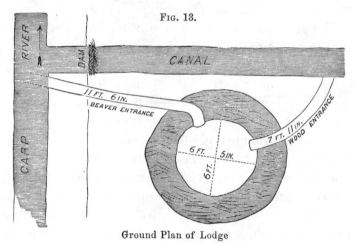

Ground Plan of Lodge

The above diagram shows the chamber and the position of the entrances.

Measurements.

Diameter of chamber parallel with canal............	6 feet 5 inches.
Transverse diameter..	6 "
Height of chamber at centre.............................	1 foot 9 inches.
Level of floor below ground.............................	6 "
Height of floor above water in entrances.............	4 "

For the purpose of ascertaining the nature of the floor we made an excavation, 1 foot and 9 inches deep, through a mass of small beaver cuttings imbedded in loam, of which it was composed, before we came to clear earth. They were mere twigs a few inches long and a quarter of an inch in diameter, and packed down in a solid mass. As the floors of beaver lodges are usually but three or four inches above the level of the water, and so near it as to become thoroughly saturated, it is extremely probable that they are, in all cases, made firm and solid in this way, partly by accident and partly by design. Without some such solidifying process these floors would soon turn into soft mire, and the chambers become uninhabitable.

The two entrances, as in the other cases, were the most interesting portions of the structure. One entered the canal, and from thence the river to go up stream; the other the river direct for going down stream. The former was nearly straight, with its bottom out to the canal a gentle slope; while the other descended quite abruptly as it emerged from the lodge, and then turning to the left, nearly at right angles, ran straight to the river. Both were neatly constructed, but one only, that which terminated in the canal, was adapted to the purposes of a wood entrance. We were able to run a pole through this passage from the point where it entered the chamber out into the canal, and obtain its length, together with its other dimensions, which were as follows:

Measurements of Wood Entrance.

Length of passage from rim of chamber to canal .... 7 feet 11 inches.
Width of same where it entered chamber...... .... 2 " 1 "
Width throughout to the canal, about............ .... 2 "
Depth of water in entrance just without chamber .... 11½ "
Roof of entrance above level of water, at same point........ 1 foot 5 "
Total height of entrance at same point.............. .... 1 " 7½ "
Depth of soil and roots above passage without lodge .... 1 " 3 "

The roof of the passage-way within the walls of the lodge, and for a short distance without, was rounded or arched quite regularly, and constructed with sticks; but for the remainder of the way to the canal it was ground excavation, the roof being strengthened by the roots of alder bushes under which it ran. After leaving the chamber, the roof of the passage-way descended so as to intersect the water at a distance of $3\frac{1}{2}$ feet, after which the passage was full of water out to the canal, which it entered 3 feet below the surface. The floor of the entrance or passage-way, just out of the chamber of the lodge, was sprinkled over with short and slender twigs of willow, about 6 inches long and $\frac{1}{4}$ of an inch thick, which were evidently designed for young beavers. They were green and fresh cuttings, some of them peeled of their bark and thrown out of the chamber, and others with the bark on ready for use. I made a small bundle of these tit-bits for young beavers, and preserved them as a memorial of this lodge.

The other, or beaver entrance, opened out from the chamber on the canal side, and, after descending for a short distance, turned abruptly to the left, after which it ran under ground nearly in a straight line to the river, as before stated.

Measurements of Beaver Entrance.

Width at edge of chamber................................	1 foot 8 inches.
Depth of water in same, at ditto........................	10 "
Height of entrance above water.........................	6 "
Total height from bottom to roof of entrance.......	1 foot 4 "
Length of passage-way..............	11 feet 6 "

Short cuttings might have been carried into the chamber through this passage, but not those of any

length.   Besides this, as they almost invariably transport their cuttings down stream, the other, from its
location, was the proper wood entrance.   As the river
was too shallow, on the lodge side, for their concealment, the beavers had excavated a channel, about 2
feet deep, in its bed for a distance of 25 feet out into
deep water.   The artificial character of this channel
was perfectly manifest.

We piled up the sticks and poles taken from this
lodge, and estimated the contents at half a cord.   It
was of the average size, and a fair specimen of these
structures.

With the minute description, now concluded, of
island and bank lodges, it will be unnecessary to
enter into details with reference to other varieties,
except to point out differences where they exist.

Fig. 14.

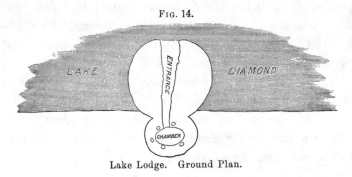

Lake Lodge.   Ground Plan.

It has elsewhere been stated that beavers inhabit
the small lakes as well as the flowing streams.   They
construct lodges upon their shores, which, as they are
usually shelving and have a hard bottom, render
some further variation in structure necessary.   The
lodge represented in the above ground plan (Fig. 14) is
situated upon the south shore of Lake Diamond, a few

rods above its outlet.   Two-thirds of it were built out upon the lake for the obvious purpose of covering the entrance as well as for its extension into deep water. It measured, on the line of the shore, seventeen feet over its summit, and twenty-four feet in the transverse direction, and was three feet and a half high. The chamber was between the five trees which were growing through the lodge and connected with the lake by a long passage-way within the lodge.   It was constructed of sticks and poles in the usual manner.   A few rods above there was another lodge built out upon the water in the same way and for the same object.   Similar lodges are found upon the shores of most of the lakes within the area embraced by the map.   They are chiefly interesting as illustrations of their capacity to vary the mode of construction of their lodges in accordance with the changes of situation.

The finest lodge I have seen was upon a grass island in Lake Flora.   It was remarkable for its regular and symmetrical proportions.   Externally it was a mass of naked poles and sticks, rather conical than dome-shaped, four feet high and sixteen feet over the apex.   Its base was smaller than usual, relatively to its height.   This lodge was the habitation of the beaver whose skeleton is represented in Plate III.   I first saw it in 1862.   In 1865 I went again to see it with the intention of obtaining a photograph, but found it deserted and going to decay.

Beavers are found upon the Missouri River from the mountains down to the mouth of the Big Sioux, along a distance of more than fifteen hundred miles, although the signs of their presence are not abundant

below the Yellowstone. Above the mouth of the last
named river their tree cuttings are seen in great numbers on the banks at intervals all the way to the

Fig. 15.

False Lodge, Upper Missouri.

mountains, with the exception of the district known
as the Bad Lands. They live in burrows in the banks,
but protect the entrances to them by a false lodge, as
shown in the figure. After the river has subsided to
its lowest level, which is shortly after the first of
September, they construct a lodge upon the bed of
the river and against its vertical bank. It is built of
sticks and poles of willow and cotton-wood, in the
precise manner of the lodges described, without being
intended for a residence, but instead of that, as a protection to the entrance to their burrow, which rises
from under this lodge back into the bank and well up
toward the surface, where the chamber or burrow is
excavated. The materials used in the construction
of this lodge furnish undoubtedly a portion of their
supply of winter wood, as well as a lodgment for
their short cuttings for the same purpose. With
the spring rise in the river most of these lodges
are swept away; but as the entrances to their bur-

rows are then deep below the surface of the water, the security of their habitations is not endangered until the river again subsides in the fall, when they are again reconstructed. I saw a number of these lodges between the Yellowstone River and the Rocky Mountains, in June, 1862, which had with-stood the great freshet of that year; and made the above sketch of one of them. The entrances or pas-sage-ways often extend back twenty feet into the bank, and each communicates with one or more under-ground chambers which are always found near the surface. Trappers who have opened them describe the chambers as small, but neatly formed and clean. Lodges are occasionally seen upon the river banks and upon the bottom lands, but from the extent of the cutting among the cottonwood-trees, which sometimes lay in piles upon each other, it is evident that most of the beavers inhabit the river banks.

Whether beaver lodges ever have more than one chamber is a question. It has been stated that two have been found, in some instances, one above the other. I have opened a large number of these lodges in dissimilar situations, and never found but one with two chambers, and these were upon the opposite sides of a fallen tree, over which the lodge was constructed. The chambers communicated with each other by water, though not directly. In some cases three or four lodges have been found in a cluster, and so near together as to have a common roof; on opening which it was ascertained that each had its separate passages to the water, and no communication with the others. They were separate lodges, built side by side, and probably at different periods; and were turned into one externally by the process of repairing in the manner previously stated. Two or three thus situated relatively are occasionally seen in the Lake Superior region. A Rocky Mountain trapper informed me that he had opened a lodge, upon one of the tributaries of the Missouri, which contained four chambers, each communicating with the other, and with the pond, and in one of which he found a quantity of cuttings stored for winter use. The other statement with reference to lodges with two chambers, one above the other, appears to be without foundation. As a general rule, the lodge has a single chamber, and where two or more are placed side by side, there is no connection between them.

In addition to the lodge, the same beavers, who inhabit it, have burrows in the banks surrounding the pond. They never risk their personal safety upon the lodge alone, which, being conspicuous to their enemies, is liable to attack. These burrows are the ultimate places of refuge to which they are more apt to retire than to their lodges, when disturbed on the land. Along their canals, also, the burrows are numerous, since while in their narrow channels they are more exposed than while in the ponds. These burrows are small underground chambers. They are entered by a passage-way, usually under the roots of a tree standing in the edge of a pond, which, with the chamber, are from ten to fifteen feet in length. As the entrances are always below the surface level of the pond, there are no external indications to mark the site of a burrow except one, and that occasional only, which will be hereafter noticed. A description of two or three of these burrows, with diagrams and measurements, will illustrate their character.

This burrow (Fig. 16) is on the east side of the lake, a few rods south of the outlet of Lake Diamond. There

FIG. 16.

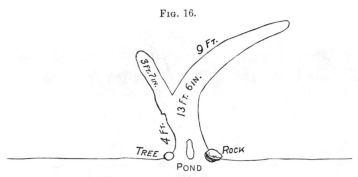

Ground Plan of Beaver Burrow at Grass Lake.

are two entrances, separated by a stone, and roofed over with roots and earth. The one upon the right side passes under the edge of a rock; the one on the left, under the roots of a tree; and both are two feet below the surface of the water. Within the distance of fifteen feet from the pond, the bank rose about seven feet above its level. The burrow rose also with the bank, so that at the distance of eight feet from its mouth, the roof of the burrow came within six inches of the surface of the ground above, and at its extreme end within three inches, the roots of the overspreading forest trees forming a covering of sufficient strength. It was evidently carried thus near the surface for the admission of air through the ground roof. The chamber, in its most capacious portion, was a foot high and twenty inches wide. With its branches it would afford ample accommodations for a beaver family. I found it accidentally by observing a small opening into it at its extreme end, which enabled me to open the remainder of it easily for the purpose of measurement. The breach previously made had destroyed it for beaver use.

FIG. 17.

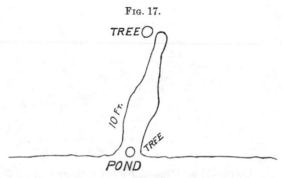

Ground Plan of second Beaver Burrow at Grass Lake.

About twenty feet above the great dam, and upon the south side of the pond, is the burrow represented in the above figure (Fig. 17). It ascends with the bank, which it enters under the roots of a tree, is ten feet long, and has a chamber twenty inches in width and a foot high. It terminates under the roots of a pine-tree, where its roof comes within four inches of the surface of the ground. It is a good specimen of the ordinary burrow.

North of the Cleveland Mine there is a natural pond, shown on the map, which will be more particularly described hereafter. The canals which enter it have a number of burrows upon their upper portions, one of which is represented in the figure (Fig. 18). This burrow is shown in Plate XVIII., and is the one nearest to the pond. It was found open at the centre and also at the extreme end. The length of the passage-way from the canal was eleven feet, and this communicated with a chamber three feet two inches by two feet and a half in ground dimensions, and about ten inches high. The roof of the latter came near to the surface, and was formed chiefly of the roots of the clump of trees under

Fig. 18.

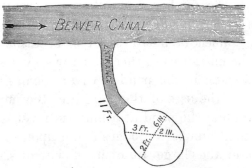

Ground Plan of Burrow on Beaver Canal.

which it was excavated. Water stood in the passage-way nearly to the chamber. It is a fine specimen of a burrow.

Fig. 19.

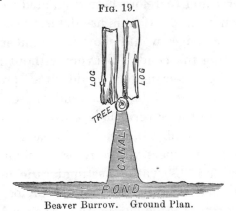

Beaver Burrow.   Ground Plan.

Burrows are often found excavated under fallen trees when lying near the pond. The above figure (Fig. 19) shows one of this description near dam No. 14. A canal about ten feet long and from three to four wide, leads up to the roots of a tree, back of which are two logs. The burrow was excavated under these fallen trees, which were much decayed, and the entrance to it was under the roots of the tree in front of them. No further description is necessary; and this, with the foregoing illustrations, sufficiently present the subject of burrows. The necessity for protecting the entrances to these burrows by a sufficient depth of water in the pond to cover them, illustrates still further the uses of the dam and the importance of maintaining the pond at a uniform level.

The small number of lodges found upon the largest ponds, and the large number of burrows, renders it probable that there are more beavers in every pond than the lodges can accommodate; and yet it is difficult to ascertain the truth of the matter. The lodges are undoubtedly warmer in the summer than the burrows, and therefore better adapted to the rearing of their young. If this use determined the number, then the lodges would show the number of families inhabiting the pond. Beavers without mates, or who have lost their mates, would, in all probability, lead solitary lives in burrows; and these, with the full families in the several lodges would, most likely, represent the number of beavers in each pond. At all events, the trappers, whose rules are founded upon experience and observation, estimate the number of beavers in each pond by the number of lodges, reckoning eight to the lodge in the Rocky Mountain region, and seven in that of Lake Superior.

In the Cascade Mountains, the beavers live chiefly in burrows in the banks of the streams, rarely constructing either lodges or dams. Upon this subject, Dr. Newberry, in his report on the Zoology of Oregon

and California, remarks: "The sides of these streams
are lined with their habitations, though we never saw
their houses, and seldom a dam; but usually their
burrows penetrated the sides of the streams, a sufficiently large and long excavation being made to form
warm, roomy, and comfortable quarters. We found
the beavers in numbers, of which, when applied to
beavers, I had no conception."[1]

The burrows of beavers inhabiting river banks are
said to be occasionally detected by a small pile of
beaver cuttings found heaped up in a rounded pile, a
foot or more high, at the extreme end of each burrow.
It is affirmed by the trappers, and with some show of
probability, that this is a contrivance of the beavers
to keep the snow loose over the ends of their burrows,
in the winter season, for the admission of air. I have
never seen these miniature lodges, and therefore cannot confirm the statement, either as to their existence
or use; but if, in fact, they resort to this expedient,
it is another reason for inferring that the lodge was
developed from the burrow with the progress of experience. It is but a step from such a surface-pile of
sticks to a lodge, with its chamber above ground, with
the previous burrow as its entrance from the pond.[2] A
burrow accidentally broken through at the upper end,
and repaired with a covering of sticks and earth would
lead to a lodge above ground, and thus inaugurate a
beaver lodge out of a broken burrow.

---

[1] Explorations for a Railroad Route, etc. to the Pacific. VI.
Zoology, 258.

[2] The Ojibwas call a burrow O-wazhé, whence the name
"wash," commonly used by the trappers to denote a beaver
burrow.

CHAPTER VI.

SUBSISTENCE OF BEAVERS.

Subsistence exclusively Vegetable—Kinds of Bark preferred—Roots of
Plants—Incisive Teeth Chisels—Their cutting Power—It diminishes with
Age—Provisions for Winter—Season for collecting—Felling Trees—
Their size—Number of Beavers engaged—Manner of cutting—Chips—
Short Cuttings—Moving them on Land—Floating them in Water—Sink-
ing them in Piles—Wood-eating—Evidence that they eat Clear Wood—
Brush-heap at Lodge restricted to Particular Places—Their Use—Ponds
in Winter—Winter Life of Beavers.

THE nutriment of the beaver is drawn exclusively
from the vegetable kingdom. They subsist principally upon the bark of deciduous trees. Where the
variety is large, they prefer, as is shown by their cuttings, yellow birch, cotton-wood, poplar, and willow.
These are their chief reliance. They also eat the
bark of the soft and bird's-eye maple, of the walnut,
and of the black and white ash, together with various
kinds of roots, such as those of the pond lily, and of
the coarse grasses that grow in the margins of their
ponds. Late in the winter they eat clear wood, and
such roots as they can reach from their burrows or
find in the banks. This subject of wood eating will
be referred to again. In the summer they rarely cut
large trees, but live upon the bark of the smaller ones,
upon willow and raspberry bushes, and upon different
kinds of roots. Notwithstanding the great abundance of food at this season of the year, they are usually the fattest in the winter.

As cutting instruments, they are armed with powerful incisive teeth, by means of which they are able to cut down forest trees of surprising size in comparison with their own diminutive forms. Their teeth are chisels in form and structure, and also in efficiency. When at the age of eighteen months, and from that on to two and three years old, their teeth, which during these periods are in a rapidly growing state, are in the best condition for cutting. After this, as they grow older, their teeth file down with constant use, and growing less rapidly, become dull and inefficient in cutting. It is said that the diminution of cutting power is so great that very old beavers are often unable to provide themselves with food sufficient for their sustenance during the winter, and, in consequence, become poor and feeble. A beaver of this description was caught, in the fall of 1864, on one of the dams of the Esconauba, and upon being shown to William Bass (Ah-shé-gos), an Ojibwa trapper extremely well versed in the habits of the beaver, he remarked that, "had he escaped the trap, he would have been killed by other beavers, before the winter closed, for stealing cuttings." Such beavers are often found dead, with gashes in their bodies, showing that they had been attacked by their associates, which occurrences the Indians explain in this way.

The thick bark upon the trunks of large trees, and even upon those of medium size, is unsuitable for food; but the smaller limbs, the bark of which is tender and nutritious, afford the aliment which they prefer. To cut down a tree, by persevering labor, in order to reach its limbs and branches, is of itself an act of intelligence and knowledge of no ordinary character. Their practice of cutting down trees is sufficiently well understood; but precise information is desirable as to the manner in which it is done, the size of the trees felled, and the way in which the limbs are reduced, removed, and stored for winter use. These topics will form the subject of the present chapter.

As beavers do not hibernate, they are compelled to provide a store of subsistence for the long winters of the North, during which their ponds are frozen over, and the danger of venturing upon the land is so largely increased as to shut them up, for the most part, in their habitations. In preparing for the winter, their greatest efforts in tree cutting are made. They commence in the latter part of September, and continue through October and into November the several employments of cutting and storing their winter wood, and of repairing their lodges and dams. These months are the season of their active labors, which are only arrested by the early snows and the formation of ice in their ponds. It is a feature of the climate of the Lake Superior region, and I presume it is equally true of that around Hudson's Bay, that the snows begin to fall before the frost has entered the ground, whence it is, that throughout the winter the earth remains unfrozen, under a deep covering of snow. In this we recognize a beneficent provision of the Creator for the welfare of the burrowing animals, without which many of them would perish. The beavers, as has elsewhere been stated, perform the most of their work at night; but they come out early in the evening, and continue at work during the early morning hours. For the remainder of the day they are rarely seen, except in regions where they are very numerous, or are entirely undisturbed by trappers. On the Upper Missouri I have seen them swimming in the river in broad day, and also basking in the sun on the tops of their false lodges under the banks. We brought down with us a young beaver caught with a scoop net, while swimming near the river bank. In the Lake Superior region I have seen them generally in the night, while watching on their dams for this purpose. By making a breach in their dams you can compel them to come out, but it will be late in the night before they show themselves, and they are so wary that it is extremely difficult so to conceal yourself in their immediate vicinity as to see them work. After ice has formed in their ponds, they retire to their lodges and burrows for the winter, and they are not seen again, either by day or night, except in rare instances, until a thaw comes, of which they take advantage to come out after fresh cuttings. It is said that the bark of their winter wood is apt to become soft and sour before spring from soakage in the pond, wherefore a mitigation of the severity of the winter, sufficient to open the ice in their ponds, is in every sense a providential relief.

In establishing their lodges so as to adapt them to winter occupation, and in the manner of providing their winter subsistence, the beavers display remarkable forethought and intelligence. The severity of the climate in these high northern latitudes lays upon them the necessity of so locating their lodges as to be assured of water deep enough in their entrances, and also so protected in other respects, as not to freeze to the bottom; otherwise they would perish with hunger, locked up in ice-bound habitations. To guard against this danger, the dam, also, must be sufficiently stable through the winter to maintain the water at a constant level; and this level, again, must be so adjusted with reference to the floor of the lodge as to enable them, at all times, to take in their cuttings from without, as they are needed for food. When they leave their normal mode of life in the banks of the rivers, and undertake to live in dependence upon artificial ponds of their own formation, they are compelled to forecast the consequences of their acts at the peril of their lives.

Before entering upon the subject of tree cuttings, it may be proper to make a slight reference to the character of the forests in the principal beaver districts referred to in these pages. On the Upper Missouri and its tributaries, cotton-wood is the prevailing tree, and willow the principal bush. In this region, therefore, as their favorite subsistence is both abundant and convenient of access, beavers have been found in the greatest numbers. Upon the Siskatchewun and its affluents, the forest growth is much the same, with a limited proportion of evergreen trees. Around Hudson's Bay and the shores of Lake Superior, the prevailing trees are the tamarack, the spruce, the hemlock, and the pine, but they are interspersed with the birch, the poplar, the maple, and other deciduous trees, and also with patches of willow upon the borders of the streams; which together furnish such an abundance of subsistence as to render them but little inferior to the first for beaver occupation. The only difference against the latter is the necessity for transporting their cuttings over longer distances. In California, Oregon, Washington, and British Columbia,

2.

I.

TREES CUT by BEAVERS

while evergreen trees are the principal forest growth, deciduous trees are sufficiently abundant for all the purposes of beaver maintenance. There was scarcely any portion of the original forest area of North America, except the exclusively pine tracts, where beavers could not sustain themselves in considerable numbers. Their greatest numbers, however, were found in those particular districts of country where the trees, whose bark was preferred, were found in the greatest profusion.

The engraving (Plate XV. Fig. 1) is from a photograph of an original specimen now in my collection. It was in the process of being cut down by the beavers in October, 1862, when my attention was called to it by some woodmen, who had observed it on the south shore of Lake Flora, near dam No. 2. I went to the place and secured it before the beavers had an opportunity to finish their work, which another night would probably have consummated, to the destruction of the symmetry of the cutting. The tree is a yellow birch, thirteen and a half inches in diameter below the incision, and twelve inches above, with a circumference of something over three feet. As the tree was green, and this part was removed before it had been exposed to the weather, the marks of the teeth are seen with entire distinctness over every part of the cut surface. The width of the incision up and down is eight inches, and it was commenced seven inches above the ground. It is evident that the process of cutting is round and round the tree continuously, and that the reduction is uniform until it is cut on all sides more than half way to the centre. After that, the remainder of the cutting varies; in some cases it is uniform until the tree falls, while in others it is the deepest on one side, toward which it is then most likely to fall; and from which the inference is drawn, with some degree of probability, that it was the intention of the beavers to fell it in that direction. Where the tree leans slightly, the deepest cutting is on the side opposite to the direction of its fall; and where it stands upon a side hill, it is often, when the tree is small, cut entirely upon the upper side. While gnawing down a tree, they sit up erect on their hind feet, which, being plantigrade, renders this posture natural and convenient for the body. Although I have not succeeded in witnessing the act, on the part of the beavers, of felling a tree, I have obtained the particulars from Indians and trappers who have. The usual number engaged in the work is but two, or a pair; but they are sometimes assisted by two or three young beavers. It thus appears to be the separate work of a family, instead of the joint work of several families. One tree of the size of this would furnish a sufficient amount of small cuttings for their winter supply. When but two are engaged they work by turns, and alternately stand on the watch, as is the well-known practice of many animals while feeding or at work. When the tree begins to crackle, they desist from cutting, which they afterward continue with caution until it begins to fall, when they plunge into the pond, usually, and wait concealed for a time, as if fearful that the crashing noise of the tree-fall might attract some enemy to the place. The next movement is to cut off the limbs, such as are from two to five and six inches in diameter, and reduce them to a proper length to be moved to the water and transported thence to the vicinity of their lodges, where they are sunk in a pile as their store of winter provisions. Upon this work the whole family engage with the most persevering industry, and follow it up, night after night, until the work is accomplished. The greatest number of beavers ever seen thus engaged by any of my informants was nine, while the usual number is much less. These somewhat minute particulars are so far important as they tend to show the existence of the family relation, as well as the number of the family; and they also have some bearing upon the question of the recognized right of property in cuttings. A fair consideration of ascertained facts tends to the inference that each family is left to the undisturbed enjoyment of the fruits of their toil and industry. The manner of reducing and removing limbs of trees will be further explained when we take up that class of cuttings.

Another and a larger tree cutting of the kind above described, I found the present season (August, 1866), and sent it to the Commissioners of the Central Park, New York. It is a yellow birch, seventeen inches in diameter below the incision, fourteen inches above, and shows a cutting entirely around the tree four and a half inches deep. The incision was not as deep relatively as in the other case; but it removed the whole of the sap-wood and a portion of the duramen. It was cut thus far in the spring of the present year, as the tree was still alive and in full leaf; and without doubt for the purpose of eating the chips, as few or none were found at the foot.

The second engraving (Fig. 2, Plate XV.) is also from a photograph of an original specimen in my col-

lection. As the tree lodged in falling, it did not break
at the point where it was cut. This tree was also a
yellow birch, and stood on the border of Grass Lake,
a few rods above the great dam. Since the deepest
incision was upon the pond side of the tree, it seemed
to have been their intention to fell it into the pond;
but their expectations in this respect, if indulged, were
disappointed; and further than this, their labor was
lost by the lodgment of the tree. It measures seventeen inches in diameter below the incision, and ten
and a half above it, with a circumference at the place
where it was made of three feet four inches. The cut
was commenced six inches above the ground, and
was twelve inches wide up and down the trunk of the
tree. This tree cutting was two years old when I
brought it away in 1861. It is quite a common practice with beavers to fell trees into ponds and lakes
for the purpose of submerging their branches, and
thus preserving them, with all their small shoots and
twigs, under water, where they may be accessible
throughout the winter under the ice. Along the
skirts of large ponds, where deciduous trees are found
growing, numbers of trees thus fallen into the pond
are seen; their conical stubs showing quite plainly by
whom they were cut down. I have a second tree
cutting precisely similar to this, the parts being un-
separated by the fall, measuring sixteen inches in
diameter below the incision, thirteen above it, and
three feet three inches in circumference at the point
where the incision was made.

Beavers occasionally cut the wild-cherry tree, although it is somewhat doubtful whether they eat its
bark. I found one of this description on the upper

part of Carp River, the present summer, which measured eighteen inches in its greatest diameter below the incision, and fourteen above. They had commenced and cut round the tree in two places higher up, finally completing the work at a third and lower place. It is an interesting specimen for this reason, although somewhat weather-worn, since it shows the appearance of a tree cutting at different stages of its depth. None of its branches were either cut or removed by the beavers. These rings show that the cutting was commenced near the close of winter, in deep snow; and that the deepest and lowest cutting was made after the snows had wasted nearly to the ground. As few chips remained, it was evident that the incision was made for the purpose of eating the wood. This specimen is now in the State Collection at Albany.

The foregoing are fair specimens, as to size, of the tree cuttings in the Lake Superior region, and are among the largest of the hard-wood trees usually cut down by the beavers. I have a number of specimens of all sizes from six to eighteen inches in diameter, all of which were cut in the same manner, and present the same external marks and conical form at the cut ends. Those described are not unusually large. I have seen many others of equal size at places inconvenient for removal. One yellow birch at the head of Lake Flora, partly cut down, measured five feet and four inches in circumference below the incision, and four feet and six inches above, with but nine inches in diameter at the centre still uncut.

The chips at the foot of a fresh cut tree are quite abundant, as well as objects of curiosity. I have an assortment of them, some of which measure three and a half inches in length, from an inch to an inch and a half in width, and about a quarter of an inch in thickness.

Fig. 20.

Beaver Chip.   Natural size.

The above representation (Fig. 20) shows the inner face of one of these chips.   Upon the end to the right are six distinct cuts, the first two of which are but half the width of a single tooth; while on the other, which is the thickest end, there are eight, some of which are, in like manner, but half the width of a single tooth.   It is made evident by running the inferior incisive teeth in a beaver's skull over these several cuts, that the upper incisors are used for holding, while the cutting is done by the inferior; and more than this, that but a single tooth is used at a time, the other following in the space made by the previous bite.   There is another fact which tends to confirm this explanation of the manner of cutting, which is that the chip is split inward toward the centre with each cut.   If both of the inferior incisors were cutting at the same time, the split would occur with each alternate cut; otherwise one of the teeth would be sprung.   These chips also show that the gnawing process is one of splitting as well as cutting.   The crowning surface of each cut is found to fit exactly the slight concavity in the inner side of the incisor. It will be observed from the sloping edges of the chip that each cut penetrated deeper than the one preceding it as they severally approach the centre, and that the split surface in the centre is less than an inch in length. From the size of this chip, and the number of distinct cuts upon it, some impression may be formed of the number and power of the bites necessary to gnaw down a tree of the diameter of either of those described; and yet it is said, by those who have witnessed the performance, that a pair of full-grown beavers will accomplish the work in two or three nights.

Cottonwood-trees are soft and easily cut. The largest trees ever fallen by the beavers are of this kind. I have seen them on the banks of the Upper Missouri twenty inches and two feet in diameter. One specimen in my collection, which I brought down this river from a point about a hundred miles east of the Rocky Mountains, measures sixteen inches in diameter, and was an ordinary specimen. It is represented in the group of cuttings (Plate XVI.), but partly concealed from view. Father De Smet, the well-known missionary to the Indians of the Columbia River, informed me that he had seen cottonwood-trees, cut down by beavers, thirty inches in diameter; and Dr. F. V. Hayden, that he had measured a cottonwood-tree, on the Yellowstone River, after it was cut down by them, of the same diameter. Lewis and Clarke, remarking upon the tree cuttings at the mouth of the same river, state that "the beavers have committed great devastation among the trees, one of which, nearly three feet in diameter, had been gnawed through by them."[1] After passing Fort Randall, in ascending the Missouri, the cottonwood-tree cuttings are seen in places in great numbers along a distance of a thousand or more miles to the mountains. At some points, as elsewhere stated, they are cut down in such quantities as to form piles of timber; but where these occur, the trees are usually small. On the Yellowstone River, where the quantity of cotton-wood is small and confined to the bottom lands, the beavers were making such havoc at the time of my visit (1862) that the Crow Indians had become seriously concerned about their own supply of wood. This may seem extravagant, and it probably was an unnecessary alarm: but it is also easy to discover that with beavers very numerous and the supply of wood limited, they might draw overlargely upon the supply.

Small trees and the limbs of large trees are cut into pieces of convenient length for transportation, and consequently must bear a definite relation to the physical powers of the animal. It is necessary to move them on land, from where they are cut, to the nearest accessible point in the pond, whence they are floated to the place where they are to be sunk to form a magazine of provisions for the winter. The larger, therefore, the limb is in diameter, the shorter must be the cutting in order to be movable. A comparison of a large number of these cuttings shows that when five inches in diameter, they are usually about a foot long; when four inches in diam-

---

[1] Travels, etc. Longman's ed., p. 146.

Plate XVI.

N°4

N°1

N°2

N°5

N°3

N°2

N°1

BEAVER CUTTINGS WINTER WOOD.

From a Photograph.

eter, they are about a foot and a half long; and when three inches in diameter, they are about two feet long. Poles from one to two inches in diameter are often found eight, ten, and twelve feet in length; and also cut up into short lengths from a few feet to a few inches long. Short cuttings of these dimensions they are able to roll for considerable distances, or drag with their teeth to the water; after which they are easily transported to the vicinity of their lodges and there sunk. I have, in my collection, a large assortment of these cuttings of every size and variety, a selection from which is represented in Plate XIV., engraved from a photograph of the originals.

The four separate pieces shown in the engraving which are marked No. 1, are bird's-eye maple denuded of bark. This portion of the tree was six feet long before it was cut into lengths, and from five to six inches in diameter. It will be observed that the cut ends are conical, showing that the beavers cut round and round, in the process of doing which it is necessary to turn the stick. One turning would probably suffice to cut a limb three inches in diameter; but one of the size of this would require several. The small tree from which these cuttings were made grew upon the border of the pond, and formed the part nearest to the root. While the remainder of the tree was cut up and removed, these were left from inability to take them away. Near the root of the tree there was a depression in the ground across which it fell, and when cut into lengths the pieces rolled down into the basin. The largest weighed eleven pounds and a half in its dry state, and the smallest six. Finding their removal impossible, they were stripped of their bark

and abandoned.   In moving cuttings of this description, they are quite ingenious.   They shove and roll
them with their hips, using also their legs and tails
as levers, moving sideways in the act.   In this manner they move the larger pieces from the more or less
elevated ground, on which the deciduous trees are
found, over the uneven but generally descending surface to the pond.   The tree cuttings are usually
within a few rods of the water, and are rarely found
at any great distance unless upon side hills which
favor their easy descent.   After one of these cuttings
has been transported to the water, a beaver, placing
one end of it under his throat, pushes it before him to
the place where it is to be sunk.   How they sink
them is a question.   The yellow birch, when fresh
cut, is of nearly the same specific gravity as water.
On trying the experiment with a piece of the size of
an ordinary cutting, I found that it would barely
float, the whole of it becoming submerged except a
small portion at one end.   It was evident that a few
hours of soakage would carry it to the bottom.   It is
sufficient to state the fact that piles of these cuttings
are found, late in the fall, sunk near their lodges in the
ponds,—except where brush piles are found, the uses
of which will hereafter be explained.   In amount
they vary from one-quarter to three-quarters of a cord,
while in occasional instances a full cord has been
found.   Pole cuttings, short bits, and brush are
dragged to the water with their teeth, and are generally moved through the water held in the same manner.   In swimming, the upper part of the head and a
small part of the shoulders only are out of water; so
that they are often seen with a stick or piece of brush

held in the teeth at one end, with the remainder
passing diagonally across the back. Captain Johnson
once saw a beaver swimming in Grass Lake, in the
daytime, with a small bundle of grass upon the top of
his head, which he was evidently transporting to his
lodge.

Beaver stick No. 2 in the engraving is a very interesting specimen, since it illustrates an intermediate
stage of the process of cutting branches of trees into
short lengths. It is a yellow birch, seven feet and a
half long, with an average of three and a half inches
in diameter. They commenced cutting it into seven
pieces, of which the first four were each about a foot
long, and the remaining three each about twenty
inches; and the work was going on at all of these incisions at the same time. Some of them were cut
about half through, the others less or more. The stick,
in other words, was ready to be turned for the completion of the work. To cut it entirely through from
the upper side would require an incision of such width
as to involve a loss of labor. Among the piles on
piles of cuttings seen and examined, I do not recol-
lect of ever finding one of hard wood of the thickness
of this cut entirely through from one side. There
was a prong at each end of this stick, the longest of
which is not seen in the engraving, which evidently
defeated their efforts to turn it over. Finding this
impossible, the stick was abandoned after stripping off
the bark on its upper surface. This specimen is interesting from the revelation it seems to make of the
manner of reducing the branches of trees. In the first
place, after felling a tree, they cut off from the trunk
such limbs as are of suitable size to be cut into lengths

for transportation, which is but a small part of a large tree.   They next trim each limb by cutting off, close to the body, the small branches and twigs, thus freeing it of brush.   There are nine such, large and small, cut off from this stick.   How the limbs are cut into sticks of the length of this I am unable to state, but it must be effected before they are brought, by the removal of the branches, prone upon the ground.   After that they can only be gnawed upon the top and sides, and the stick must be turned to complete the work. Whenever, from any cause, they are unable, as in this case, to turn it over, they are forced to abandon it, or finish their labor in an unusual manner.   That they rarely fail is shown by the scarcity of these abandoned cuttings.   I have found but three, two of which are in my collection, and the third was left to be brought in, but the person sent after it was unable to retrace the route.

The short cutting, No. 3 in the engraving, was taken from the top of the lodge at dam No. 14.   Both ends are conical, showing that it was turned while being gnawed.   There are two extra cuts, which on close examination show the same fact.   The only explanation which can be offered for these extra incisions is that the wood itself was eaten.   Stick No. 4, which is a poplar, is marked in precisely the same way.   These apparently unnecessary gnawings are often found on beaver cuttings.   No. 5 is the stub of a small tree, with two deep incisions around it, while it was taken off at a third place above.   These are the only evidences found upon the cuttings themselves that they ever eat clear wood.   It was stated by some of the early writers that the beaver subsisted upon wood as well as bark,[1] but the former fact appears to have been overlooked in the more recent articles upon this animal, until the statement became general that he lived upon bark and the roots of certain plants. The three beavers sent down for dissection last winter were taken in February and March, at the time when, their store of provisions being the lowest, they might, if ever, be expected to eat clear wood. Dr. Ely found their stomachs filled with lignine, with a slight intermixture of the tendrils of forest trees, and no perceptible remains of bark. The comminuted particles were so clearly of wood as to leave no doubt upon the question. The contents of the cæcum disclosed the same fact, as the digestive process simply removed the saccharine materials from the wood. At the same time the beavers were in excellent condition. Trees are often found in the spring gnawed around, and no chips at the foot. It was evident from the leaves that the work was done after the sap had started, and for the purpose of eating the wood. Additional evidence, tending to confirm the fact of wood-eating, may be derived from a comparison of the amount of bark upon the usual stock of winter cuttings with the necessary wants of a beaver family of six or eight individuals. It would afford to each but a small amount of sustenance.

While it is generally understood that beavers never eat the bark of evergreen trees, for which they have an aversion, they sometimes cut them down; and it may be done for the purpose of eat-

---

[1] M. Sarrasin, Histoire de l'Académie Royale des Sciences. Année 1704.

ing the wood. Dr. Newberry, in his Report referred to (*supra*, p. 165), remarks as follows upon the tree cuttings in the Cascade Mountains of Oregon: "From the point where their burrows terminate in the water, trails lead off to the thickets of willow or pine, where the beavers find their food. These thickets exhibit the most surprising proofs of the power and industry of these animals; whole groves of young pine-trees cut down within a few inches of the ground, and carried off bodily. * * * We often saw trees of considerable size cut down by the beaver; the largest of which I noticed was a spruce pine, twelve inches in diameter." In the Lake Superior region no species of evergreen tree is ever cut by them; except occasionally a young spruce, and in these cases the Indians affirm that they are cut down for the gum exuded from the tree. A Missouri trapper informed me that he had seen pine-trees that had been cut down by beavers, but he observed, that he never could find a place where a limb or a twig had been cut off from such a tree. There is a possibility that the evergreen trees, referred to by Dr. Newberry, were cut down by the beavers to obtain the nutritious mosses which grow upon certain species of these trees in great profusion; or for the sweet gums they afforded. Upon the pines west of the mountains there is a moss, growing as a parasite, which the Indians collect in large quantities and bake in ground ovens for winter food. It is cooked or baked in the same manner as the Kamash, which is one of their staple articles of consumption. A "moss glue," as it is commonly called, is thus obtained, which is both palatable and nutritious. The inner bark of the gum-pine tree also, is sweet flavored, and used by the Indians for food. Undoubtedly the beavers of the west coast have special inducements to attack the evergreen trees which do not exist in other parts of their habitat.

Pole cuttings of different lengths are often found in their piles of winter wood, but they are generally cut for present use. Fresh cuttings are rarely found between the commencement of vegetation in the spring and the first appearance of frost in the fall. When the trapper begins to find them, he regards it as a sign that they have commenced their fall work.

After their cuttings of various lengths and sizes have performed the first office for which they were collected and stored, they are in the condition to be most useful for repairing their lodges and dams. Most of the sticks and poles found upon the tops of their lodges and upon the lower faces of their dams show conclusively that they were first cut and stored for winter subsistence, then carried into the lodge and the bark eaten off, after which they were thrown out into the pond, to be again gathered and applied to the purposes named. This is not always the case with respect to their lodges, some of which I have found covered with a mass of poles of black alder, with the bark on; upon their dams, also, brush and drift-wood are often found; but these cuttings are the usual materials used for repairing both.

There is another class of brush cuttings, the principal object and use of which are involved in some doubt. In streams having considerable volume, which are liable to rise suddenly after rains or thaws, and develop currents more or less strong, a brush-heap (Fig. 21) is almost universally found sunk in the pond

immediately against, or slightly above each lodge.
There is a strong current, at such times, in Carp River
below dam No. 30, and in the Esconauba below dam
No. 13.   On the other hand, these brush piles are
rarely, if ever, found connected with lodges situated
upon the margins of ponds formed by dams across

FIG. 21.

Brush-heap near Lodge.

small brooks, or near island lodges in large ponds,
or near the lake lodges.   In the ponds of the small
streams there is little or no current, and none that
is perceptible in the small lakes.   As a confirmation of the supposed relation between these currents
and the brush heaps, the latter were found connected with all of the lodges on the Carp below the
point named, while none were to be seen near the
lodges in Grass Lake, nor in the pond at the Long
Dam, nor at any of the lake lodges.   The same is

equally true with reference to the four lodges on the margin of the natural pond hereafter described.

The brush-heap represented in the figure was in front of the lodge at dam No. 34. It was simply a pile of brush, composed of alder bushes and the small branches of deciduous trees, sunk to the bottom of the pond in water about four feet deep, with a portion of the pile rising above the surface. To form these heaps, they tow in the brush to the place, piece by piece, and sink it in some way in a well-compacted pile, which after a short time becomes firmly anchored in the mud below. A Missouri trapper informed the author that he had seen beavers, while performing this work, swim to the place towing a piece of brush, and then, holding the large end in their mouths, go down with it to the bottom apparently to fix it in the mud-bottom of the pond. An ordinary pile covers an area from ten to fifteen feet in diameter, and rises a few feet above the surface of the water, and contains the substance of half a cord of wood.

Both the Indians and the trappers regard these brush-heaps as their winter supply of provisions. Whether the old brush is removed each fall, and its place supplied with fresh, I have not been able to ascertain with any certainty, but it is very doubtful. I have seen the same brush piles at the same lodges in different years, on the Carp, the brush itself being old and decayed; but without knowing whether the lodges were still occupied. In any event it would be necessary to replenish the supply at times, to make good the waste by decay. While the brush was fresh they would be certain to use it for food, but whether it is their supply for the winter, is made doubtful by the presence of short cuttings lodged here and there in the pile. Having in repeated instances seen and pulled out of these brush-heaps short cuttings of the kind found in their store piles in the large ponds and lakes, with the bark still upon them, the fact of their presence suggested the probability that the principal object of these brush-piles was to afford a safe lodgment for short cuttings, upon which they mainly rely. Without some such protection they would be liable to be floated off by the strong currents, and thus be lost to the beavers at the time when their lives might depend upon their safe custody. A resort to a brush-pile, anchored in the bed of the channel in the manner described, as a means to the safety of their winter wood, displays remarkable forecast and intelligence. It may also throw some light on the false lodges of the Upper Missouri, which may have been constructed in part for a similar object. Whether this is the true explanation of their object is not entirely certain; but it seems to be extremely probable.

The otter is a rapid and splendid swimmer, possessing such agility of movement that he is able to catch the quickest fish. It is doubtful whether the beaver is quick enough in his motions, were he inclined to adopt this mode of subsistence. There is no evidence that he ever attacks or feeds upon fish. When domesticated he will eat some kinds of animal food; but he prefers farinaceous substances, and soon develops a special fancy for sugar.

The flesh of the beaver has no particular excellence to attract the epicure. It is used acceptably, however, in the same forms as the flesh of other animals.

The tail, which is composed largely of dense, fatty tissues, is regarded as a delicacy.

It is rather remarkable, on general considerations, that the shallow ponds made by beaver dams do not freeze to the bottom during the cold winters of the high northern latitudes. The fact that they remain unfrozen to this extent, even around Hudson's Bay, is well established. Captain Wilson informed me that he had found open water along the crest of the dam at Grass Lake, and generally at the lodge before described, in the coldest part of the winter, the thermometer in this region standing at an average of 5° below zero for weeks together. There are special reasons for this, among which is the deep covering of snow throughout the winter, which protects the water from the severe temperature of the atmosphere. The first fall of snow lies in the pond partly congealed, and afterward freezing at the surface, bears up the subsequent deposits. From this, or some other cause affecting the temperature of the water, the ice formed is not always strong enough in the coldest weather to bear up the weight of a man. Another curious fact observed by the trapper is, that thin ice is usually found over their piles of winter wood. As these ponds are rarely over six feet deep in any part of their area, the consequences of their wood becoming ice-bound would not be less fatal than the formation of solid ice in the entrances to their lodges. There are undoubtedly local causes affecting the temperature of ponds and of their different parts, such as springs rising through their beds with their waters at a relatively higher temperature, of the knowledge of which the beavers avail themselves in selecting the places of deposit for their winter subsistence, as well as the sites for their habitations. Strangely as it may appear to us, the winter life of the beaver, while shut up in the seeming darkness of a pond covered over with its white mantle of ice and snow, is made a season of security, of comfort, and of pleasure. Thus we see, on every hand, how the Divine Author of existence has hedged about the lives of these remembered creatures with His protecting care.

NOTE.—It is a peculiarity of the languages of our Indian nations that, while they are barren of terms to express metaphysical or abstract conceptions, they are opulent in terms for the designation of natural objects, and for expressing relative differences in the same object. In the Ojibwa, for example, there are different names for the beaver according to his age, and compound terms to indicate sex, as follows:

Specific name,	Ah-mik'.
Year old and under,	Ah-wa-ne-sha'.
Two years old,	O-bo-ye-wa'.
Full grown, or old,	Gĭ-chĭ-ah'-mik.
Male beaver,	Ah-yä-ba-mik'.
Female beaver	No-zha-mik'.

Their terms for the works of the beaver are the following : O-ko'-min, beaver dam; Wig-e-wam', beaver lodge; O-wazhe', beaver burrow; O-de-nă-o'-nane, beaver canal—literally, "made channel to travel in;" O-dă-bc-naze', lodge chamber—literally, "lodging place;" Pä-pä-num-wad', snow chimney over lodge—literally, "where they let off their breath." They have names, also, for the different kinds of cuttings; but they are descriptive rather than specific terms.

(a, as in ale; ä, as in father; ă, as in at; i, as in ice; ĭ, as in it.)

CHAPTER VII.

BEAVER CANALS, MEADOWS, AND TRAILS.

Beaver Canals—Their Extraordinary Character—Originated by Necessity—
Their Uses—Evidences of their Artificial Character—Canals at Natural
Pond—Their Form and Appearance—Canal on Carp River—Use of Dams
in same—Canal across Bend of Esconauba—Same across Island in Pond
—Beaver Meadows—How formed—Their Extent—Beaver Slides on
Upper Missouri—Scenery on this River—Bluffs of Indurated Clay—Bad
Lands—White Walls—Game—Connection of River Systems with Spread
of Beavers.

IN the excavation of artificial canals as a means for
transporting their wood by water to their lodges, we
discover, as it seems to me, the highest act of intelligence and knowledge performed by beavers. Remarkable as the dam may well be considered, from its
structure and objects, it scarcely surpasses, if it may
be said to equal, these water-ways, here called canals,
which are excavated through the low lands bordering
their ponds for the purpose of reaching the hard wood,
and of affording a channel for its transportation to
their lodges. To conceive and execute such a design
presupposes a more complicated and extended process of reasoning than that required for the construction of a dam; and, although a much simpler work
to perform, when the thought was fully developed, it
was far less to have been expected from a mute animal.

When I first came upon these canals, and found
they were christened with this name both by Indians

and trappers, I doubted their artificial character, and supposed them referable to springs as their producing cause; but their form, location, and evident object showed conclusively that they were beaver excavations. They are not mentioned, as far as I am aware, in any of the current accounts of this animal, for which reason, as well as their extraordinary character, they are deserving of more than a general notice.

From the preceding engravings an impression has been obtained of the character of the forest in the vicinity of dams and ponds. It will be observed that the tamarack and spruce are the prevailing trees upon the borders of the streams. These evergreen trees are themselves indicative of swamp lands. Both the Esconauba and the Carp flow through low grounds, which, widening out in places into flats, are invariably covered with these trees; with the exception of the areas of the beaver meadows. Birch, maple, poplar, and ash are found upon the first high ground; but often at the distance of several hundred feet from the original channel of the stream. In some places these rivers cut the high banks, thus bringing the deciduous trees within reach; but the latter are some distance back at the greater proportion of the ponds shown on the map. It is one of the principal objects of dams on the small streams, which are without defined banks, to flood the low grounds with a pond, and thus obtain a water connection with the first high ground upon which the hard wood is found. Where the pond fails to accomplish this fully, and also where the banks are defined and mark the limits of the pond, the deficiency is supplied by the canals in question. On descending surfaces, as has elsewhere been stated,

Plate XVII.

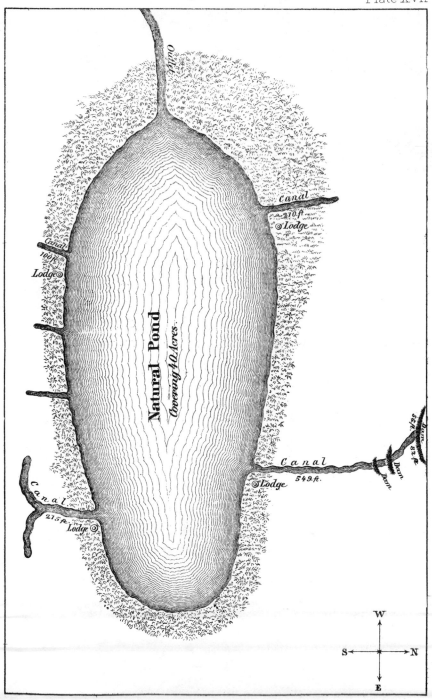

Outlet

Canal
210.ft
Lodge

Canal
100.ft
Lodge

Natural Pond
Covering 40 Acres.

Canal
549.ft
Lodge

Dam
82.ft
Dam
36.ft
Dam

Canal
215.ft
Lodge

W
S —— N
E

NATURAL POND and BEAVER CANALS

beavers roll and drag their short cuttings down into the ponds.   But where the ground is low, it is generally so uneven or rough as to render it extremely difficult, if not impossible, for the beavers to move them, for any considerable distance, by physical force. Hence the canal for floating them across the intervening level ground to the pond.   The necessity for it is so apparent as to diminish our astonishment at its construction; and yet that the beaver should devise a canal to surmount this difficulty is not the less remarkable.

The area represented by the map is not more abundantly supplied with dams, lodges, and burrows than with artificial canals.   It contains within its limits nearly every variety of the works of the beaver found in North America, some of which, as the Grass Lake dam, are unequaled in their magnitude and completeness.   Beaver canals are very numerous within this area.   Many of them are small and unimportant; but the great length of some of them is the striking feature which invests them, as artificial works, with a high degree of interest.

Immediately north of the Cleveland Iron Mine there is a natural pond (Plate XVII.) covering about forty acres of land.   It is bordered on all sides, except at its outlet, with rising ground at the distance of a few hundred feet from its margin.   The intermediate ground is level, and rises but a few inches above the surface of the pond.   On this low land there is first a border of moss turf entirely skirting the pond, and spreading out in different places from fifty to two hundred or more feet.   Without this, tamarack, spruce, and pine are found; and upon the rising ground, birch, ash, and maple. The pond is shallow, and thickly sprinkled over in the summer with water lilies; while in the moss turf, the unique Pitcher-plant (*Sarracenia Purpurea*) grows in the greatest profusion. This turf, which is saturated with water, and yields under the feet, spreads out like a carpet on the skirts of the pond. These particulars have been mentioned to show that there was not a spot of solid earth impinging upon the water in which the beavers could construct a burrow. It is well known that they never risk their personal safety upon the lodge alone, which is conspicuous to their enemies, but rely upon concealed burrows as the places of final resort. In addition to the principal use of a canal to reach by water the hard-wood lands, it was also necessary to their inhabiting this pond that they should be able, by its means, to reach burrowing ground.

These canals are about three feet wide and about three feet deep, with a depth of water varying from fifteen to thirty inches. They are made by excavation. The earth, which is more or less soft from saturation, is removed by being thrown out on either side, or carried out into the pond. In some places it appears to have been placed on the bank, but nearly all of these canals are so old that no signs can now be observed of the places where the excavated materials were deposited. Their artificial character is demonstrated by other proofs. In the first place, they are filled with water from the ponds up to the first of the dams, which are sometimes built across them; and where there are none, then to the end of the excavation. The banks, in the second place, are vertical, showing none of the marks of water flowing in a

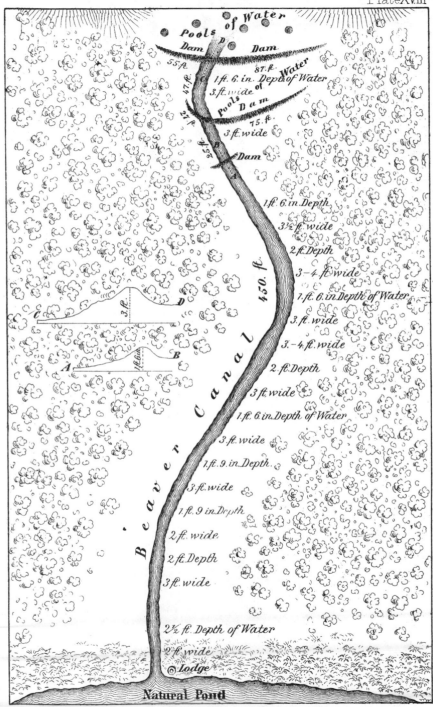

BEAVER CANAL North Side

small stream.   In the third place, they often terminate in dry hard earth at the foot of the rising
ground.   There is not, in the fourth place, the slightest current in these canals showing that they are fed
by springs.   In the fifth place, surface water, filtering
through grounds substantially level, never could cut
such uniform, and, much less, such deep channels.
And in the sixth and last place, roots of trees, four
inches in diameter, are found cut off and removed to
afford an unobstructed channel.   In like manner,
alder bushes, which branch low, as well as send out
strong roots, are found cut off in large numbers where
they overhang and line their borders.   An inspection
and comparison of a number of these canals leave no
doubt whatever of their artificial character.

The first canal to be described, and which is shown
in Plate XVIII., is on the north side of the pond represented in the preceding plate.   For the distance
of four hundred and fifty feet it is cut through level
ground, and filled with water from the pond.   There
are knolls or hummocks scattered over the surface in
which tamarack and spruce trees are rooted; but
there is no perceptible ascent until the first dam is
reached, when there is a rise of about a foot.   The
banks of the canal, which are vertical, rise a few
inches above the level of the water with which it is
filled.   Up to this dam it is perfectly evident that the
water in the canal is supplied from the pond.   Twenty-
five feet above there is a second rise of about a foot,
and here we find a second dam, extending over seventy-
five feet beyond the canal on one side, and twenty-
seven on the other.   As here used, these dams are
exceedingly ingenious.   They were designed to receive

and hold the surface water from rains, as well as that passed down by drainage from the high grounds, after which it was collected by filtration, in the channel of the canal which is sunk about three feet below the level of the surrounding ground. At the distance of forty-seven feet from the second, there is a third and much larger dam, one hundred and forty-two feet long, constructed in a semicircle, with its arms pointing out toward the high ground, and designed for the same object. It collects the surface water in pools, here and there, but fails to form a pond for want of sufficient water. With this dam the canal terminates. At this point the hard wood is reached, at the distance of five hundred and twenty-three feet from the pond. A B in the diagram represent a transverse section of the first dam, on the line of the canal; and C D, the same of the third. The crests of these dams where they cross the canal are depressed, or worn down, in the centre, by the constant passage of beavers over them while going to and fro, and dragging their cuttings. This canal, with its adjuncts of dams and its manifest objects, is a remarkable work, transcending very much the ordinary estimates of the intelligence of the beaver. It served to bring the occupants of the pond into easy connection, by water, with the trees that supplied them with food, as well as to relieve them from the tedious, and perhaps impossible, task of moving their cuttings five hundred feet over uneven ground, unassisted by any descent. As an effort of free intelligence to surmount natural obstacles, it is one of the highest achievements of this animal. The width and depth of the channel at different points are sufficiently shown upon the ground plan.

Plate XIX

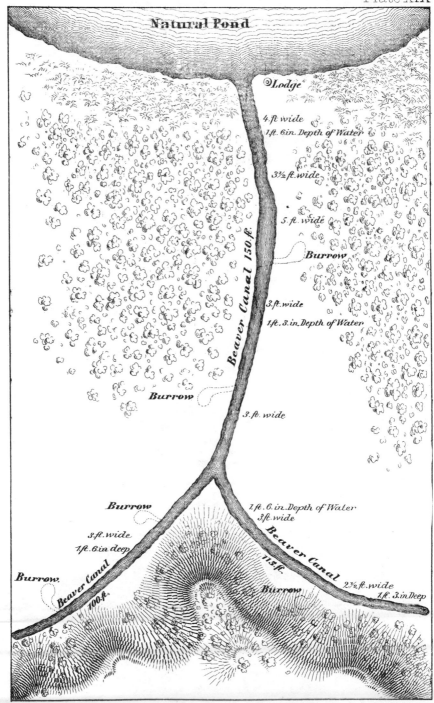

Natural Pond

Lodge

4 ft. wide

1 ft. 6 in. Depth of Water

3½ ft. wide

5 ft. wide

Burrow

Beaver Canal 150 ft.

3 ft. wide

1 ft. 3 in. Depth of Water

Burrow

3 ft. wide

Burrow

1 ft. 6 in. Depth of Water

3 ft. wide

3 ft. wide

1 ft. 6 in. deep

Beaver Canal

115 ft.

Beaver Canal

Burrow

2½ ft. wide

1 ft. 3 in. Deep

Burrow

Beaver Canal

100 ft.

Burrow

BEAVER CANAL South Side.

Not the least interesting fact connected with this canal is that of the great amount of labor necessary for its excavation. It must have required many years of continuous effort before it was brought into its present completed condition, both as to length and depth. The canals are most likely cleaned out and deepened from time to time, as materials from the surface fall into them and obstruct the channel. The bottom was covered with fine fibres and tendrils of tree roots, and with decayed leaves, which made it soft and yielding to the depth of a foot below the apparent bottom.

There are several canals connected with this pond, of which the four largest commence near the four lodges situated upon its borders. It will be sufficient to describe one of those remaining, taking that immediately opposite on the south side of the pond (Plate XIX.). This canal is also excavated through the low ground, and is filled to its extreme ends with water from the pond. At the distance of one hundred and fifty feet it reaches the first rise of ground, and the hard-wood land, where it branches into two canals, one of which is continued for one hundred feet, and the other for one hundred and fifteen feet along the base of high and dry ground, covered with deciduous trees. Both branches terminate with a vertical cut in dry sandy soil, and are carried through the same low ground as the main trunk, the surface rising but a few inches above the level of the pond. Of its artificial character there can be no doubt. The measurements are given upon the ground plan.

This canal passed a number of knolls surmounted with trees, under many of which burrows had been excavated. Evidences of this underground work were apparent in many places. One of these burrows, that nearest to the pond, is described with a diagram (*supra*, page 163).

At the distance of about seventy feet from the pond, this canal widens out to five feet, and then bears a little to the left. The engraving (Plate XX.) is from a photograph taken from this point, and looking down toward the pond. It shows the pond and about seventy-five feet of the canal. The lodge is mostly concealed behind the clump of small trees upon the right. The engraving is inaccurate in one respect. It shows the ground too much elevated above the level of the water in the canal.

There is one feature of this canal deserving of attention. After the rising ground, and with it the hard-wood trees, were reached at the point where it branched, there was no very urgent necessity for the branches. But their construction along the base of the high ground gave them a frontage upon the canal of two hundred and fifteen feet of hard-wood lands, thus affording to them, along this extended line, the great advantages of water transportation for their cuttings. If we are to regard these extensions as a further expression of their appreciation of the uses of a canal, it must increase our estimate of their powers of reflection. "Instinct," as that unfortunate and blundering term is understood by those who comprehend its meaning, would have fully performed its office when the canal had been carried to the point of contact with the high ground. Any progress of the work beyond this must be referable to the exercise of a free intelligence.[1]

---

[1] The lodges upon this pond were of the usual size, measuring from fourteen to sixteen feet over their summits, and from three

Plate XX.

From a Photograph.

P.S. Duval Son & Co Philᵃ

BEAVER CANAL   South Side

There is an extensive canal on Carp River a short distance below the bend represented in Plate XIV. It runs through low, swampy ground, which is covered, for one-quarter of its length, with a thicket of alder so dense that it was difficult to follow the channel for the purposes of measurement. The river, which at this point is a hundred feet wide, more or less, is bordered with alder and cranberry bushes, and with a forest of tamaracks. Back of these, some six hundred feet, is the first rising ground covered with deciduous trees; to reach which the canal was constructed. At the distance of one hundred and eleven feet from its commencement in the river there was a rise in the surface level of about a foot, which made necessary either a dam, or an additional foot of excavation, to furnish a sufficient depth of water. A dam twenty-five feet long, across the canal and the grounds adjacent, was the expedient adopted. The second level of the canal, thus raised a foot above the first, continued one hundred and seventy-eight feet, where a second rise occurs of about the same amount, and where a second dam was constructed thirty feet long. As the ground on both sides of the canal was swampy, with water in pools here and there, it was only necessary to excavate a channel of the requisite depth to obtain a sufficient supply of water by filtration from the adjoining lands. Up to the first dam the canal was filled from the river, and consequently varied in depth with the rise and fall of the stream; but above this, where it

---

feet to three feet six inches in height. The chamber of the lodge at the canal last described was four feet nine inches in its largest diameter, four feet six inches in its transverse, and one foot three inches high.

depended upon the dam, and the source of supply
before named, it was uniformly about eighteen inches
deep. From the second dam the canal continued at a
foot higher level for the distance of two hundred and
ninety feet, where it terminated at the base of the
hard-wood lands at a distance of five hundred and
seventy-nine feet from the river. Its average width
was about four feet, and it had an unobstructed channel of about eighteen inches deep from one end to the
other, with the exception of the dams. The run-ways
of the beavers over these dams were very conspicuous. They were shown, as in the other cases, by a
depression in the centre formed by traveling over
them in going up and down the canal. At the mouth
of the canal the river was not deep enough for a
beaver to swim below its surface out into the stream.
To obviate the difficulty, a channel, twenty-five feet
long and a foot or more deep, was excavated in the
bed of the river far enough out to carry them into
deep water. The materials were thrown up in an
embankment on the side below the excavation, apparently lest the current of the stream should carry
them back into the channel. The excavation and the
embankment, which were plainly to be seen side by
side, the latter in places coming up to the surface of
the water, presented another striking illustration of
the industry as well as intelligence of the beaver.

It is manifest from the form and general appearance
of this canal (Plate XXI.) that it is artificial. In addition to the uniformity and depth of its channel, its
vertical banks, the absence of a current, the sources
whence the water is obtained, and its actual use as a
channel for the transportation of wood cuttings, there

Plate XXI.

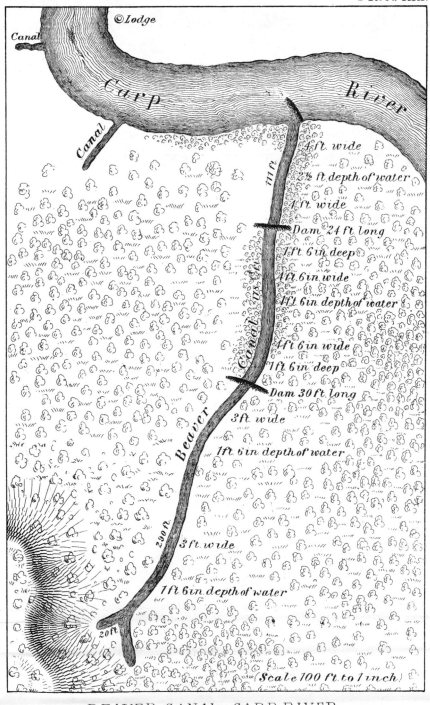

BEAVER CANAL, CARP RIVER.

is still other evidence tending to the same conclusion. Along the canal there are roots from two to four inches in diameter cut off at the bank on opposite sides, below the surface of the water, and removed. Alder bushes in great numbers, even when branching across the canal several inches above the ground, are found cut off to free the channel from obstructions. Besides these several considerations, the canal terminates in dry ground; and the intermediate space through which it is carried is of such a character as to preclude the possibility of the formation of such a channel by natural causes.

This canal may be regarded as typical of these works. They are usually cut through low, swampy ground where the supply of water is obtained by filtration from the adjacent lands, after forming a channel for its reception. With dams at each change of level to prevent the channel from drawing off the water, they can be carried as far as pools of surface water can be found.

It is not uncommon to find, at bends in streams, canals cut across the neck, apparently to shorten the distance in going up and down by water. One of this kind has been shown (Plate XIV.) in connection with a lodge. There are a number of these canals within the area of the map, three of the largest of which are shown in sections 4 and 28. The engraving (Plate XXII.) is from a photograph of one on the section last named, and it is introduced to show the beaver meadows on the Esconauba as well. It is a view across a bend in this river, showing the stream in the foreground passing by from right to left, and again in the background flowing in the opposite direction. The canal is excavated across the neck, and appears in the right side of the engraving. It is one hundred and eighty-five feet long, three feet wide, and about fifteen inches deep. When the dam below (No. 14) was in repair and the pond full, it would be about four feet wide and three feet deep. No other object for these excavations can be assigned, except to shorten the distance in going up and down the river. There was no hard wood in its vicinity. Alder bushes were growing on both sides of the canal, which were cut away on one side to show the water within it. The evidence is less conclusive that these excavations are artificial than in the case of the canals before described.[1]

In some cases similar excavations are made across islands in their ponds, where they are long, for the obvious purpose of saving distance in going around. In the Chippewa River, in Lower Michigan, there is a pond, covering several hundred acres of land, formed by a beaver dam, in which there is a low island of firm earth nearly a mile in length. Across this island there are two such canals about five hundred feet long, excavated by the beavers for the purpose of a water transit over the island. They were described to me, with their dimensions, by the Rev. Mr. Johnson, for many

---

[1] The Ojibwas discriminate this variety of canal from the other, and call it *o-ne-ge'-gome* (from *nee-geek'*, otter), signifying "otter crossing," from the use the otter is known to make of them. The otter is a "gay and festive" animal. He does not slide down hill upon the frozen snow after the fashion of the Polar bears described by Dr. Kane; but, coiling himself up in the form of a hoop, with his tail in his mouth, he will roll down a hill upon the snow-crust with great velocity. Father De Smet, before referred to, witnessed this performance of an otter in Washington Territory.

Plate XXII

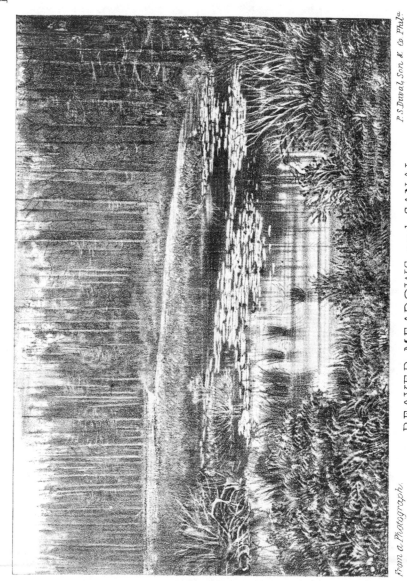

From a Photograph.

BEAVER MEADOWS and CANAL.

P.S.Duval Son & Co Philª.

years a missionary among the Ojibwa Indians, who went upon the island and examined them. Beaver excavations on a large scale are very common in districts favorable for their occupation, and they are greatly diversified in character. At the upper end of the principal pond at the gorge, where the series of dams are found, there is a canal two hundred and fifty feet long, which enters the pond where it is too shallow for a beaver to swim below the surface of the water. To correct this inconvenience a channel was excavated in the bed of the pond for about fifty feet in length, the materials from which were thrown up on either side.

Beaver meadows are properly among the works of the beavers, although consequences, merely, of their labor for other objects. Where dams are constructed, the waters first destroy the timber within the area covered by the ponds. When the adjacent lands are low, they are occasionally overflown after heavy rains, and are at all times saturated with water from the ponds. In course of time, the trees within the area affected are totally destroyed; in place of which a rank, luxuriant grass springs up. A level meadow, in the strict and proper sense of the term, is thus formed; although much unlike the meadow of the cultivated farm. At a distance they appear to be level and smooth; but when you attempt to walk over them, they are found to be a series of hummocks formed of earth and a mass of coarse roots of grass rising about a foot high, while around each of them there is a narrow strip of bare and sunken ground. The bare spaces, which are but a few inches wide, have the appearance of innumerable water-courses through which the water passes when the meadows are over-flowed. A beaver meadow, therefore, may be likened to the face of a waffle-iron—the raised eminences of which represent the hummocks of grass, and the indentations the depressions around them for the passage of water. In Plates IX. and XXII., which are engraved from photographs, a small portion of the beaver meadows are shown.

The amount of lands in a beaver district thus turned into meadows is large, when the conditions under which they are produced are considered. On the Carp and Esconauba Rivers, within the area of the map, there are about ninety acres, in the aggregate, of beaver meadows; the situation and boundaries of which are indicated by dotted lines. There are other districts, particularly on the main branch of the Esconauba, where the amount is much larger. These meadows are very common in the vicinity of beaver dams. When iron mining operations were first commenced in the Lake Superior region, the grass upon these meadows was the main reliance of the miners for hay for their winter stock. In 1865, Captain Johnson, superintendent of the Lake Superior Mine, cut fifty tons of hay upon a single beaver meadow on the main branch of the Esconauba.

In addition to the nutriment which the roots of these grasses afford to the beavers, the meadows themselves are clearings in the wilderness, by means of which the light, as well as the heat of the sun, is let in upon their lodges.

Beaver trails are quite numerous, as well as conspicuous, along the margins of their ponds. They show their run-ways back into the woods, and the

Plate XXIII.

BEAVER SLIDES

lines on which they move their cuttings into the ponds.   They are narrow, well-beaten paths for a short distance from the ponds, but soon lose their distinctness and disappear altogether.   They are chiefly interesting as indications of their numbers, and of the long periods of time each dam has been maintained, and each pond inhabited.

On the Upper Missouri we meet with another form of trail, which is called a "beaver slide."   It is designed to maintain, as well as afford, a ready connection between the river and its banks.   On both sides of this river, for miles together, the banks are vertical, and rise, at ordinary stages of the water, from three to eight feet above its surface.   It would, consequently, be impossible for the beavers to get out of the river upon the land except by excavating a passage way through the bank, from the river to the surface, or by the construction of the inclined or graded way, known as a "beaver slide."   The latter expedient was adopted and made the ordinary run-way to and from the river, and the bottom lands upon its border.   They are simple excavations in the bank, in the form of a narrow passage-way, inclined at an angle varying from 45° to 60°, so as to form a gradual descent from a point a few feet back of the edge of the bank to the level of the river.   Several of them are often seen in the bank, within ten feet of each other, as shown in the Plate.   (Plate XXIII.)[1]   They are first seen near the

---

[1] In the foreground in this engraving is shown the "Bull Boat" of the Upper Missouri, used by the Mandans, Minnitares, Crows, and Blackfeet, for crossing the river.   It is made of a single raw hide of a buffalo, unhaired and stretched over a dome-shaped frame of splints.   It is safe, convenient, and portable ; and it will carry two persons.

mouth of the Big Sioux River, from which point to the mountains they are observed in great numbers, in places where beavers are most numerous. They furnish another conspicuous illustration of the fact that they possess a free intelligence, by means of which they are enabled to adapt themselves to the circumstances in which they are placed.

This great river, which has been so frequently referred to in these pages, presents to the tourist many striking features. I am tempted to make a digression for the purpose of noticing a few of them. It runs for three thousand miles through the great central prairie area of the continent without being interrupted by a waterfall, or traversed by a mountain chain. It is a great river from its mouth to the Falls of the Missouri, which are within the Rocky Mountain chain; and it is navigable at certain seasons by steamers of the first class, within forty miles of the falls. In width it varies from a mile and a half to a third of a mile, rarely contracting its channel within a quarter of a mile when its banks are full. Its current, which is rated by river men at from four to five miles per hour, exceeds, in rapidity, that of any other navigable river within the United States. By means of its powerful current it is able to hold in suspension the great amount of earthy materials that impart to its waters their deep yellowish color. From this circumstance, also, it derived its aboriginal name, *Ne-sho'-ja*, which, in the dialect of the Kaws, signifies "the muddy river."[1]

---

[1] "With reference to the range of the Missouri between low and high water, but little can be said. It is about thirty-five feet at the mouth; twenty feet at St. Joseph's, Missouri; and still

Its "bluffs" testify to the long series of centuries during which this river has flowed from the mountains to the sea, and measure the enormous amount of solid materials which it has transported to the Mississippi and thence to the Gulf. For the first thousand miles these bluffs are, upon an average, upwards of four miles apart; for the second thousand, upwards of three miles; and for the remainder of the distance to the falls, upwards of one. They bound the valley excavated by the river, and mark the limital range of its flow. The tops of the bluffs, which are on a level with the prairies, are from fifty to one hundred and fifty feet above the level of the river, from its mouth to the confluence of the Yellowstone; while above the latter point they rise three hundred feet high and upwards for miles together.

The lands between the bluffs are level, rising but a few feet above the river, and are called "Bottom

---

less above, being at Fort Benton only about six feet. Ice dams in the spring sometimes occasion great local rises.

"Its high water width, for so long a river, is remarkably uniform. In the vicinity of Fort Benton it varies from five hundred to one thousand feet. Near the mouth of Milk River it has increased to fifteen hundred feet. Below the Yellowstone it is about two thousand feet. From this vicinity the river gradually attains an average width of about three thousand feet, which it holds for some six hundred miles to its mouth.

" Its annual discharge is about four trillions of cubic feet, or about one-fifth of that of the Mississippi.

"At Fort Benton it is two thousand eight hundred and forty-five feet above the Gulf, and at its mouth, three hundred and eighty-one feet."—*Physics and Hydraulics of the Mississippi River.* Published by the War Department, 1861, p. 61.

The June rise of the Yellowstone is about ten days in reaching St. Louis, or in moving a little over two thousand miles.

Lands." It is a striking fact with reference to these lands, that they have been literally made by the river to the depth of its channel from bluff to bluff; and that they are still undergoing the process of being cut away and reformed with each successive flood. Although the river to-day cuts against one of its bluffs, while the opposite one may be four miles distant, the time has been when it also impinged on the other,— having removed in its course all the intermediate soil to the depth of its channel. As it cuts away on one side, it throws up materials on its receding bed in the form of a sand-bar, which is afterward raised by the slow process of surface deposits by successive floods to the common level of the bottom lands. With every change of level in the river it shifts its channel more or less, as the direction and force of the pressure upon its banks change with the rise and fall of the stream. The rapidity with which this river, when in flood, cuts away its banks, which it is seen are sedimentary, is quite remarkable. It is not uncommon for a farmer on the Lower Missouri to lose forty acres of his farm in the bottom lands in a single night. At such times there is a constant splash of earth falling into the river, carrying with it the tallest cottonwood-trees, whose age measured the interval since the river, cutting its way in the opposite direction, had cast up the sand-bar upon which they afterward took root. I have seen trees falling in, one after another, while still others in a leaning position were just ready to follow. The mud deposited on their foliage soon brings them to anchor, after which they are stripped, in course of time, of both limbs and bark; and thus, with one end imbedded in mud and the other rising toward the surface of the water and pointing down stream, become the "snags" which have made this river famous for its steamboat disasters.

The river banks are usually from five to eight feet high when the channel is full, and always vertical. Any person falling into this river, in time of flood, is pretty certain to be drowned, unless he can reach a sand-bar, or the side opposite the one against which the current is running.[1]

From the mouth of the Missouri to Kansas City, there is a belt of forest on both sides of the river several miles wide; but above this point the belt contracts rapidly in width, the prairie coming occasionally to the bluffs, as at Fort Leavenworth and at Omaha. Above the last-named place the forest continues to decrease to the confluence of the Big Sioux River, after which, for the remainder of the distance of about two thousand miles to the mountains, it is confined to the bottom lands and the declivities of the bluffs. All without is open prairie, with the exception of narrow belts of forest along the margins of the tributary streams. For the last fifteen hundred miles the bottom lands are but partially wooded; and

---

[1] Where the channel is narrow and the current swift and full, the most powerful swimmer is unable to keep himself above the surface of the water, its whirling and eddying motions tending to draw him under. In 1862, I saw five men drown at mid-day in this river just below Fort Benton, which is but thirty-six miles below the Falls of the Missouri. Six men were capsized in a rapid in a small boat, and were one after the other soon drawn under. Of these, four came to the surface once, and again went under; three came up a second time, and one a third. He alone was saved, by means of a small boat, which went to their relief within two minutes of the accident.

the country, in other respects, is unfavorable for settlement.

The scenery upon the Missouri is monotonous until the confluence of the Yellowstone is approached. This is owing to the fact that at the river level we are shut in from the magnificent summer landscape of the prairies, of which the eye never wearies; and are confined to the narrow range of the bottom lands and bordering bluffs, which have few attractive features. One of the most remarkable regions of the earth is thus traversed without being seen. From the old village of the Mandans, and particularly above the Great Bend of the Missouri, the scenery changes and assumes more imposing forms. First there are high banks of indurated clay, seamed with lignite, which rise three hundred feet high and assume grotesque architectural forms from the effects of rain and frost. These, with more or less uniformity in appearance, border the river for five hundred miles until the Bad Lands are entered, which, commencing about fifty miles above the confluence of Milk River, continue for upwards of three hundred miles. The "Bad Lands" (*mauvaises terres*), so called, are sterile, rounded mud hills, of a dingy-brown color, thickly studded together, and rising, with deep chasms between, two hundred or more feet high. They are composed of adhesive clay, which, softening to a considerable depth under every rain, are destitute of every species of vegetation except an occasional sage-tree or dwarf cedar, and a straggling cactus. This assemblage of conical hills presents the most dreary landscape within the limits of our Republic, the deserts of the Colorado Basin not excepted. Silence and desolation reign throughout their area. They form a narrow belt along this portion of the Missouri, from which they stretch southward across the Yellowstone, and terminate in the Black Hills in the central part of Nebraska.

About one hundred miles from the foot of the Rocky Mountains we find the most remarkable formation upon the river, and the most striking scenery upon its borders. Lewis and Clark, who passed through this region in 1805, called this formation the "White Walls"—a not inapt designation. Prince Maximilian, in his "Travels in North America," also describes them; but any description, however minute, must fail to convey more than a faint general impression of their actual appearance. They are continuous for about forty miles, first appearing as the north bluff of the river, then upon both sides, and afterward on the north side alone. The river cuts through the formation, which is a whitish friable sandstone, so slightly cemented that small pieces are readily pulverized with the fingers, and yet it retains the form of solid rock. Its opposite bluffs here approach within half a mile of each other; and rising about two hundred feet high, are buried but a few feet below the level surface of the prairie. The extraordinary appearances of these "walls" are the effects, in a great measure, of frost and rain, which, having disintegrated portions of the rock, have wrought out the marvelous results presented to the eye. A steep bank first rises from the river, which is composed of the comminuted materials of this rock, colored a dingy brown by washings from the soil above. This, ascending about a hundred and fifty feet, at an angle of 60° or more, is destitute of vegetation, and has a smooth, uniform surface. Out of this bank rises the "White Walls" in perpendicular cliffs from fifty to seventy feet high. In some places, masses of this rock abut against the face of the bluff; in other places, detached masses are exposed on two and sometimes on three sides; and in still other places, solitary walls, in the form of masonry, rise in stupendous magnitude. Ravines here and there break through the formation at right angles with the river, exposing two and sometimes three sides of a great square; while in other places there are wide openings in the rock, more or less parallel, which assume somewhat the appearance of great streets. To complete the illusion, there are rents in some of the narrow walls having the semblance of gateways, doors, and windows. The effects of atmospheric causes in disintegrating this unequally cemented sandstone have been extremely curious, giving rise to every conceivable form. Buttresses, turrets, pinnacles, and spires meet the eye on every side, together with massive walls, rent and perforated, and standing like piles of masonry. In the distance the effect is truly imposing, suggesting very naturally the presence of great cities in ruins.

Some of the detached masses have been christened by tourists, among which are the "Castle," the "Cathedral," and the "Steamboat." The last is a huge pile of whitish rock, exposed on three sides for about five hundred or more feet, and, rising about sixty feet in height, presents the general form of a Missouri steamer, with its saloon deck, smoke-stacks, and pilot-house traced in dim outline.

In addition to the white sandstone, of which nine-tenths of this formation is composed, there is another stone of a reddish-brown color, the nature of which I was not able to ascertain, which assumes not less remarkable forms. It crops out in the form of narrow, long, and low stone walls, with horizontal lines of stratification or seams distinctly visible; and vertical rents here and there, from top to bottom, which give to it the appearance of dry stone walls. In some places, gateways through them, formed with the most perfect regularity, are seen. These brown-stone walls run parallel with the river in some places, and in others diagonally up its banks.[1]

In Arabia Petræa there is a white wall formation very similar to the one here imperfectly described. In future years, when the Upper Missouri region becomes more accessible, a summer expedition to the "white walls" will abundantly reward the tourist.

This river is also celebrated for its game. All of the principal animals of the North American Continent are found upon its banks. The buffalo, elk, red and black-tailed deer, antelope, grizzly and black bear,

---

[1] Lieutenant Grover, after first referring to the "white walls," speaks of this brown rock as volcanic. "The bluffs," he remarks, "are now more abrupt, and crowded the river; colonnades and odd detached pillars of partially cemented sand, capped with huge globes of light brownish sandstone, tower up from their steep sides to the height of a hundred feet or more above the water. Then the action of the weather upon the bluffs in the background has worn them into a thousand grotesque forms, while lower down their faces seams of volcanic rock from three to six feet thick, with a dip nearly vertical, and no uniform strike, beaten and cracked by the weather, rising from six to eight feet above the surface, run up and down the steep faces and projecting shoulders of the cliff—a most perfect imitation of dry stone walls."— *Physics and Hydraulics of the Mississippi River*, p. 58.

beaver, and the gray wolf are seen from the mouth of Cannon-ball River, where game first becomes abundant, through all the intermediate region to the mountains, with the exception of the Bad Lands.

Buffaloes are the most numerous, and are often seen in herds of several thousands. They are easily shot from the deck of a steamboat, while swimming across the river. However eager a person may be for buffalo-shooting, he will find it in such ample measure on this river that he will finally put aside his gun from mere weariness.[1]

The grizzly bear is the great animal of North America, not excepting the buffalo or the moose. We first saw this monster among the "white walls," galloping along the sloping banks beneath them. His bulky and powerful form gave him a dangerous as well as commanding appearance.

Among the lesser animals upon this river is the prairie dog, a rodent resembling the squirrel. We stopped at one of their "villages," as a collection of their burrows is familiarly called, and were not a little surprised at the number and spread of their habitations.

The antelope is the most beautiful animal of the plains. We often saw them in small herds of one or

---

[1] When the first pair of buffaloes had been shot and taken on board the steamer, at the time I went up the river, the mate called upon the trappers on board for volunteers to dress the animals. Two men stepped forward, one of them a Frenchman, as might have been expected, but the other, strange to say, was a Greek, born at Athens, as he afterward informed me. For two years he had been pursuing the vocation of a trapper in the Rocky Mountains. He found his way to New Orleans in a merchant vessel, and thence went to the mountains as an adventurer.

two hundred.   Their flesh, upon which we occasionally feasted, is superior to that of the elk or the buffalo.   Elks were frequently seen in small herds of twenty or thirty.

Another characteristic animal of the Upper Missouri is the mountain sheep. They were formerly found as low down as the confluence of Cannon-ball River, but now they are rarely seen below the Bad Lands. We first saw them among the "white walls," in flocks of from ten to twenty.   They are of a brown color, somewhat larger than the common sheep, and of timorous disposition.   Along the faces of the steepest cliffs, where the slightest footing can be had, they run with assurance and rapidity, working their way up through places apparently impassable.

FIG. 22.

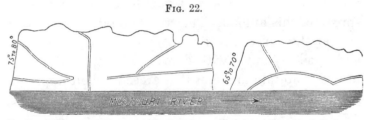

Trails of Mountain Sheep on Bluffs near confluence of Muscle Shell River.

Above the "white walls," where the bluffs rise in places three hundred feet high, the footprints or trails of the mountain sheep are very frequently seen on their steep declivities. A representation of these trails is given in the figure (Fig. 22).   The banks rise precipitously, apparently at an angle of 70° or 80°, with a smooth surface and devoid of vegetation.   No animal found in the region, except the mountain sheep, could either ascend or move in a horizontal line upon such bluffs and maintain his footing.   These footprints appear to be a series of alternating footholds sunk in the bank by long use, rather than continuous depressions in the form of a sunken trail. Their lines along the bluffs can be seen as distinctly in the clear atmosphere of this region, for a quarter of a mile, as a chalk line upon a black-board immediately before the eyes. The preceding diagram, in two sections, is from a rough sketch made while we were passing the bluffs at the distance of a few hundred feet. It seems probable that the mountain sheep resort to these precipitous banks for safety as well as rest, since while upon their dizzy declivities they could enjoy the consciousness of perfect security.[1]

From this long digression I return once more to the beaver, to make a brief reference to the connection of the great river systems of North America with the spread of this animal. The true habitat of the beaver is near the sources of streams, where they are small and easily spanned with dams. This transfers them to the mountain and elevated areas as their appropriate home. And yet, as they are migrating animals,

---

[1] The least reputable animal of the Missouri is the gray wolf, the largest of his genus in North America, and the most insatiable of the carnivorous genera. They are very numerous, following the buffalo in their migrations, and preying upon their young as well as upon the wounded and decrepid. The wariness of the wolf was well illustrated to us, one day, by his manner of drinking. We saw one jump down the bank of the river, which was about five feet high, upon a piece of fallen earth just above the water, and lap the water for about five seconds, and then jump up again upon the bank to see whether any one was approaching. After this he returned and drank again for the same length of time, and again ascended the bank to repeat his observation. These proceedings were repeated six or eight times before his thirst was satisfied.

they have but to surrender themselves to the current of the rivers, the Missouri for example, to propagate themselves over a large part of the United States. With this river, and commencing at its source, they could reach, in time, every part of the area between the Alleghany and the Rocky Mountains: and in like manner with the Siskatchewun, commencing their spread from the same mountains, they could reach the chain of lakes, the St. Lawrence, and all their tributaries upon a line of thousands of miles. The wide habitat of the beaver is thus explained by his aquatic habits and the remarkable connection of the river systems of the continent.

CHAPTER VIII.

MODE OF TRAPPING BEAVER.

Other Habits of the Beaver—Indications of Age—Tame Beavers—Nursed
by Indian Women—Building and Repairing Dams—Great Beaver Districts—Hudson's Bay Company—American Fur Company—Private Adventurers—The Steel Trap—Trapping Season—Trapping at the Dam—
At the Lodge—Traps sprung—Whether the Beaver when caught bites off
his Leg—Trapping under the Ice—Catching in a Pen—Trapping Bank
Beavers—Catching in Burrows—Trappers as a Class—Custom of hanging up Skulls—Statistics of Fur Trade—Early and Recent Exportations—
Immense Numbers of Beavers.

BEFORE taking up the subject of trapping, there are
a few remaining facts relating to the habits of the
beaver which it may be well to embody in a general
statement. His personal acts, as far as they can be
ascertained, are not less essential to the completeness
of his natural history than his works, or his anatomical structure. Our knowledge of these acts, although
more ample than in relation to most animals, is
still very limited; wherefore each additional item
must be considered in the light of a substantial gain.
Some of the facts about to be stated are upon the authority of the Missouri and Lake Superior trappers,
others were obtained from Indian sources, and the remainder were derived from personal observation.

The beaver, in moving, never steps backward, but
turns round, as his tail drags on the ground. While
walking, his back arches slightly; when standing still,
its curvature is much increased. In running, his

quickest movement is by a gallop, or a series of jumps, which take him along, notwithstanding his clumsy frame, at a rapid rate. When swimming with a part of his head out of water, the tail is extended motionless behind; but when he is entirely under, and swimming at the most rapid rate, it is swung from side to side with a peculiar diagonal stroke; that is, it is raised in a partly vertical position, and then moved upward and to the side, when the relative position of the edges of the tail are reversed, and it is swung in the opposite direction. It is the precise movement by which a boat is sculled with an oar. I have not seen this tail movement, but make the statement upon the authority of Indians by whom it has frequently been observed. By means of his tail used as a scull, and his webbed hind feet, the propelling power of the beaver in swimming is very great. They carry small stones and earth with their paws, holding them under the throat, and walking on their hind feet. Large stones, weighing five or six pounds, of which size they are found on dams, they push along in different ways—with the shoulder, with the hip, and with the tail. They work the tail under a stone, and give it a throw forward. In moving materials of various kinds they are very ingenious and persevering. It is said by the trappers, with how much of truth I cannot affirm, that they will place earth and sod upon each other's backs and tails, to be thus transferred to the dam. They handle a stick with their paws as dextrously as a man would with his hands, turning it at pleasure while cutting it in two or eating off the bark. Taking one end of a short cutting in their teeth, and rising up on their hind feet so as to bring it across their back, they will carry it, with the opposite end dragging on the ground, for a considerable distance, walking nearly erect on their hind feet. Their tracks in the snow are often seen, with the marks of a bush or limb by their side, showing that it was held in the mouth and passed across the shoulder, the ends dragging on the snow upon the side opposite to that on which it was held. They have also been seen swimming in their ponds, carrying small branches in the same manner.

In cutting down trees, they either sit or stand upon their hind legs, and placing their fore feet against the tree, gnaw round and round, making the first incision about three inches wide and an inch deep, and each successive one wider and deeper until the tree falls. I have found these trees in all stages of their progress in cutting. Three beavers have been seen at work together gnawing at the same tree, which is as many as could conveniently find a place. With this number, two nights at most would give ample time to fell a tree a foot in diameter. After the tree falls, they retire for a short time, until the woods are again still, when the whole family come out and commence cutting off and reducing the limbs to short lengths to be carried to the pond, and thence to the winter pile. A small portion only of the limbs of a large tree are used. They select such as are most convenient for cutting and removing, or are preferred for other reasons. Small trees, a few inches in diameter, are removed bodily. The number of trees of different sizes cut down each season in a well-stocked beaver district is surprisingly great. In places they obstruct the passage through the woods, although this occurs infrequently. While the surveys on the Marquette and Ontonagon Railroad were progressing, a small party encamped upon the main branch of the Esconauba, near its source, counted nineteen treefalls, which they heard in a single night, between the hours of seven and twelve o'clock. Along the margins of streams inhabited by beavers, the stubs of trees cut down by them are very numerous. They are met at almost every step. This might be expected, since a number of years are required to obliterate the evidences of their work. Many trees partially cut and abandoned are also found, as well as many that have lodged in falling.

The usual number of beavers in a litter, as elsewhere stated, is from three to five, but it is occasionally greater. William Bass, before mentioned, found eight young beavers in a foetal state in one female, and eight young beavers born alive in a single lodge. He had also found six young ones a number of times, and all the numbers below this down to a single young beaver. With reference to the duration of their lives it is difficult to ascertain any facts tending to establish its limit. There are no indications to be found on their teeth by which their age can be determined; but their tails grow stout with age, and become grayish or light colored on the under side. Their teeth file down and lose their sharpness, and they become lean and their flesh tough as they grow old; but these are relative indications only. Bass informed me that he once caught a part of a beaver's foot in a trap, taking four of the five claws; and that eight years afterward he caught a beaver in the same trapping district with the corresponding foot mutilated in

a manner so exactly agreeing with it that he felt per-
suaded it was the same beaver. This would have
made him not less than eleven years old. He had
also seen others apparently several years older than
this. From such imperfect data as they possess, the
Indians believe he lives from twelve to fifteen years.

Young beavers are easily domesticated; and although active and mischievous, they are affectionate
and harmless. When captured very young, the Indian women, if they desire their preservation, nurse
them until they are old enough to feed upon bark. At
six weeks of age, a young beaver will wean itself and
take to bark. When brought up in an Indian family
they become very much attached to all its members,
and are entirely contented in their domesticated condition. A Missouri trapper mentioned to me the circumstance of a young beaver captured by his partner,
and nursed by the wife of the latter, who was an Indian woman, that followed them on their trapping
rounds, wherever they went, for several successive
years. They shifted their camp frequently, and
moved long distances, always taking the beaver with
them as one of the family. When they commenced
breaking up their camp he understood the movement
immediately, and showed, by unmistakable signs, his
desire to accompany them. After securing two packs
upon a horse, he was placed on top, between them,
which was his usual place, and rode for miles, from
camp to camp, on many different occasions. Whenever they stopped, he fed himself upon bark, but he
would eat their food as well. He soon manifested a
great passion for sugar, and whenever it was shown
to him he was extremely troublesome until his desire

was gratified. He was particularly attached to the half-blood boy with whom he was nursed and grew up—following him on all occasions wherever he went. He was also a great favorite in the camp of the trappers, as the care taken of him sufficiently shows.

Beavers are often seen sunning themselves on the bank of a stream, lying side by side, but head and tail: their relative positions seeming to indicate a double degree of watchfulness. When they come out of the water and intend to rest, they first dry or drip themselves; after which they comb the hair about their heads with their paws, and with the extra claws on the hind feet they comb each side of their bodies alternately. Occasionally they indulge themselves at play, for which a formal preparation is made. After selecting a suitable place upon dry ground near the pond or stream, they void their castoreum here and there upon the grass, and, in the musky atmosphere thus created, spend some hours at play or basking in the sun.[1] The trappers call these play-grounds "Musk Bogs." Two or three of them are often seen at play in the water—diving, swimming around, and ducking each other.

In building a dam in deep water they commence with brush, preferring alder, from the small amount of its foliage, which they cut on the adjoining banks, and move by water, holding it by their teeth, to the place selected. The brush is arranged in parallel courses, as near as may be, lengthwise with the flow of the

---

[1] The castoreum sacs are inclosed in muscular cavities, so that a portion of their contents can probably be voided at the pleasure of the animal.

stream, and with the large ends facing the current. It is begun literally at the surface of the water, and the first courses are sunk to the bottom by successive deposits upon them. I have seen such dams when first commenced, and when the brush filled but a small part of the channel.

At first the brush makes a loose dam, through which the water flows without sensible obstruction; but when the materials, by their increase in quantity, begin to check the flow of the water and to experience, in consequence, an increase of pressure, they commence carrying in and depositing upon them earth, sods, and stones, for down-weight to anchor them, as well as to fill up the interstices. The first season the beavers content themselves with a low dam, rising about a foot above the original level of the water, and afterward raise it from year to year until it reaches its natural limitations. In this manner the small dams on the main branch of the Esconauba, near its sources, were constructed. For several miles this stream passes through comparatively level land, with a channel about thirty feet wide and from one to two feet deep, and with defined banks about three feet high. Dams are found at short intervals upon its entire course, and also upon its small tributaries; but those upon the former are short, low, and inferior structures. Beaver meadows border this river continuously for miles. As places of concealment, they are equivalent to thousands of burrows. These meadows show of themselves how completely the stream has been appropriated, in past times, for beaver habitation.

The persevering industry of beavers in repairing their dams is well established. Many successive

breaches must be made in these structures before they
abandon the work of their restoration; and even after
deserting the place, either they or other beavers are
sure to return when circumstances become favorable.
The instances are rare in which they are seen, for
any length of time, while engaged upon this work.
Captain Daniel Wilson informed me that he had seen
beavers at work on the Grass Lake dam, making
ordinary repairs, on several different occasions, while
watching at night for deer, in one of the trees growing in its crest. They came down to the dam singly,
and swam along its line from one end to the other.
When any work seemed to be needed, each one, upon
his own motion and without any concert with others,
devoted himself to the task of setting it right. They
brought sticks in their mouths, and mud with their
paws held under the throat. When these were arranged and the mud deposited upon them, they gave
the latter a heavy stroke with the tail to pack it
firmly in its place. Four or five beavers came down
each night, at intervals of half an hour apart; each
and all of whom performed more or less work upon
the dam, and did it in the same manner. One night,
while I was watching upon the same dam, the first
beaver made his appearance about eleven o'clock, and
swam across the pond near the crest of the dam, coming within a few feet of the place where I was partially concealed. Having discovered the intrusion, he
went under immediately, giving the alarm signal with
his tail. After this he went behind the grass island
upon which the lodge represented in Plate XIII. is
situated, and repeated these signals at intervals for
more than an hour; thus preventing other beavers

from showing themselves that night near the dam. By cutting their dams and lowering their ponds, they are easily compelled to come out of their lodges to discover the cause. But it is not as easy to witness, undiscovered, the process of their repair. When a branch of the Marquette and Ontonagon Railroad was extended to the Esconauba River, in 1862, dams number 11 and 12 were cut through, and abandoned in consequence by their proprietors. Two years afterward, this end of the road being disused, a pair of beavers returned to the lower pond and repaired the dam. With the hope of witnessing the process of repairing a dam, several large openings were made in it to draw off a part of the water; a scaffold was erected in one of the trees overlooking these breaches, and at nightfall my friend Johnson and myself were established in this lookout for the night. About one o'clock, two beavers came down together to ascertain the cause of the lowering of their pond, and to repair the mischief; but they discovered us in our imperfect concealment, when within a few feet of the dam, and avoided coming any nearer. They remained swimming about the pond, with a part of their heads above the water, for about an hour, and being afraid to undertake the work, they then retired. In the clear atmosphere of this region you can almost read print by the light of the moon. The ripples in the water, made by the beavers, were seen by us before the animals themselves were discerned. These two were probably the sole occupants of the pond, where they had shortly before established themselves for the winter. Their presence also tends to show that they live in pairs and families, and not in colonies or communities.

It has elsewhere been stated that beavers never eat the bark of evergreen trees, although they cut down pine and spruce in certain places. Pine-trees have been found cut down in Oregon, without showing a limb or a twig removed. They cut the fir-tree, commonly called the balsam-fir, in the Lake Superior region, generally taking the smallest. I have short cuttings of this fir—single cuttings made from single young trees, trimmed of their branches. The Indians affirm that they are cut for the balsam. Whether beavers eat it, my informants were unable to state; but they believe it is used to heal their wounds; with how much of truth I cannot say. There is no doubt that evergreen trees are cut for some other purpose than their bark, but with what object appears to be as yet unknown; unless it be for their gums and mosses, as elsewhere suggested.

A knowledge of the habits of beavers is necessary to the trapper to enable him successfully to pursue his vocation. During the aboriginal period, this animal was of no use except for his flesh, which was not of much request; and the Indians had no method of taking him except by the bow and arrow. After the colonization of North America commenced, a new value was given to the beaver for his fur, which was chiefly used, as is well known, for making hats. From their excessive numbers and wide distribution, their pelts were among the first, and for a number of years the largest, exportations of the colonists. The settlers as well as the Indians united in the business of trapping, which they pursued with such diligence that, about the year 1700, beaver pelts ceased to be exported, to any considerable extent, from the New

England and Middle States. At this early period, their numbers had become so greatly reduced by capture and dispersion that the business of the trapper, within these areas, ceased to be remunerative. In the regions around Hudson's Bay and Lake Superior; upon the head waters of the Missouri and Siskatchewun, and upon the Columbia and its tributaries, it has continued through all the intermediate period to be, and still is, a profitable vocation. After the substitution of silk for fur in the manufacture of hats, the value of beaver peltry greatly declined; thus affording a respite to this persecuted animal, under the effects of which he is now increasing in numbers in certain localities. This is particularly the case on the Upper Missouri and in the great forests around Lake Superior: but it is not at all probable that they will ever recover, in any locality, their former numbers. In 1862, beaver pelts were worth, at Fort Benton, on the Upper Missouri, one dollar and a quarter per pound against seven and eight dollars per pound fifty years ago. They are now worth two dollars per pound on the south shore of Lake Superior. An ordinary pelt weighs from 1½ to 1¾ pounds.

The Hudson's Bay Company, chartered May 2d, 1682, and the American Fur Company, organized in the early part of the present century, have been the principal organizations engaged in the fur trade in North America. Instead of ravaging their districts, as the colonists did, they early adopted a protective system, not only with reference to the beavers, but also to other fur-bearing animals, that their numbers might not become exhausted. Among other regulations of the Hudson's Bay Company, an interval of five years is allowed to elapse, after a season's hunt in a particular beaver district, before it is again resumed. While these companies have prosecuted their operations upon a vast scale, they have by no means enjoyed a monopoly of the business. Private adventurers in large numbers have engaged in trapping, and followed it year after year as a regular pursuit. Our Indian nations, also, whose territories produce fur-bearing animals, trap more or less for the means of subsistence. Within our national limits there are hundreds, and even thousands of men, who now make trapping their exclusive business.

As success in trapping depends very much, as before remarked, upon the knowledge the trapper has of the habits and mode of life of the several animals he seeks to capture, an examination of the methods resorted to in trapping beavers will develop some of the habits of this animal not before introduced. It is for this reason exclusively that the subject will be considered.

FIG. 23.

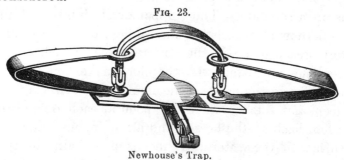

Newhouse's Trap.

The steel trap came into use when the systematic pursuit of the fur-bearing animals commenced. Its form is well known. The most perfect instrument, however, is of recent introduction, and is known as the "Newhouse Trap," of which the foregoing cut is a representation.

The jaws are smooth, and spread six inches and a half, of the size best adapted for taking beavers. Its chief merits, as an improvement upon the old form, are said to consist in such an adjustment of the form of the jaws, and of the bow of the spring to each other, and the further adaptation of the power of the spring to both, as to secure in the highest degree the two qualities of a good catcher and a sure holder. These traps are used without bait, and operate on the principle of an inadvertent tread upon the pan.

The trapping season commences about the first of November and ends about the first of April, during which period the different fur-bearing animals are in the best condition with respect to their fur. But it is pursued more or less at all seasons of the year, by persons who are more reckless of the waste of animal life than the regular trappers. In the spring, summer, and fall, the usual place of setting traps for beavers is upon the dam. The trapper avails himself of the well-known habit of this dam builder to repair at once any breach made in the structure, over which his supervision is constant. He therefore makes one or more openings in the crest of the dam, four or five inches deep, and sets a trap in the pond at each one, about a foot back of the breach and a few inches below the surface of the water. By means of a chain the trap is then secured to a stake driven into the bed of the pond, about four feet back of the trap and out in the pond, where the water is of some depth. When a beaver ascertains that the level of his pond is subsiding, which is shown by the fall of the water in the lodge entrances, he goes to the dam, after night has set in, and commences its repair. While thus engaged, he is in constant danger of springing the trap by stepping on its pan inadvertently. If taken by either of the fore feet, he is very apt to break the bones in turning around the trap, thus freeing himself; but if caught by either hind leg, his case is hopeless. He immediately plunges into the deep water of the pond, where his course is soon arrested by the stake and chain. It is a part of the trapper's merciless plan to drown the animal, for the double purpose of preventing him from breaking away and of saving his body under water, where it will be inaccessible to beasts of prey. To accomplish this end, two contrivances are resorted to, of which the most simple is an extra stake set a short distance beyond the first, around which the beaver is quite certain to coil the chain, and thus drown himself, in his attempts to escape; and the other is the pole-slide. A dry pole, ten or twelve feet long, with a prong at one end to prevent the ring of the chain from slipping off, is secured to the bank or dam by a hook driven down into the ground near the trap. The small end of the pole—the ring being run up to the large end near the hook—is then immersed in the pond as far out as it will reach. When a beaver is caught, he dives and swims in the direction to which the pole leads, the ring sliding down to the end. In the deep water thus reached, the weight of the chain and trap, by which his motions are embarrassed, prevents his rising to the surface, and he is soon an unresisting victim of the trapper's art.

Captain Wilson, before referred to, on one occasion

set three traps in this manner on the Grass Lake dam, using stakes instead of the pole-slide, with the following results. Two days afterward he found, on going to the traps, the three breaches fully repaired. Two of the traps held each a beaver, and both drowned; but notwithstanding the calamity that had befallen them, other beavers had finished their work. The third trap had disappeared from sight. He found the chain still held by the stake, which showed, on running it up, that the trap was buried in the breach made in the dam, under the materials used in its repair. Upon drawing it out, he discovered a duck in the trap, which had been caught and drowned, and that both the duck and the trap had been carried by the beavers into the breach and there buried.

Trapping at the lodge is another of the common methods. Two parallel rows of stakes are driven in from the mouth of each entrance for some distance out into the pond, thus forming two narrow channels, through one of which the beavers must pass to enter the lodge. A trap is set in each passage-way, and secured by a chain and stake in the usual manner. In Fig. 11, *supra*, page 149, these rows of stakes are shown. Traps set in this way are often found sprung and empty, which has given rise to an opinion, more or less prevalent among the trappers as well as the Indians, that they are deliberately sprung by the beavers. There is not only no foundation for this conceit, but, on the contrary, the beaver is a remarkably dull animal with reference to precautions against the trap. A sufficient explanation is probably found in their manner of disposing their fore feet while swimming, which are pressed back against the body, so that in passing over the trap the abdomen instead of the feet comes in contact with the pan, causing the trap to spring. As the trap cannot hold upon a broad flat surface, the beaver escapes.

There is another belief, universally adopted by both Indians and trappers, which also admits of question, namely, that when a beaver is caught by either fore leg, he bites it off and thus frees himself from the trap. Beavers are frequently taken with one and sometimes both fore legs gone, and others with the hind feet mutilated in various ways. Two of the three beavers sent down to me from Lake Superior last winter, for the purpose of dissection, had lost each a fore leg, one the right and the other the left, apparently cut off close to the shoulder, with the stumps perfectly closed over with skin and healed. The beaver represented in Plate I. is one of them, and has his lost leg restored by borrowing the remaining one of his neighbor. A beaver was taken on the Upper Missouri, in 1860, with but one perfect foot remaining. Both fore legs were wanting, and one of the hind feet was in part cut off. Captain Wilson caught a beaver on the Esconauba River, in 1862, with but one perfect foot, and that, one of the fore ones, by which he was captured. The other fore leg was gone, apparently cut off close to the shoulder, and the stump healed; one hind foot was cut off across the middle of the webbed portion; and the other diagonally across the same, leaving one toe and its claw. This beaver had evidently been caught four times in traps, from three of which he had escaped. Trappers expect to lose most of the beavers

taken by the fore leg,—that is, they catch a foot instead of the animal,—and they endeavor so to set their
traps that the hind feet will be most likely to tread
upon their pans. The true explanation of their ex-
trication from traps, when caught by the fore legs, is
probably found in the relative smallness of the bones
of these legs, and in their frantic efforts to escape.
Running around the trap would easily snap them off,
after which the rending of the skin would be quickly
effected. That such is the true explanation, receives
confirmation from the fact that the tendons of the leg
are usually found pulled out from the shoulder, and
still attached to the foot in the trap; which would
have been severed by the teeth before the bones of
the leg, had the beaver attempted to bite off the
latter.

Beavers caught in traps, and not drowned, sometimes become entirely tame from the effects of exhaustion. Mr. Atchinson, before mentioned, informed
the author that he once found a beaver alive in his
trap, and completely tamed. He said, to use his own
language, "that it looked at him with such an entreat-
ing and submissive expression, that he could not find
it in his heart to kill him." He resolved to save his
life, and take him to the museum at Marquette. On
placing his hand upon the beaver's head, and passing it
along his back, the latter showed no disposition to bite,
or aversion to this familiarity. After taking him out
of the trap, he held and fed him in his lap; and then
carried him on his back for sixteen miles, through
the forest, to the railroad station. The journey
proved too rough for the exhausted beaver, and he
died the following morning. This tameness was un-

doubtedly the result of physical exhaustion, which deprived the animal of all power of resistance, as well as carried him beyond the sensation of fear. Rarey's system of taming horses is founded upon the same principle. [1]

In the winter, which is the season for trapping, after the ponds are frozen over and the beavers are housed for the winter, other methods are resorted to, among which is the following: the trapper selects a place in the vicinity of a lodge, cuts a hole through the ice, and puts down into the pond a fresh-cut pole of birch or poplar about ten feet long. While the small end is pushed out into the water, the large end is securely fastened in the edge of the bank, and a trap is set immediately under the place where it is secured. This fresh cutting the trapper knows will

---

[1] That great fear will produce nearly the same results is shown by the peaceful gathering together of different species of wild animals in South America, when the annual rains deluge the pampas. Upon this subject Lieut. Gibbon remarks: "The Indian builds his hut on those elevated places which remain islands. When the great floods of water come down, crickets, lizards, and snakes crawl into his thatched roof; and droves of wild cattle surround his habitation. Armadillos rub their armor against the pottery in the corner of his hut, while the tiger and the stag stand tamely by. The alligator comes socially up, when the 'gran bestia' seats himself on the steps of the door. The animal family congregate thus strangely together under the influence of the annual deluge. Those of dry land meet where the amphibious are forced to go; and as the rains pour down, they patiently wait. Birds fly in and light upon the trees and top of the hut, while fish rise out of the rivers and explore the prairie lands. The animals begin to seek a place of refuge in the month of January, when the soil becomes gradually covered."—*Exploration of the Valley of the Amazon*, Part II. p. 253.

soon be discovered, and seized with avidity for transportation to the lodge. When a beaver has thus
found it, and ascertained that it is fast at one end, he
follows it up for the purpose of cutting it off—very
naturally desiring to secure the whole of the stick.
This brings him immediately over the trap; and if the
trap is judiciously placed, it will be next to a miracle
if the unsuspecting victim does not step upon its pan
before the stick is severed. This has always been
found one of the most successful methods of trapping.
After a trap has been set in this way, the trapper
throws snow into the hole cut through the ice, to
hasten the freezing over of the opening, and leaves
the place to quiet until his next round among his
traps brings him again to the spot.

Another method, of Indian invention, and which,
for its deliberate wickedness, surpasses all others, if
the business itself admits of gradations in cruelty, consists in staking around the pile of winter wood of a
beaver family, for the purpose of forcing the whole of
them, one after the other, by hunger, into the death-
pen thus contrived for their ensnarement. By sounding on the ice, they are able to discover where these
piles are deposited; after which stake-holes are cut
through the ice, and dry stakes are driven in so as to
form a palisade entirely around their stock of winter
provisions. On the line of their run-way from the
lodge to this pile one of the stakes is pulled out, and
a light, dry twig is put down loose in its place. When
these arrangements are completed, the trapper rolls
himself up in his blanket and lies down upon the ice
to watch for a movement of the twig, which must occur whenever a beaver enters the inclosure. If he is

fortunate in point of time, that is, if there is a present want of a cutting at the lodge, he has but a short time to wait. A beaver goes out from the lodge to bring back a cutting from the pile, and, finding a barrier around the magazine, he seeks and finds the only opening left, through which he passes into the inclosure. As he enters, the light twig is moved, disclosing to the trapper above his presence within the pen; whereupon the latter restores the stake to its place, and the fate of the luckless beaver is sealed. When he finds his return to the lodge cut off, he swims around the circuit of the stakes until he comes back to the place where he entered, and there resigns himself to death. After he is drowned, the trapper takes him out of the pond, removes the stake, restores the twig, and again lies down to wait the coming of the second beaver. The same necessity which sent out the first soon sends out another upon the same errand, to experience the same fate. One after the other the remainder of the family, under the pressure of the same hunger, and perhaps to discover the cause of the absence of those who went before them, go forth from the lodge and enter the fatal prison-house of the trapper. It is said that if he takes the first beaver by this device, it is almost certain that he will capture the entire family. The drawback to this manner of entrapping is the danger of alarming their fears by the presence of the palisade around their pile of cuttings, at which, if the first beaver turns back, the rest will keep at a distance. It is further stated that they invariably drown at the stake where they entered.

In trapping bank beaver, they use various kinds of scents to attract them to the place where the trap is set, which is usually near the bank, and a few inches below the surface of the water. Gum camphor is one, a piece of which is inserted in the split fork of a stick, and the latter is then set in the bank so as to bring the camphor immediately over the trap, but above the water. A beaver, when he scents the pungent odor of the camphor, follows it up until he discovers the substance; whereupon he rises up to reach it, in doing which he is liable to step on the pan of the trap with his hind foot, and thus pay for his curiosity with his life. Trappers also use castoreum, cinnamon, cloves, and oil of juniper for the same purpose. Cloves and cinnamon are dissolved in alcohol and made into a kind of paste, which, when smeared over a stick adjusted in the same manner, is found to answer equally well as a bait. Traps are also set, at a venture, upon their run-ways, particularly on their solid-bank dams, which always, by some depression, show where they pass in going up and down stream. When set in such places, it is necessary to make a slight excavation for the reception of the trap, and to cover it with leaves. They are also set in the water at points where the land juts out into the pond, along which beavers are apt to pass in going up or down the pond. Whenever the trapper discovers a trail, or well-marked line on which beavers travel, either on land or in the water, he avails himself of the knowledge to conceal a trap under their footsteps.

Another method of catching beavers where they are very numerous, is to drive them from their lodges to their burrows, and having closed the entrances, to open the burrows and pull them out with hooks or by hand. This mode of hunting them was formerly practiced extensively in the Hudson's Bay territory. The Indians ascertained the situation of their burrows by sounding the ice along the margins of the ponds with ice chisels, the sound of the stroke revealing in some way the presence of a chamber in the bank. After the burrows were found, an opening was made in the ice over the mouth of each entrance, for the double purpose of discerning by the movement of the water when a beaver had entered, and of closing it up behind him. The next step was to stake across the stream, where it entered the pond, to prevent their escape out of the pond. After these preparations were completed, and a person was stationed on the ice near each entrance, the lodges were broken open to drive out their inmates and force them to take refuge in their burrows. As soon as the motion of the water showed that one or more of them had entered a burrow, its mouth was closed, and every one thus entrapped was sure to be taken. After they were thus locked up, the next movement was to open their burrows from above, whereupon, without resistance, they were captured and dispatched. Hearne, from whose work the above account is taken, remarks: "When their houses are broken open, and all their places of retreat are discovered, they have but one choice left, as it may be called, either to be taken in their houses or their vaults; in general they prefer the latter; for where there is one beaver caught in the house, many thousands are taken in their vaults."[1]

When beavers are shot in the pond, they sink to the bottom and are thus lost, for which reason the gun is

---

[1] Hearne's Journey, etc., p. 235.

rarely used in the beaver hunt. West of the Rocky Mountains, however, where the ponds are shallow and small, and the danger of losing the animal after being caught in a trap is greater, the gun is often used. Robert Meldrum, for many years a trapper in this mountain region, and now one of the factors of the American Fur Company, informed me that when he hunted beaver west of the mountains he preferred the gun for the reasons stated. He mentioned that on one occasion he found three lodges on a pond upon one of the tributaries of the Columbia, where he "shot twenty-one beavers and left three." His estimate of the total number was upon the assumption of eight to a lodge, the well-known rule among Rocky Mountain trappers. It is amusing to find how systematic this class of men become in their calculations.

Trappers often associate for the purpose of extending their operations over a larger area, in which case they establish and provision camps, and assign the several branches of the work to different persons. When two or more are engaged in the same vicinity, and not associated, they adopt certain independent lines or routes, so that neither may interfere with the other. It is a custom among the trappers of the Rocky Mountains to recognize in each other proprietary rights in certain beaver districts. When a trapper finds a new stream well stocked with fur-bearing animals, it takes his name, and is regarded as his exclusive range so long as he chooses to occupy it. Among such of the Ojibwa Indians on Lake Superior as engage in trapping, there is a similar custom. They divide the principal districts among themselves, after which each leaves to the others the undisturbed enjoyment of their respective beats. Each trapper, or family, or association, therefore, has a special round, upon which they make repeated expeditions during the season of the hunt. On the first journey, they carry in and distribute their traps, select and provision their camps, and prepare generally for an arduous winter's work. A single trapper can manage from fifty to seventy traps upon a line thirty or forty miles in circuit. At regular intervals, the traps, after being set, are visited, the captured animals removed, and the traps reset. This round of the traps, with the curing of the skins, fills out their time, and furnishes systematic employment for the season.

The life of the trapper, although one of hardship and privation, is full of adventure. They lead, to a greater or less extent, a life of solitude in the trackless forests, encountering dangers of every kind, enduring fatigue and hunger, and experiencing, in return, the pleasures, such as they are, afforded by the hunt. As a class they are generous, reckless, and intelligent, and very companionable. From their relations to each other of their adventures, and of their observations upon the habits of animals, a kind of "animal lore" has been developed and propagated of very ample fullness and range, which, in course of time, may be considered worthy of perpetuation in written form. Their conclusions are not always veritable, as they are prone to be over-credulous; neither are their speculations always sound; but in both they display much acuteness and ingenuity. The regular trappers are an original and peculiar class of men, whose tendencies of mind have led them away from human society, into a life substantially with the wild animals, and with Nature in her most rugged forms. Many of them, by natural endowments, were deserving of a higher destiny.

It is one of their customs, and one which served me a useful purpose, to hang up the skulls of captured animals upon bushes and limbs of trees on the lines of their routes. This practice is alluded to by Samuel P. Ely, Esq , in the following letter, which I take the liberty to insert for its humorous reference to this custom. Having written to him for some beaver skulls to complete my collection, his answer came under date of February 26, 1866, as follows: "I can obtain the skulls, and have arranged with two different trappers for thirty each. If they both fulfill their engagements, your craniology of the beaver will be unimpeachable. Accompanying them will be an occasional mink, otter, and lynx skull, which may be useful for purposes of comparison. It is fortunately quite easy to procure these skulls. It appears that a custom is quite prevalent among trappers to hang up, among the bushes on their line, the skulls of the animals whose fur and flesh they have appropriated; and it is nothing more than the collection of them on one of their tours to get thirty or forty specimens. Since nothing of this kind is done without motive, I present you gratuitously my theory on that point. 1st. It is subjectively encouraging to the trapper, when the hunt fails him for a time, and his traps are empty, to look upon the memorials of his past success.

" 2d. It is objectively calculated to produce on the living animals, which also view these relics, a feeling of resignation to the fate, which, once deemed finally inevitable, they are the less careful to avoid.

"It is interesting, however, that so remarkable a custom should furnish immediately such a mass of materials for scientific investigation. Think of sixty skulls off-hand? They are promised to me without fail. Do not, however, count them already sure, because these sons of the forest, as a general thing, fail to apprehend the relation between a promise and its fulfillment, which the more civilized man finds it convenient to observe."[1]

The number of beavers taken during a season's hunt varies, of course, with the skill of the trapper and the supply within his district. On the south shore of Lake Superior, an Indian family of four effective persons will capture from seventy-five to one hundred and fifty, if their hunting grounds are well stocked. Fifty and a hundred are not an uncommon number.[2] But the business must be assiduously followed to secure any degree of success.

The statistics of the fur trade sufficiently prove that beavers existed in immense numbers in different parts of North America at the several epochs of their settlement. A brief reference to some of the figures will make this apparent. In 1624, the Dutch West

---

[1] It is proper to add that the promise was amply redeemed by the production, in due time, of forty skulls.

[2] John Hutchins, a famous trapper, now residing in Manlius, New York, estimates the number of animals he has caught in traps, or taken in other ways in the course of his life, as follows: "one hundred moose; one thousand deer; ten caribou; one hundred bears; fifty wolves; five hundred foxes; one hundred raccoons; twenty-five wild-cats; one hundred lynx; one hundred and fifty otters; six hundred beavers; four hundred fishers; mink and marten by the thousands, musk-rats by the ten thousands."— *Newhouse's Trapper's Guide*, p. 64.

India Company exported from New Amsterdam four hundred beaver skins, and thus inaugurated this trade with the New World. This number had increased by 1635 to fourteen thousand nine hundred and eighty-one. During the ten immediately previous years the whole number exported was eighty thousand one hundred and eighty-three.[1] Each pelt was then worth about two dollars and a quarter. The trade steadily increased until the dominion of the Dutch ended, in 1664. Beaver pelts were then a measure of value, and formed a part of the currency; and the beaver himself was adopted for the central symbol in the seal of the province. Their furs continued, under English rule, to be the chief article of export from New York until the year 1700, after which the exportation declined rapidly, and soon became extinct. In 1687, Thomas Dongan, governor of the province of New York, remarks in an official letter as follows: "We find this year that the revenue is very much diminished, for in other years we were used to ship off for England thirty-five or forty thousand beavers, besides peltry; this year only nine thousand and some hundreds, peltry and all."[2] Again, in November, 1700, Governor Bellomont wrote to the lords of trade in equally discouraging language: "The beaver trade here and at Boston is sunk to little or nothing, and the market is so low for beaver in England that 'tis scarce worth the transporting. I have been told that in one year, when this province was in possession of the Dutch, there were sixty-six thousand beaver skins exported from this town; and this last year there was

---

[1] Natural Hist. New York, Pt. I., Zoology, p. 73. De Kay.
[2] Colonial Hist. New York, iii. 476.

but fifteen thousand two hundred and forty-one exported hence."[1] During the same periods, large numbers of beaver skins were exported from Delaware, Maryland, Pennsylvania, and Virginia, and from New England. In the early part of the last century the trade ceased within these portions of the United States.

Shortly before the year 1800, American enterprise was directed to the fur trade on the Northwest Coast, and the several organizations which sprang up were finally merged in the American Fur Company, whose field of operations was upon the head waters of the Columbia, the Yellowstone, and the Missouri, and the shores of Lake Superior. This company is still engaged in the general business, but the amount of beaver skins now obtained is comparatively small. Formerly it was large, but the statistics of their trade are not within my reach.

The Hudson's Bay Company has been the most important and efficient organization in North America for the capture of the fur-bearing animals. Possessing exclusive jurisdiction over an immense area, of little value for settlement, but of great value for the production of fur, they have enjoyed a monopoly of this trade for nearly two centuries. Their exportation of beaver skins alone has often exceeded a hundred thousand per annum. In 1743, one hundred and fifty thousand were received at Rochelle and London, the greater portion of which was from the Hudson's Bay territory and the Canadas. From the recent catalogues of the sales of this company, it appears that they sold at their houses in Edinburgh and

---

[1] Colonial Hist. New York, iv. 789.

London, in January and August, 1854, five hundred and nine thousand two hundred and forty beaver skins; in January and August, 1855, sixty-two thousand three hundred and fifty-two; and in January, 1856, fifty-six thousand and thirty-three;[1] making in the aggregate the enormous number of six hundred and twenty-seven thousand six hundred and twenty-five beaver skins in the course of two and a half years. It is to be inferred that the large number sold in 1854 was the accumulation of a few previous years, and that the numbers sold in 1855 and in the first half of 1856 show the average annual production at this late period.

The foregoing statistics are sufficient to indicate the numerical extent to which the species had become developed and increased in North America, as well as to mark the areas in which they were the most abundant. A statement before made may be here repeated, that the beaver, with his life, has contributed in no small degree to the colonization and settlement of the British Provinces and the United States.

Having in the preceding pages discussed the principal questions with reference to the beaver and his works, it is proposed, in a final chapter, to consider some of those relating to Animal Psychology. Although a digression from the main subject to one entirely independent, the two are strictly correlated. It must be the ultimate result of investigations concerning the habits and lives of animals to raise Animal Psychology to the rank of a science, by affording

---

[1] Schoolcraft's Hist., Cond., and Pros., of the Indian Tribes, vi. 728.

the necessary materials for solving questions relative to the mental qualities of the mutes.

NOTE.—In closing these pages upon the works of the beaver, I desire to make special mention of my friend, William Cameron, of Marquette, to whom I am indebted for my first acquaintance with the beaver lore of the trappers. Although I have not ventured to use it, except with caution, I have found it useful in the progress of this investigation. A quarter-blood Ojibwa, and the son of one of the factors of the Hudson's Bay Company, Cameron married an Ojibwa woman, adopted the customs of her nation, and is now drawing near the end of a long life spent on the shores of Lake Superior. As a voyageur, he has traversed the continent to the Pacific coast; as a trapper, he has explored the great forests around Lake Superior, as well as portions of the Hudson's Bay Territory; and lastly, as a soldier in the army of the United States, he has served his country with fidelity. A thoroughbred woodman, an honest and most unselfish man, he is every way a clever companion. I shall ever hold him in pleasant remembrance as one of those eccentric and unspoiled children of nature whom we occasionally meet with in the journey of life.

CHAPTER IX.

ANIMAL PSYCHOLOGY.

Inquiries proposed—Whether the Mutes possess a Mental Principle— Whether its Qualities are similar to those manifested by the Human Mind—Whether the Differences are of Degree, or of Kind—Considerations from Structural Organization—The Principle of Life—Memory—Reason —Imagination—The Will—Appetites and Passions—Lunacy of Animals —General Conclusions.

THE popular mind has always been in advance of the metaphysicians with reference to the mental endowments of animals. For some reason there has been a perpetual hesitation among many of the latter to recognize, in the manifestations of the animal mind, the same characteristics that are displayed by the human intellect: lest the high position of man should be shaken or impaired. Besides this, the connection in man between the intellectual faculties and the moral sense is found to be so intimate, that the concession of the former has seemed, to cautious minds, to draw after it the necessary admission of the latter. In attempting to escape this imaginary dilemma, the metaphysicians have been betrayed, as it would seem, into a false position. This is shown by the invention, in modern times, of a vague, not to say fictitious, principle, with which all animals have been arbitrarily endowed for the government and maintenance of their lives. There can be no objection to the use of this principle, which is termed "instinct," to explain, or rather to leave unexplained, certain mental phenomena exhibited equally by man-kind and the inferior animals, so long as it is restricted to those mental processes which are beyond the reach of consciousness. But the attempt to explain all the mental phenomena manifested by the mutes by means of an arbitrary term is an evasion of the true question involved. It would be difficult, in right reason, to discover the slightest tendency to lower the personal dignity of man, or to alter in the least his responsibility to God, by recognizing the existence in the mutes of a thinking self-conscious principle, the same in kind that man possesses, but feebler in degree; nor even by conceding their possession of a moral sense, although, so far as our present knowledge extends, it is so faintly developed as scarcely to deserve the name. Man, at least, should neither admit nor deny the moral sense to the lower animals because of the supposed bearing of such an admission upon his own relations to the Supreme Being. The question of the degree and kind of their mental endowments should stand upon its own basis, and be resolved upon its own merits. I trust the sensibilities of no one will be disturbed by this method of introducing the subject of Animal Psychology; and that the subject may be considered unaffected by external complications, and be studied independently upon its own authoritative facts.

When the Creator brought into existence the various species of animals, He intrusted to each individual being the care of his own life. As a principle of intelligence was indispensable to capacitate each one to maintain and preserve that life, we find each individual endowed with a mental or spiritual essence which is distinct from the body, but associated with it in a mysterious manner. It requires no argument to prove that the mutes possess a principle of intelligence which performs for them the same office in governing their conduct that the human mind does for man. When the existence of mind in the mutes is recognized, the qualities it manifests become the subject of investigation. As we know nothing of the ultimate nature of the human mind, so in like manner we know nothing of the ultimate nature of the animal mind; but since the former manifests certain faculties, as memory, certain passions, as anger, certain appetites, as hunger, and puts forth a certain power, the will,—the true inquiry is, whether the latter manifests certain faculties, as memory, certain passions, as anger, certain appetites, as hunger, and puts forth a certain power, the will? If the affirmative is found to be true as to each of these propositions, then the next question must be, whether any difference in kind can be discovered between the memory of a man and the memory of a mute; between the anger of the one and the anger of the other; the hunger of the one and the hunger of the other; or the will of the one and the will of the other. Unless some real and determinate difference can be found by which to differentiate the qualities of the animal mind from those of the human mind, it must necessarily follow that the mute and the man are both endowed with a similar mental principle; and that man owes his superior dignity not to the exclusive possession of this principle, but rather to its enjoyment in a higher, more ample, and more distinguishing degree.

It is one of the extraordinary features of this Divine gift that it is capable of adaptation to so many, and to such diversified organisms; and not less remarkable that it should still reveal the fundamental similarities of a common principle through all its ramifications, so far as we are able to observe its manifestations. Our knowledge of the lives of the higher animals is extremely limited, and founded upon observation alone; while of the inferior species it is next to nothing. The discussion of the subject of Animal Psychology is, therefore, necessarily limited to the higher animals, and to such facts, with reference to these, as are well authenticated and universally admitted. Any argument which passes beyond the range of ascertained facts is incapable of proving or disproving any proposition.

Neither is it desirable to perplex ourselves with the question, whether or not the mutes possess a conscience, or the moral sense. While a negative declaration proves nothing, an affirmative assertion is without support in existing knowledge. The prior question, in point of time, is concerning their mental endowments.

It is equally unnecessary to discuss the grounds of the artificial distinction which is made between the appetites and passions on the one hand, and the intellectual powers on the other. The concession of the former to the mutes in common with mankind, and the withholding of the latter as an independent and distinguishing gift, is an assumption which tends to mislead without advancing the true inquiry. The passion of anger and the pain of hunger can only be predicated of a mental principle, of which they are manifestations as absolutely as memory or imagination. Indeed, it is an axiom in moral as well as in intellectual science, that pain and pleasure are experienced in the mind, and not in the organs of the body. When, therefore, we find the phenomena of pleasure and pain displayed by individuals of every species, and to be essentially the same in kind among them all, it leads to the same general conclusion; namely, that all living creatures possess a similar mental principle. This leaves the question of difference in degree, which was rendered necessary by difference in species.

I propose to submit, in a brief form, a series of considerations or arguments based upon the structural organization, and authenticated acts, of the higher animals, tending to show: first, that they possess a mental principle; secondly, that the qualities which it manifests are essentially the same as those displayed by the human mind; and lastly, that the difference between these qualities, and, inferentially, between the principles they respectively represent, is one o. degree and not of kind. The discussion, to be brief, must necessarily be general; and it is entered upon rather for the purpose of offering suggestions upon branches of the subject, than of treating it systematically as a whole. I have neither the facts nor the ability to prepare a treatise upon this important but difficult theme.

I. *Structural Organization.* It has been demonstrated, by anatomical comparisons, that the structural organization of the vertebrate animals conforms to a general plan, the fundamental features of which run through all the species, genera, orders, and classes of this branch of the animal kingdom. The several species thus stand in fixed relations to each other, and are all bound together by the common creative thought which is incorporated in the diversified forms of the individual representatives of each. Man, therefore, is not permitted to overlook the fact that he is a constituent member of this vertebrate branch; and although endowed, relatively, with the highest capacities, and invested with the highest organization, he cannot free himself from the bond by which its several members are indissolubly united.

Among the conspicuous features of this plan of structure is the brain, which is enveloped in a skull, and placed in immediate connection with the organs of sense. The nervous system, of which the brain is the centre, is universally regarded as the seat of the mental principle. Since all the vertebrate animals possess both the one and the other, they are all alike raised to the first condition necessary for the manifestation of intelligence. In the next place, they all agree in the possession of the organ of vision, located in the head in immediate connection with the brain; of the organs for smelling and hearing (with the exception perhaps of some species), similarly placed, and holding similar relations to the brain. Besides these, are the senses of taste and touch. These several senses, operating through similar mechanisms, have but one office, that of communicating impressions of external objects to the brain for the information of the mental principle. By their means a second condition of intelligence is secured; namely, perception. Without one or more of these senses, which are the instruments of perception, the bare continuance of animal life would be impossible; and yet, without the presence of a mental principle to take cognizance of the impressions thus conveyed, their object would necessarily be defeated.

These intimacies of structure are particularly remarkable among the mammals. The office and functions of the several bones and muscles of the animal frame are much the same in the different species. So the nervous system, which is centralized in the brain, is distributed throughout the body in such a manner that the relative position as well as functions of its several parts are similar, if not precisely the same, in all. The several ganglia are found in the same connection with the nerves of sensation and of motion, and performing the same offices in a similar manner. Such minute differences as exist find their explanation in the special adaptation of each animal to his sphere of life. In like manner, the circulating system is constructed upon the same general plan, employing the same organs, with slight variations of form. The same is equally true of the organs of respiration and of the digestive apparatus. One nomenclature suffices for the minutest subdivisions of the mammalian form. The anatomist traces, with facility, this conformity of structure through all the diversities which specific difference creates. Such modifications of particular organs as occur are seen to be necessary to meet special exigencies, such for example as relate to subsistence and to motion. Thus, the organs of respiration admit of considerable diversity in size and form, according to the amount they are required to furnish. Birds need a large quantity of respiration to give to their muscles the strength, and to their bodies the lightness necessary to flight; whence they have not only a double circulation of the blood, and an aerial respiration, but they also respire by other cavities besides the lungs. In most animals the quantity of respiration is moderate, because they are formed to walk rather than to run; in reptiles, which are formed to creep or hop, it is lower still; while in fishes it is least of all, since they are suspended in a medium of nearly their own specific gravity, and require but little muscular strength for motion. These differences are chiefly produced by variations of the same organs. From the fact that the vertebrate animals share a common typical structure, a strong presumption arises that they also share a common principle of intelligence.

This presumption is materially strengthened by other considerations. The structure of the higher animals leads directly to the inference that each of their organic forms was designed to be actuated and governed by a thinking principle; a principle not only capable of receiving impressions conveyed by the organs of sense, but also of making a rational use of the perceptions which these organs were designed to throw perpetually under its cognizance. To deny the existence of the principle, or its power to act, is a denial of the obvious purpose of the elaborate mechanism of the animal frame.

From every point in which the structural relations of the vertebrate animals are considered, a common plan of creation is not only seen, but this, in turn, becomes deeply significant upon the question of similar mental endowments. These intimacies of structure are the foundation of corresponding intimacies in the principle of intelligence by which they are actuated.

II. *The Principle of Life.* Life in all its forms is a mystery. As a formative power, it builds up the infantile body from weakness into maturity and strength. It maintains a perpetual conflict with the elements of disorder and decay until the organism in which it dwells breaks up, or wears itself out. Is death the destruction of this principle? or is it immaterial, and expelled, like the spirit, from the body? If it be a principle, and, therefore, immaterial, it would be difficult to show that the living and thinking principles are separate and distinct entities. It seems to be more than surmisable that the two are identical. It is I—the spirit—which lives, and not the body, which is material. If life comes of the union of body and spirit, then it is not an entity, but a result; and all there is of life is the life of the spiritual essence, or of the principle of intelligence.

Vegetable life cannot be compared with animal, because the former, to omit other differences, is without self-consciousness. Will it be said that the mutes are without consciousness? It is answered that consciousness is an inseparable and essential quality of the mental principle. When a beaver stands for a moment and looks upon his work, evidently to see whether it is right, and whether anything else is needed, he shows himself capable of holding his thoughts before his beaver mind; in other words, he is conscious of his own mental processes.

The possession of the principle of life by the higher animals, from its most robust to its most sensitive forms, draws after it whatever this principle may represent.

III. *Memory.* The mind is known by its qualities exclusively.

As a principle, or essence, it is not divisible into parts, or faculties, or organs, each having an independent existence. "The utmost ingenuity," says Abercrombie, "has not been able to advance a step beyond the fact that the mind remembers, reasons, imagines; and there we must rest contented."

It cannot for a moment be doubted that the animal mind remembers, and that it displays this quality as purely and as absolutely as the human mind. Memory, then, must be conceded to be one of its qualities. Its quickness or slowness, its retentiveness or weakness, are wholly immaterial. It is sufficient that the animal mind is able to recall a former perception, or previously known fact, and to have treasured it during the interval. The inference that follows from the recognized possession of a principle capable of remembering is very important. Memory is one of the qualities by which the existence of the human mind is demonstrated. By the same quality the existence of a corresponding principle in the mutes is also established. If a comparison of the two acts of remembrance show them to be in all respects similar, then the two principles of which they are manifestations are, inferentially, the same in kind. The difference is indeed immense between the memory of a familiar object, or even of a series of antecedent facts, which a mute may exhibit, and that powerful memory in man, which not only is able to hold the facts of universal knowledge, but also to reproduce the process of reasoning, by which the great truths of science have been demonstrated. This difference, however, is immaterial, since it is one of degree, and not of kind. As there is a gradation of its power among the individuals of the human species, so there is undoubtedly a similar gradation among the several species of the vertebrate animals.

"Memory," says Sir William Hamilton, "is an immediate knowledge of a present thought, involving an absolute belief that this thought represents another act of knowledge that has been." As the mind is a unit, the whole mind remembers, and not one of its fractional parts. If the power to remember were removed from the mental principle, it would become powerless, and perhaps be overthrown. The past, in such a case, would be utterly lost, the present vanishing with every instant, the future inconceivable, and the external world a blank. On the other hand, let any created being possess, in addition to the senses, a something capable of remembering, and it has more than the power to remember; it has, with it, a capacity to know, to understand, and to reason. That something is the mental principle. Every other inference is excluded. Knowing the qualities of this principle as it exists in the human species, and conscious of its unique and extraordinary character, when we find the mutes in possession of a something which displays the same qualities, the philosophical axiom at once suggests itself, namely, "that a plurality of principles is not to be assumed, when the phenomena can possibly be explained by one."

IV. *Reason or Judgment.* The mutes perceive external objects in the same manner that we do. After admitting that no distinction can be found between their manner and our own of acquiring a knowledge of external things, through the organs of sense, it has been denied that they are able to make a rational use of the perceptions thus obtained. Their acts, in innumerable instances, are seen to be acts of intelligence and knowledge, such as a man would perform under similar circumstances, and yet, there is an unwillingness to recognize in them the results of deliberate processes of reasoning, followed by an exercise of the will. A large class, it is true, acknowledge some reasoning powers in the mutes, but under such qualifications, limitations, and restrictions, that, in effect, it denies to them the possession of a free intelligence. The real question is practically evaded. Their acts should be tested by the same analysis which is applied to human acts, and full credence be given to the results. As we cannot place ourselves in personal connection with the animal mind and thus obtain their testimony concerning their mental processes, we are remitted to their personal acts. Upon these, however, a judgment can be formed as definitely as one man can pronounce upon the act of another man. While this method is not as irrefragable as an appeal to consciousness, it is one upon which mankind act implicitly in their own affairs.

"Reason," says Abercrombie, "consists in comparing and weighing facts, considerations, and motives, and deducing from them conclusions, both as principles of belief and rules of conduct." * * * * "It is the exercise of mind by which we compare facts with each other, and mental impressions with external things." There are many simple forms of reasoning; such as the relation of cause and effect; the comparison of one fact with another, and drawing an inference therefrom; and the separate consideration of the several qualities of an object. It will be sufficient for the present purpose to take a few of the more simple acts of animal intelligence, and test them by the ordinary standards by which human reasoning is measured and determined.

Anecdotes of the intelligent conduct of animals are innumerable. They are not only constantly appearing, and arresting attention, but a sufficient number of instances to illustrate the subject are within the personal knowledge of every individual. It will not be necessary, therefore, to seek a large number of cases, or to choose such as are the most remarkable. Such only will be selected as tend to illustrate particular forms of reasoning.

It is said that a dog, when attempting to track his master by the scent of his footsteps, will, if he finds the road branching, turn up one branch, and failing to find his scent, will then return and go up the other without putting his nose to the ground. It shows he drew the inference that because he did not take the one branch, he must necessarily have taken the other. The act being conceded, the interpretation given becomes an unavoidable conclusion.

Again, a dog will open a gate with his paw, a self-taught act. From the fact that he applied the means to effect the end, the inference arises necessarily that he understood the connection between the means and the end. This is, pure and simple, a case of reasoning; and, more than that, a kind of reason which can only be predicated of a thinking principle. The following artifice for catching fish, resorted to by the tiger of the Amazon, is related by Herndon. It involves the same form of reasoning, but covers a wider range of facts. "An enormous tiger," he remarks, "was extended full length upon a rock level with the water, about forty paces from me. From time to time he struck the water with his tail, and at the same moment raised one of his fore paws and seized a fish, often of an enormous size. These last, deceived by the noise, and taking it for the fall of fresh fruit (of which they are very fond), unsuspectingly approach, and soon fall into the claws of the traitor."[1] This self-taught device, founded upon a practical knowledge of the habits of fish, displays the operation of unfettered reason. If an analysis of the act were made for the purpose of discovering the mental processes involved, the formula and the result would be precisely the same as if it had been a human act. Reasoning upon the relations of causation must be of perpetual recurrence in the lives of animals. It is not conceivable that they could maintain their existence from day to day without this mental power.

Dr. Kane relates a somewhat similar artifice of his dog Grim to escape duty in harness. "Grim," he says, "was an ancient dog: his teeth indicated many winters, and his limbs, once splendid tractors for the sledge, were now covered with warts and ringbones. Somehow or other, when the dogs were harnessing for a journey, 'Old Grim' was sure not to be found; and upon one occasion, when he was detected in hiding away in a cast-off barrel, he incontinently became lame. Strange to say, he has been lame ever since except when the team is away

---

[1] Valley of the Amazon. Part I., 312.

without him."[1]   How came Grim, it may be asked, to understand the relation between sound legs and the sledge? and beyond that, to feign lameness as an excuse from duty?   To reach this final device required a lengthy process of reasoning, as well as a recognition of the sense and justice of his master, upon both of which he intended an imposition.   To say the least, these acts transcend the supposable powers of "an agent which performs ignorantly and blindly a work of intelligence and knowledge."[2] They can only be explained as the operations of a free intelligence.

The works of the beaver afford many interesting illustrations of his intelligence and reasoning capacity.   Felling a tree to reach its branches involves a series of considerations of a striking character.   A beaver seeing a birch-tree full of spreading branches, which to his longing eyes seemed quite desirable, may be supposed to say within himself: "If I cut this tree through with my teeth it will fall, and then I can secure its limbs for my winter subsistence."   But it is necessary that he should carry his thinking beyond this stage, and ascertain whether it is sufficiently near to his pond, or to some canal connected therewith, to enable him to transport the limbs, when cut into lengths, to the vicinity of his lodge.   A failure to cover these contingencies would involve him in a loss of his labor.   The several acts here described have been performed by beavers over and over again. They involve as well as prove a series of reasoning

---

[1] Arctic Explorations, i. 149.
[2] Sir William Hamilton's definition of " Instinct."

processes undistinguishable from similar processes of reasoning performed by the human mind.

Again, the construction of a canal from the pond across the lowlands to the rising ground, upon which the hard wood is found, to provide a way for the transportation of this wood by water, is another remarkable act of animal intelligence. A canal is not absolutely necessary to beavers any more than such a work is to mankind; but it comes to both alike as the result of progress in knowledge. A beaver canal could only be conceived by a lengthy and even complicated process of reasoning. After the conception had been developed and executed in one place, the selection of a line for a canal in another would involve several distinct considerations, such as the character of the ground to be excavated, its surface, elevation above the level of the pond, and the supply of hard wood near its necessary terminus. These, together with many other elements of fitness, must be ascertained to concur before the work could be safely entered upon. When a comparison of a large number of these beaver canals has demonstrated that they were skillfully and judiciously located, the inference seems to be unavoidable that the advantages named were previously ascertained. This would require an exercise of reason in the ordinary acceptation of the term.

And this leads to another suggestion. Upon the Upper Missouri these canals are impossible, from the height of the river banks; and besides this they are unnecessary, as the cotton-wood, which is the prevailing tree, is found to the edge of the river. While, therefore, canals are unknown to the Missouri beavers, they are constantly in use among the beavers of Lake Superior. On the other hand, the "beaver-slides" so common and so necessary on the Upper Missouri, are unnecessary, and therefore unknown, in the Lake Superior region. Contrary to the common opinion, is there not some evidence of a progress in knowledge to be found in the beaver canal and the beaver-slide? There was a time, undoubtedly, when the canal first came into use, and a time, consequently, when it was entirely unknown. Its first introduction was an act of progress from a lower to a higher artificial state of life. The use of the slide tends to show the possession of a free intelligence, by means of which they are enabled to adapt themselves to the circumstances by which they are surrounded. In like manner it has been seen that the lodge is not constructed upon an invariably typical plan, but adapted to the particular location in which it is placed. The lake, the island, and the bank lodge are all different from each other, and the difference consists in changes of form to meet the exigencies of the situation. These several artificial works show a capacity in the beaver to adapt his constructions to the particular conditions in which he finds himself placed. Whether or not they evince progress in knowledge, they at least show that the beaver follows, in these respects, the suggestions of a free intelligence.

"Instinct," says Dr. Reid, "is the habitual power of producing effects like contrivances of reason, yet so far beyond the intelligence and experience of the agent, as to be wholly unexplainable by reference to them." Habitual acts can only be understood from human experience. Acts to be performed habitually or mechanically must first be learned by an exercise of intelligence. It is a very unsatisfactory explanation of the works of a beaver, to affirm that he was endowed at his birth with a mechanical skill which, by the laws of mind, must be acquired by experience. An assertion that the acts of a beaver in felling a tree, in constructing a dam, or in excavating a canal, are beyond his intelligence, is mere assumption, as well as a contradiction of terms. This conclusion flows legitimately from the original blunder of attempting arbitrarily to endow animals with a supernatural principle, which enables them to perform ignorantly and blindly works of intelligence and knowledge. While this mysterious "agent" performs its office intelligently, the animal is a mere machine, according to the theory of Descartes. In other words, he is made a dwelling for a principle of intelligence; but this principle being superior to, and in some way independent of, the mute, holds no other relation to him than that of master and guide. Can anything be found in the whole range of human speculation more feeble than this expedient of human reason to explain a class of phenomena as simple as the simplest in the natural world?

The practice of beavers, while moving their short cuttings by water, of placing one end against the throat and pushing it from behind, of carrying mud and stones under their throats, holding them there with the paws, and of packing mud upon their lodges and dams by a stroke of the tail, have elsewhere been explained. They are severally intelligent acts, performed sensibly and rationally. Their method of shoving or rolling the larger billets of wood with their hips is even more ingenious. The little ants resort to a similar expedient to move bits of grain, but shove them with their shoulders. Their ingenuity and intelligence attracted the attention of ancient observers, several of whom recognized in them the possession of a mental principle.[1] Cicero says of the ant, who excels the beaver in systematic industry: "In formicam non modo sensus, sed etiam mens, ratio, memoria."[2] Personal labor of every kind and description depends upon, as well as evinces, the continuous operation of a mental principle.

Many animals, among which the beaver and the ant are good examples, provide a store of provisions for their sustenance during winter. This act shows a forecast of the future. To satisfy present hunger is a simple act of intelligence; but to anticipate distant wants and provide for them is a much higher act of knowledge. What motive could induce the mutes to make such provision unless they knew, or had

---

[1] Ac veluti ingentem formicæ farris acervum
quum populant, hiemis memores, tectoque reponunt:
it nigrum campis agmen, prædamque per herbas
convectant calle angusto; pars grandia trudunt
obnixæ frumenta humeris; pars agmina cogunt,
castigantque moras; opere omnis semita fervet.
                                VIRGIL, ÆNEID, iv. 402.

Ac si quis comparet onera corporibus earum, fateatur, nullis portione vires esse majores. Gerunt ea morsu. Majora aversæ postremis pedibus moliuntur, humeris obnixæ. Et iis Republicæ ratio, memoria, cura.
                                PLINY, NAT. HIST., Lib. xi. c. xxxvi.

The ants are a people not strong, yet they prepare their meat in the summer.   PROVERBS, xxx. 25.

[2] De Nat. Deorum. Lib. iii. c. ix.

learned by experience, that winter followed the summer, and that the preservation of their lives required the accumulation of a surplus of food? The possession of a thinking principle renders all of these acts perfectly intelligible as well as simple; and without it they are wholly incapable of a rational explanation.

The beaver, in a comparative estimate, is a low animal in his structural organization, as has been shown. He lives upon the coarsest food, is slow of motion upon land, of low respiration, monotrematous, and aquatic. His vision is short in range, and his brain is without those convolutions which are regarded as indications of mental power. In the great catalogue of animals, which is constructed upon the basis of anatomical structure, he rises no higher than the rat, the porcupine, or the squirrel. There is no reason for supposing that he is more intelligent than any other rodent of a corresponding grade. And yet by his sagacity, his industry, and his artificial erections, he has raised himself to a very respectable position, in human estimation, for intelligence and architectural capacity. It is because he needs these erections to promote his comfort and safety that man is able to follow the evidences of his skill and intelligence, and to become satisfied of their extraordinary character. If then an animal, with such an inferior organization, manifests so large an amount of mental capacity, of how much more must those be capable whose organization is found to be so much superior!

There is no doubt that the highest forms of intelligence among the mutes are to be found in the carnivorous animals. As an order they live pre-eminently by their wits; and they are unquestionably endowed with mental capacities, of higher relative power, to enable them to maintain their existence. The propagation and perpetuation of their species to the present time, testifies to the continuous triumph of their superior intelligence over the feebler capacities of the non-carnivorous mutes upon whom they subsist. They are able to endure hunger and fatigue, to wait and watch for prey, and to invent and practice many artifices for the capture of the latter. Many of them have great physical strength, a large brain, powerful respiration, and remarkable fleetness of foot. Their personal appearance commands both respect and admiration. Who ever looked into the clear round eye of a lion, without being impressed with the thought that there was a quick intelligence and a powerful will behind it, which, in the open plain or in the thicket, it would be hard to deceive and difficult to overmatch!

The carnivorous animals construct nothing, save a burrow or a den. Their personal acts, which have never been carefully studied, furnish, therefore, the only sources of information concerning their mental endowments. But enough of these have been witnessed and authenticated to illustrate the subject. It will be sufficient for the present purpose to introduce one or two cases.

The fox, when pursued, often takes to the bed of a shallow stream to conceal his footprints and suppress his scent; or runs back upon his own track for some distance, and then, making a long leap at a right angle, changes his direction. These devices were well adapted to embarrass and foil his pursuers. It seems to be an unavoidable inference that the fox understood the means by which he was followed, and that he possessed sufficient acuteness, as well as subtlety of mind, to counteract, in these ways, the danger. These expedients presuppose a consciousness of peril, which of itself involves a knowledge of antecedent occurrences; and the execution of the device shows deliberation, conclusion, and an exercise of the will. The acts themselves are unexplainable except as manifestations of a free intelligence.

This animal, whose cunning is proverbial, has been known to simulate death, to secure his deliverance, under circumstances somewhat trying to his fortitude. A fox one night entered the hen-house of a farmer, and after destroying a large number of fowls, gorged himself to such repletion that he could not pass out through the small aperture by which he had entered. The proprietor found him, in the morning, sprawled out upon the floor apparently dead from surfeit; and taking him up by the legs carried him out, unsuspectingly, and for some distance to the side of his house, where he dropped him upon the grass. No sooner did Reynard find himself free than he sprang to his feet and made his escape.[1] He seemed to know that it was only as a dead fox that he would be allowed to leave the scene of his spoliations; and yet to devise this plan of escape required no ordinary effort of intelligence, while its execution rather taxes our confidence in his possession of such steadiness of

---

[1] This incident was communicated to the author by Coral C. White, of Aurora, New York, who carried out the fox. His veracity is unimpeachable.

nerves. A man placed in similar circumstances, and resorting to a like expedient, would be conscious of several distinct processes of reasoning. It is difficult to perceive how these processes could be possible, in either case, except by the agency of a mental principle, or how they could differ as modes of thought.

The several acts of the mutes here cited, as illustrations of the exercise of reason, can be fully explained as manifestations of a thinking principle. When the possession by them of such a principle is recognized, all difficulties vanish; and their conduct appears in an intelligible light. It also follows that their intelligence must necessarily be free to act within the range of its powers. In this discussion the relative strength of their mental capacities is left out of view, as immaterial. Compared with those of the human intellect they are feeble and slight, but within their several spheres of life and action they are ample for the promotion of their individual happiness.

V. *Imagination.* Whether the animal mind exhibits the quality of imagination it may be difficult to substantiate. Although it is one of the highest qualities of the mental principle, yet it is manifested in many simple forms. The playfulness of childhood, which is also commonly exhibited by the young of animals, is superinduced, seemingly, by the pictures or images formed in the mind by the fancy or imagination. This faculty, Kames observes, "is the great instrument of recreation." If an attempt is made to explain the songs of birds, it will be necessary to resort to imagination, since the art itself is imaginative. Animals are known to dream from physical indications during sleep, and dreams are the works of memory and imagination. Too little is known of the lives of animals to show whether they possess this quality in any sensible degree.

VI. *The Will.* A doubt has been entertained whether the mutes possess a will, like the will of man, because responsibility must follow its exercise. Their own lives, at least, are intrusted to their keeping, the preservation of which is the highest form of responsibility. With a free volition, they rise up or lie down; they go or come; they play or quarrel, they bark, or mew, or sing; and they lie in wait for prey, or seek it by long excursions. These several acts are performed under the influence of motives, and were preceded by an exercise of the will. Unless the mute has a free choice between alternative courses, one of which may lead to danger and the other to safety, his conduct would be unintelligent. He might lose his life at any moment. The will is that mental power that sets the body in motion to execute a resolution previously reached by a process of reasoning. It is the power which adopts and executes the conclusions of the judgment. Unless a difference can be discovered in the quality of the will, as displayed by the mutes and by mankind, there is no means of distinguishing one from the other, except in the degree of its strength and persistency. A will, also, presupposes the existence of a mental principle, of which alone it can be predicated.

VII. *Appetites and Passions.* The mutes have the appetites and passions in common with mankind. No difficulty has ever been found in conceding a community of characteristics in these, the inferior, manifestations of the mental principle. While they differ in

the degree of their strength, some of them are undoubtedly wanting among the lowest grades of the
vertebrate animals. As a portion of them excel mankind in the acuteness of the senses, by means of which
the feebleness of their mental powers is supplemented,
so in some of the appetites and passions they may
possess a delicacy of sensibility of which the human
species are incapable. In their affections for their
young, and for their mates (among such as pair), the
highest evidence of their sensibility is found. They
also display courage, fidelity, and gratitude, and to
these, perhaps, in some rare instances, benevolence
may be added. For the possession of these qualities,
which are undistinguishable from the corresponding
qualities manifested by the human mind, and for the
beautiful illustrations of maternal affection which
they display, they are entitled to our regard.

Captain Stansbury gives the following account of a
blind pelican upon one of the islands of the Great
Salt Lake of Utah: "In a ramble around the shores
of the island, I came across a venerable looking old
pelican, very large and fat, which allowed me to approach him without attempting to escape. Surprised
at his apparent tameness, we examined him more
closely, and found that it was owing to his being entirely blind, for he proved to be very pugnacious,
snapping freely, but vaguely, on each side, in search of
his enemies, whom he could hear but could not see.
As he was totally helpless, he must have subsisted on
the charity of his neighbors, and his sleek and comfortable condition showed, that like beggars in more
civilized communities, he had 'fared sumptuously every
day.' The food of these birds consists entirely of

fish, which they must necessarily obtain from Bear River, from the Weber, the Jordan, or from the Warm Springs on the eastern side of Spring Valley, at all of which places they were observed fishing for food. The nearest of these points was more than thirty miles distant, making necessary a flight of at least sixty miles to procure and transport food for the subsistence of their young. Immense numbers of young birds were huddled together in groups about the island, under the charge of a grave looking nurse or keeper, who, all the time that we were there, was relieved from guard at intervals as regularly as a sentinel."[1]

Incidents illustrative of this class of qualities could be multiplied to an indefinite extent. They tend in a

---

[1] Stansbury's Salt Lake, p. 193. Another incident related by the same writer, expressive of the maternal solicitude as well as intelligence of the pelican, is worth repeating. "Rounding the north point of Antelope Island, we called at the little islet, to which we had given the name of Egg Island, to look after our old friends, the gulls and pelicans. * * * One poor fellow, about four inches long, driven by the extremity of his fear, took to the water of his own accord, when he was swept out by the current to the distance of two or three hundred yards, and seemed quite bewildered by the novelty of his situation. As soon as he was discovered by the old birds, who hovered over our heads in thousands, watching our proceedings with great anxiety and noise, one—the parent, we judged, from its greater solicitude—lighted down by its side, and was soon joined by half a dozen others, who began guiding the little navigator to the shore, flying a little way before him, and again alighting, the mother swimming beside him, and evidently encouraging him in this, his first adventure upon the water. The little fellow seemed perfectly to understand what was meant, and when we sailed away, was advancing rapidly under the convoy of his friends, and was within a few yards of the shore, which he doubtless reached in safety."—Ib. p. 207.

striking manner to show the uniformity of the operations of the mental principle throughout the animal
kingdom.

VIII. *Lunacy of Animals.* Under the preceding
heads we have discussed a small number out of the
great body of facts which tend to establish the existence of a thinking reasoning principle among the
mutes; and also tending to show that the qualities
manifested by it cannot be distinguished from the corresponding manifestations of the human mind, except
in the degree of their strength. Cases have occurred
among animals where their mental powers were overthrown, and lunacy supervened, furnishing the same
external indications which follow the overthrow of
the human intellect, so that the animal has been seen
in both conditions, when in the full possession of his
faculties, and when their functions have been suspended. Dr. Kane relates several cases in point among
his dogs, occasioned by the absence of light during the
long arctic winter while he was ice bound in the far
north. He remarks as follows: "The mouse-colored
dogs, the leaders of my Newfoundland team, have for
the last fortnight been nursed like babies. No one
can tell how anxiously I watch them. They are kept
below, tended, fed, cleansed, caressed, and *doctored*,
to the infinite discomfort of all hands. To-day I give
up the last hope of saving them. Their disease is as
clearly mental as in the case of any human being.
The more material functions of the poor brutes go on
without interruption; they eat voraciously, retain
their strength, and sleep well. But all the indications beyond this go to prove that the original epilepsy,
which was the first manifestation of brain disease

among them, has been followed by a true lunacy. They look frenziedly at nothing, walk in straight and curved lines, with anxious and unwearying perseverance. They fawn on you, but without seeming to appreciate the notice you give them in return; pushing their heads against your person, or oscillating with a strange pantomime of fear. Their most intelligent actions seem automatic; sometimes they claw you as if trying to burrow into your seal skins; sometimes they remain for hours in moody silence, and then start off howling as if pursued, and run up and down for hours. So it was with poor Flora, our 'wise dog.' She was seized with the endemic spasms, and after a few days of violent paroxysms, lapsed into a lethargic condition, eating voraciously, but gaining no strength. This passing off, the same crazy wildness took possession of her, and she died of brain disease (arachnoidal effusion) in about six weeks."[1]

This account is so full and specific that it needs no comment. Such a case of lunacy was only needed to complete the analogy which seems to be sustained in every other of the more common manifestations of the animal and of the human mind.

From the foregoing but most incomplete and imperfect consideration of some of the branches of the subject of Animal Psychology, it would be venturesome to urge any other than the more simple conclusions. Two or three only will be suggested.

In the first place, the term "instinct," to explain the intelligent acts of animals, should be abandoned. This term was an invention of the metaphysicians to

---

[1] Arctic Explorations, i. 157.

assert and maintain a fundamental distinction between the mental principle of the human species and
that of the inferior animals. With its multiform defi-
nitions, and with the repeated enlargements of its
signification, it is wholly incapable of explaining the
phenomena of animal intelligence. As a vain attempt
to embody a system of philosophy in a definition, it
has proved a failure, as might have been expected.
When carried to its legitimate results, it endows every
animal with a supernatural principle, and makes
each of his intelligent acts little short of a miracle.
As a term or invention it is *functus officio*. With its
disuse the subject of Animal Psychology is freed from
all extraneous embarrassments, and the mental phenomena manifested by the mutes can be investigated
and explained on philosophical principles.

In the second place, we are led to recognize in the
mutes the possession of a free intelligence. In other
words, that they are endowed with a mental principle
which performs for them the same office that the
human mind does for man; that this principle is free
to act in view of motives and premises; and that it is
ample in measure to enable each animal, within his
sphere of action, to preserve his life and govern his
conduct. This conclusion seems necessarily to follow
from their possession of the organs of sense, from
their manifestation of the appetites and passions, and
from their ability to perceive, to remember, to reason,
and to will.

And in the third and last place, as we are unable,
in similar specific acts, to find any difference in kind
between the manifestations of perception, appetite
and passion, memory, reason and will on the part of

a mute, and the corresponding manifestations on the part of a man, we are led to the conclusion that the difference is one of degree, and not of kind; and therefore that the principle from which they emanate is the same in kind, but bestowed in different measure, to adapt each species to its particular mode of life.

This theory, when rightly considered, is neither novel nor subversive of moral truth. The general intelligence of mankind, which embodies, in a greater degree than is usually supposed, the highest sense of the human understanding, never adopted the speculations of the metaphysicians with reference to the endowments of the inferior animals. On the contrary, it has ever been disposed to recognize in them the possession of a rational, thinking principle, as free to act as the mind of man. To this view later writers are drawing sensibly nearer. Among the number, Max Müller has quite recently put forth some very sensible observations. "I mean," he remarks, "to claim a large share of what we call our mental faculties for the higher animals. These animals have *sensation, perception, memory, will,* and *intellect*—only we must restrict intellect to the interlacing of single perceptions. All these points can be proved by irrefragable evidence. * * * There are, no doubt, many people who are as much frightened at the idea that brutes have souls, and are able to think, as by 'the blue ape without a tail.' * * * It does not follow that brutes have no souls, because they have no human souls. It does not follow that the souls of men are not immortal, because the souls of animals are not immortal; nor has the *major* *premiss* ever been proved by any philosopher, namely, that the souls of brutes must necessarily be destroyed and annihilated by death. Leibnitz, who has defended the immortality of the human soul with stronger arguments than even Descartes, writes: 'I found at last how the souls of brutes and their sensations do not at all interfere with the immortality of human souls; on the contrary, nothing seems better to establish our natural immortality than to believe that all souls are imperishable.'"[1] To nearly the same effect, Agassiz had previously expressed himself. "When animals fight with one another," he says, "when they associate for a common purpose, when they warn one another in danger, when they come to the rescue of one another, when they display pain or joy, they manifest impulses of the same kind as are considered among the moral attributes of man. The range of the passions is even as extensive as that of the human mind, and I am at a loss to perceive a difference in kind between them, however much they may differ in degree, and in the manner in which they are expressed. * * * This argues strongly in favor of the existence in every animal of an immaterial principle similar to that which, by its excellence and superior endowments, places man so much above animals. Yet the principle exists unquestionably, and whether it be called soul, reason, or instinct, it presents in the whole range of organized beings a series of phenomena closely linked together; and upon it are based not only the highest manifestations of mind, but the very permanence of the specific

---

[1] Science of Language. Scribner's ed., lec. ix. p. 349.

differences which characterize every organism. Most of the arguments of philosophy in favor of the immortality of man apply equally to the permanence of this principle in other living beings."[1]

With two or three further suggestions this discussion will be concluded. It cannot be said that the views, herein presented, tend to lower the personal dignity of man; but, on the contrary, they rather serve to distinguish his position. His great superiority is abundantly assured by the bestowment of the highest structural organization, of the fullest mental endowments, and by the possession of articulate speech. The distance which separates him from the highest of the mutes is sufficiently immeasurable to relieve his pride from all sense of humiliation from the consciousness of sharing the principle of intelligence with the latter. Sidney Smith has touched this point with his satirical pen in the following language: "I confess I feel myself so much at ease about the superiority of mankind—I have such a marked and decided contempt for the understanding of every baboon I have ever seen—I feel so sure that the blue ape without a tail will never rival us in poetry, painting, and music, that I see no reason whatever that justice may not be done to the few fragments of soul and tatters of understanding which they may really possess." The mental principle here derided, while its possession is admitted, has, nevertheless, the inherent dignity of which a thinking principle cannot be divested. By his pre-eminent endowments, man stands at the head of the animal kingdom, the great

---

[1] Nat. Hist. U. S., i. 64.

exemplar of this principle, and separated by a wide interval from its other possessors. The separation is as marked and real as could be desired. But it is doubtful whether he possesses the sum of the powers of the principle called mind. It is precisely here, as it seems to the writer, that God has revealed a feature in the plan of creation not less wonderful than the original conception of a mental principle. Having called into existence this marvelous principle, and created a series of organic forms, He apportioned it among them all in such measure as to adapt each individual being to the sphere of life in which he was designed to move. The widest possible range for the exercise and development of mind was thus provided. A full comprehension of its powers and capacities must therefore be sought in its varied manifestations by the several species. It is not probable that the whole of its powers are possessed by any species: but rather that in their totality they are to be found among the members of the animal kingdom as a whole. A true system of mental philosophy, therefore, cannot be developed until all the manifestations of this principle are comprehended.

The hiatus between man and the nearest species below him in the scale of intelligence is so wide as to disturb the symmetrical gradation of the several orders of animals. We can neither conjecture that some intermediate order has fallen out of existence, nor assume the permanent degradation of any existing species; but, on the contrary, it seems to have been a part of the original plan of creation that man should stand without a compeer or contestant, the indisputable head of the series of organic forms, and the recipient, in the largest measure, of the gift of the mental principle. Some explanation of his excessive superiority may be found in the progress he has made since his emergence from his primitive condition. For ages, the bounds of which are unknown, mankind were immersed in a barbarism the depths of which can be but feebly conceived. They were without arts, without agriculture, without flocks or herds, depending chiefly upon fish, and the spontaneous fruits of the earth for subsistence. There are glimpses afforded to us, here and there, of a state of society in which the family relations were unknown, and in which violence and passion reigned supreme. The contrast between such a condition of mankind, and that of the present time, is so great that it is difficult to recognize in these primitive barbarians our lineal progenitors. Out of that condition man has struggled through a long and painful experience until he has been finally rewarded with the amenities of civilization. Language has been the great instrument of this progress, the power of which was increased many fold when it clothed itself in written characters. He was thus enabled to perpetuate the results of individual experience, and transmit them through the ages. Each discovery thus became a foundation on which to mount up to new discoveries. With the knowledge he has gained, and the elevation he has experienced, it is now difficult to realize the low condition from which his line of advancement commenced. Portions of the human family are still found in the darkness of ignorance, and in the feebleness of mental imbecility; and yet, although the distance of their intellectual separation is very great, it is much less than that between the latter and the most intelligent of the inferior animals. The difference expresses the superiority of his structural organization and of his mental endowments.

On the other hand, can it be truly affirmed that the inferior animals have been stationary in their knowledge from the commencement of their existence? This conclusion should not be over-hastily assumed. Within the period of human observation, their progress has seemed to be inconsiderable—but yet not absolutely nothing. For example, dogs under training have developed special capacities, such as the pointer and the setter, and have transmitted them to their offspring. This shows not only progress, but that of so marked a character as to work a transformation in the characteristics of the animal. Many animals, as the elephant, the horse, the bear, and even the hog—the type of stupidity—have been taught a variety of performances, under the stimulus of rewards, of which they were previously ignorant. These examples, however, are less important than the knowledge acquired by undomesticated animals, and transmitted, as a part of their experience and knowledge, in the species in which they were acquired. Of this kind are the several varieties of the beaver lodge and dam, and the development and perpetuation of the idea of a beaver canal. When careful and patient investigation has been made of these several subjects, the results will materially modify, in all probability, our present impressions.

Finally, is it to be the prerogative of man to uproot and destroy not only the masses of the animal kingdom numerically, but also the great body of the species? If the human family maintains its present hostile attitude toward the mutes, and increases in numbers and in civilization at the present ratio, for several centuries to come, it is plain to be seen that many species of animals must be extirpated from the earth. An arrest of the progress of the human race can alone prevent the dismemberment and destruction of a large portion of the animal kingdom. Domestication or extermination is the alternative already offered not alone to species, but to families and orders of animals. It may be that this result was never intended in the councils of Providence. It is not unlikely that God has adjusted a balance among the several orders of animals which cannot be overthrown except at the peril of the aggressor; and that in some mysterious way this balance is destined to be preserved. The present attitude of man toward the mutes is not such, in all respects, as befits his superior wisdom. We deny them all rights, and ravage their ranks with wanton and unmerciful cruelty. The annual sacrifice of animal life to maintain human life is frightful, if considered only with reference to its excess beyond our reasonable wants. When the Creator made man omnivorous, He designed his use of animal food. It is not sentimentalism but rather sense, to say that he should exercise the right with reason and forbearance. When we claim that the bear was made for man's food, we forget that man was just as much made to be food for the bear; and that our right to eat the bear rests upon no higher sanction, than his coequal right to feast upon our flesh if he overcomes in battle. Man's dominion over the mutes is in virtue of his superior endowments; but it is equally clear that the great Author of existence designed the happiness of the smallest and least endowed of all His creatures as completely and as absolutely as He did the happiness of man. If we recognize the fact that the mutes possess a thinking, and reasoning, and perhaps an immortal principle, our relations to them will appear to us in a different, and in a better light.

APPENDICES.

A.

DR. W. W. ELY'S NOTES ON CHAPTER II.

B.

SAMUEL HEARNE'S ARTICLE ON THE BEAVER.
From Hearne's Journey, etc. Lond. ed. 1795, p. 226.

C.

BENNETT'S ARTICLE ON THE BEAVER.
From Gardens and Menagerie. Zoolog. Soc'ty. Quadrupeds. I. 153.

NOTE.

THE annexed articles by Hearne and Bennett, Appendices B and C, are the best and most authentic extant upon the beaver. They have been made the foundation of the later accounts of this animal which are found in the Encyclopedias, and in current works on Natural History. It was their brevity, and consequent incompleteness, which induced the publication of this work, for the purpose of furnishing a more detailed exposition of the habits of the beaver, and of his artificial erections.

APPENDIX A.

I. *Measurement of skulls—in inches and hundredths of an inch. From No. 7 to 41, American skulls from the region near Lake Superior. No. 7284, American skull from the Upper Missouri. No. 1072, Young American skull from New York. No. 6564, European skull from River Elbe, Germany.*

	7	20	21	33	36	40	41	7284	1072	6564
From anterior margin of intermaxillary to occipital crest	5·35	5·36	5·34	5·42	5·16	5·72	4·13	5·85	4·61	5·12
From tip of nasal to occipital crest	5·20	5·20	5·20	5·22	5·06	5·54	4 02	5·67	4·45	5·05
Width across zygomatic arches	3·88	3·78	3·78	3·87	3·67	4·08	2·89	4·03	4·18	4·30
Width from outer borders of auditory tubes	3·05	2·89	2·98	2·91	2·85	3·06	...	3·00	2·55	2·45
Length of nasal bone	1·76	1·90	1·87	1·75	1·66	1·91	1·26	2·10	1·64	2·00
Width of nasal bone	·51	·52	·52	·52	·45	·52	·41	·57	·45	·54
Narrowest part between orbits	·88	1·06	1·00	1·02	·96	1·04	·79	1·02	·87	1·02
From incisors to anterior margin of incisive foramen	·83	·81	·90	·72	·67	·81	·57	·85	·63	·52
Length of incisive foramen	·45	·49	·31	·50	·49	·54	·30	·60	·50	·52
From incisors to palatal foramen	2·36	2·38	2·38	2·35	2·19	2·44	1·58	2·38	2·00	2·01
From incisors to anterior margin of molars	1·71	1·79	1·76	1·62	1·59	1·76	1·24	1·90	1·52	1·50
From incisors to posterior margin of palatal bone	2·98	2·91	2·93	2·96	2·82	3·11	2·20	3·18	2·65	2·76
From palatal arch to occipital foramen	1·65	1·66	1·55	1·54	1·46	1·75	...	1·78	...	1·45
Height of occipital foramen	·70	·62	·60	·58	·60	·65	...	·62	...	·67
Width of occipital foramen	·73	·67	·70	·72	·77	·76	...	·73	...	·72

288   APPENDICES.

II. *Differences between the European and the American Beavers.*

If naturalists have found it difficult to agree as to the proper classification of the beaver, they have been scarcely less troubled to decide whether the beavers of the Old and the New World constitute one or more species. Some reference to this subject might be expected in a work like the present; and in order to limit the discussion I propose to examine only the views given by Dr. Brandt, as being the latest and most elaborate, and probably the most conclusive, that can be adduced in favor of the diversity of species.

In a series of essays published in the "Memoires de l'Académie de St. Petersbourg," Brandt has discussed many questions relating to the beaver with great ability and thoroughness of investigation. His conclusions on the point before us are expressed in the following summary:

"1. From the investigations of Kuhl, Oken, and previously of Brandt and Ratzeburg, no outward characteristic appears affording evidence of a specific difference.

"2. That in respect to the relative size of the body, the American beaver, from previous experiences, does not differ from the European in any essential particular, and probably not at all.

"3. That in respect to the relation of the head-, ear-, foot-, and tail-formation, no distinctive characteristics have yet been discovered. ·

"4. That, on the other hand, by the comparison of eight skulls of the European beaver, with five skulls of beavers from the northwest coast of America, manifold constant differences, in part very striking, become apparent between the beavers of the Old and New World.

"5. That many of the differences in these skulls involve also variations in the external structure.

"6. That, finally, the well-known histological variation in the castor sacs, which exists between the beavers of the Old and the New World, and also the difference in the appearance of their secretion, seem to establish a specific difference between the two." P. 62.

Excluding then, as we may do, all but the two points named,

viz., the differences observed in the skull, and in the castoreum organs, it remains to inquire whether these variations are constant and essential, and such as characterize species, or only varieties.

The fact that the beavers of the Old and the New World present certain points of difference in the skull formation is not to be denied, and the attempt has been made to eliminate those which are considered unessential from those which possess an invariable character in the two races, so as to establish just grounds for the specific distinction. It is important to realize the tendency to variation which exists in the cranial structures, and I therefore quote from Brandt, from an article "Upon the variation of particular bones of the Beaver Skull," op. cit. p. 67.

"If we have the opportunity of comparing with each other a large number of skulls of one and the same species, we not unfrequently learn, on closer inspection, that no one of them agrees perfectly with the others, but that all show more or less striking variations. These variations are often so considerable, that if we thus examined but two or three skulls, we should have no hesitancy in deciding, according to the prevailing method of determining zoölogical species, that there was a specific difference in the animals to which such skulls belonged. The examination of a larger number of beaver skulls convinced me how erroneous would be a conclusion drawn from the examination of a small number of specimens.

" The following remarks, therefore, have only for their object to name the variations which I have seen occur in the skulls of the species CASTOR, and to show that it is only by several, or better, by many specimens of one and the same species, that we can with any degree of certainty determine the boundaries of such species."

In the comparisons made by Brandt of European and American beaver skulls, he refers to eight of the former, and five of the latter variety. We have, in our collection, over ninety skulls of the American beaver from the region near Lake Superior, and through the kindness of Prof. James Hall, of the New York State Museum, and Prof. Spencer F. Baird, of the Smithsonian Institution, I have had the opportunity to examine skulls from other American localities, in all over one hundred specimens. Prof. Baird has also favored me with a European skull, No. 6564, from the Smithsonian Institution.[1]

By comparing the skulls of this extensive series with the descriptions given by Brandt in the following article, I find that many more resemblances may be traced between the European and the American beaver than he has observed, thus reducing the amount of constant differences between the two varieties.

We give the translation of the whole of his article in which the two kinds of skulls are compared, adding to the sections the results obtained by an examination of the skulls of the American series referred to above.

"Mémoires de l'Académie de St. Petersbourg, VI. Série, p. 53.

"§ 1. Superior aspect of different beaver skulls.

" If we examine the skull of the European and of the American beaver, we notice the following special differences:

"1. The portion of the frontal bone lying between the arches of the eyebrows, in all the European skulls is shorter and broader, much broader than long; but in the American, narrower and somewhat longer (quite as broad as long); so that the middle transverse diameter of the anterior portion of the frontal bone— that part lying between the eyes—is in the American skulls nearly or quite as long as the arch of the eyebrows; but in the European it appears longer than this."

This is true generally of the American skulls; but in six specimens the average length of the eyebrow portion is $81'''\frac{2}{3}$, and the average width of the middle portion is $1'' 08'''\frac{1}{3}$, being an excess of width of $26'''\frac{2}{3}$.

" 2. In the European skulls the arches of the eyebrows are shorter, and their posterior tubercles, opposite the highest point of the malar bone, are strongly developed. In the American, on the contrary, the posterior eyebrow processes, only indicated, sometimes scarcely indicated at all, or at least but slightly developed, can be seen back of the highest point of the malar. The anterior eyebrow process is in all the European skulls likewise stronger than in the American."

The highest point of the malar in American skulls is in advance of the posterior processes; but in one skull (No 20) it is on a line

---

[1] I am also indebted to Prof. Baird for the use of several works, relating to the beaver, from the Smithsonian Institution.

with these processes, as in the European variety. In the older and larger American skulls, both processes are strongly developed, particularly the anterior. In many skulls the posterior processes are as strongly marked as in the European skull. In the young New York skull they are even stronger than in the young and larger European skull.

"3. The snout, measured from the inferior orbital opening to the inferior corner of the nostril in two European skulls of equal size (Nos. 56 and 186 of the Kiew Col.), is broader and somewhat longer than in an American skull of equal size in the Academic Museum.

"4. The nasal bones show the greatest variations. Their length in all the European is much above one-third the length of the skull, measured from the incisor teeth to the crista occipitalis; while, on the contrary, in the three larger of the American skulls the length of the nasal bones is only a little if any over one-third, and the smallest not even one-third the length of the skull. The nasal bones of the six older skulls lying before me of the European beaver are therefore longer, and extend more or less far posteriorly, i.e. more or less beyond the anterior prominence of the arch of the eyebrows, so that they (the nasal bones) lie with their posterior borders nearly or quite opposite the middle of the margins of the orbits. In a young Polish beaver (No. 57 of the Kiew Col.) they reach, however, only to the anterior third of the orbital ring (note — our Caucasian skull can serve as an example of strong lengthening of the nasal bones) — and in our young Lapland beaver they lie nearly as in our California beaver skull, opposite only the circumference of the anterior border of the orbital ring. In none of the five American skulls, lying before me, on the contrary, do the nasal bones extend beyond the anterior prominence of the eyebrows. In nearly all the skulls of the European beaver, compared with the five American ones lying before me, the nasal bones are in form longer in the middle and posterior, however, in general narrower, so that their breadth in their middle varies between one-fourth and one-fifth of their length, while in our five American skulls the breadth of their middle portion attains to between one-third and one-fourth of their length. Although the nasal bones of the American beaver are thus on the whole broader, still they vary less in this respect than in their lesser length. The external border of the nasal bones of the European beaver is not so strongly curved as in the American. Two of the European skulls, however, approach quite to the American in this respect. The superior surface or the anterior half of the nasal bones is in six of the European skulls pretty plane; in two of the others, on the contrary (Nos. 51 and 1955 of the Kiew Col.), as in all the five American, it is strongly convex. In regard to the character (or relation) of the nasal bones, there remains, therefore, in consequence of the preceding remarks, only their more considerable length in comparison with the skull as a mark of the European beaver; since the greater lengthening posteriorly of the nasal bones cannot be so rigorously proven in all European beavers, especially not in our Lapland specimens. It is possible, however, that the nasal bones are less prolonged posteriorly in younger animals than in fullgrown, so that in this way the full-grown European might be recognized by its posteriorly prolonged nasal bones. Confirmatory of this view are the following facts : 1. That in all of the six old skulls lying before me of European beavers, the posterior extremities of the nasal bones reach more or less far posteriorly, and that this happens in a young skull of the Kiew Collection (No. 57), the length of which is four lines greater than that of the one from Lapland ; and 2, that in one very young American skull, the nasal bones extend backward somewhat less relatively than in the full grown."

It is in respect to the nasal bones that the greatest difference has been observed between the European and the American beavers. The most striking obvious difference being the backward extension of the nasals in the European variety. In extreme cases, their posterior margins are found behind the middle of the margin of the orbital ring; and over the anterior margin of the upper molars—a point probably never reached by the nasals in the American skull; but this feature of the European skull is not constant. Brandt has not found it in the Polish and the Lapland beaver, and he expressly yields the point as to its being a characteristic mark of the European variety; it cannot, he says, "be rigorously proven in all European skulls." In the New York skull the nasals are elongated as represented in the Polish skull. It does not appear that the lengthening of the nasals in the American skull is invariably due to age—since their proportional length, in some young skulls, perhaps equals that of older specimens. The form of these bones, *i.e.* their width and convex outer margin, differ much in American specimens. Having examined this subject with much care, Brandt concludes in respect to the nasal bones, that there remains "*only their more considerable length in comparison with the skull as a mark of the European beaver.*"

I have carefully examined over one hundred skulls in reference to this point, the measurements being made with callipers, the length being estimated from the inferior border of the intermaxillary to the occipital crest in the median line.

In six American skulls the average length is $5''$ $39'''\frac{1}{6}$. The average length of the nasals is $1''$ $80'''\frac{5}{8}$, an excess of $13'''\frac{1}{2}$ over one-third the length of the skull.

In three skulls having an average length of $4''$ $42'''$, the length of the nasals is $1''$ $58'''\frac{2}{3}$, making the excess over one-third $34'''$.

In seven skulls whose length respectively is $5''$ $10'''$, $3''$ $95'''$, $5''$ $10'''$, $5''$ $13'''$, $4''$ $94'''$, $5''$ $13'''$, $5''$ $17'''$, the excess of length of the nasals over one-third the length of the skull is $63'''$, $34'''$, $30'''$, $42'''$, $46'''$, $51'''$, $47'''$.

In the New York skull, No. 1072, in which the backward projection of the nasals resembles some of the European skulls, the excess over one-third is but $11'''$. In the European skull, No. 6564, in which the backward projection of the nasals appears to have its maximum, this excess is $29'''$, which is much less than in many American skulls. We must conclude, therefore, that the backward projection of the nasals, and their greater proportionate length as compared with American skulls, are not constant and distinctive features of the European variety.

"5. The frontal portion of the lachrymal bone of the American beaver is more triangular, posteriorly twice as broad as anteriorly, and smaller than in the European; it is also nearly limited to the space between the malar and frontal bones; since it impinges only with its anterior border-like narrow end upon a small process of the upper jaw, or even only approaches it. In the beavers of the Old World, however, the larger, more quadrangular, anteriorly and posteriorly equally broad frontal portion of the lachrymal bone lies not only between the malar and frontal bones, but is united in similar extent equilaterally with the superior maxillary."

I find American skulls in which the upper surface of the lachrymal bone has the quadrangular form, as broad anteriorly as posteriorly, and united as in the European skull, to the intermaxillary, while in the greater number of instances the description above given is found to be correct.

"§ 2. Anterior aspect of the skull.

"On the closer study of the beaver skull anteriorly, we learned that in all the examined skulls of the European beaver the nasal opening appears triangular, inferiorly narrow, and hence more or less pointed; while the lateral margins, raised like a crest, and bounding it inferiorly, approached each other at a more or less acute angle. In the American skulls, on the contrary, the nasal opening has a quadrangular form, and appears below only a little narrower than above; while the lower ends of the crest-like ridges of the lateral margins are nearly parallel, and curved inward but little."

The tendency to the quadrangular form of the nasal opening in the American beaver, and to the triangular form of the European, is evident. Yet there are American skulls where the form of the opening is nearly if not quite as triangular as in the European.

"A comparison of the both equally large European skulls with the American skull of equal size of the Kuprianow skeleton, showed that the inter- and inferior maxillary, together with the incisor teeth, are strikingly broader in the European, but somewhat lower than in the American skull. So much so indeed that the breadth of the American intermaxillary is to that of the European as 9 : 13, nearly as 3 : 4. The breadth of a single incisor tooth of the upper jaw in the European beaver is something more than one-third the breadth of the anterior inferior border of the intermaxillary, while each single upper incisor of the American beaver is equivalent in breadth to one-third the transverse diameter of the inferior border of the intermaxillary."

In the measurement of five skulls I find the breadth across the incisor portion of the intermaxillary to average 88''', and the average width of a single upper incisor to be 30'''. In five other skulls the intermaxillary width is 78''', and the width of an incisor is 27'''. In another skull the intermaxillary width is 91''', and the width of the incisor is 32'''. This is "something more than one-third."

" § 3. Lateral aspect of the beaver skull.

"A comparison in profile of the two European skulls mentioned above (Nos. 55 and 186 Kiew), with a skull of equal size of the Kuprianow skeleton, gave the following results:

" 1. As has already been mentioned above, a straight line drawn from the anterior extremity of the nasal bone to the crista occipitalis, shows no essential difference between the American (of Kuprianow) and the two European skulls of corresponding size. The same result is also furnished by a comparison of all the other European and American skulls.

" 2. The zygomatic process of the superior maxillary appears on the external surface of that portion lying up near the superior maxillary process of the malar bone, in the European at least half as broad, generally more than half as broad as the adjacent end of the superior maxillary process of the malar bone, and in fact even in the younger specimens (also in No. 57 Kiew, and in our Lapland skulls).

"In all of the three larger American skulls the zygomatic process of the superior maxillary lying near the anterior and upper malar bone, attains to only about one-quarter the breadth of the upper end of the superior maxillary process of the malar bone, and appears, at least in its middle and upper portion, only as a border, a condition especially noticeable in our smallest American skulls, in which even the lower end of the zygomatic process of the superior maxillary appears like a border."

In five American skulls the zygomatic process of the superior maxillary equals, or exceeds in breadth, one-half the width of the corresponding portion of the malar.

" 3. The nasal process of the intermaxillary of the older and old European skulls, in which the posterior ends of the incisors appear to extend less high than in the older American, is provided with a longitudinal depression of greater or less size running from before backward, above the posterior ends of the upper incisors where they are located in the skull, which depression is also present in the very young American skulls in which, in variation from the three larger American skulls lying before me, the posterior ends of the incisors go backward in a straighter direction than in the European skulls of different ages.

" 4. The malar bone of the European appears in general higher in the middle of its broader portion.

"5. The ridge formed by the parietal and frontal, behind and below the posterior tubercle of the eyebrow arches, in the European skull, is more considerable, and enters into combination with a ridge elevating itself out of the squamous portion of the temporal, which ridge in the American is generally wanting, or only indicated."

Brandt's largest American skull was but a medium sized one, measuring 5″ 24‴ by 3″ 60‴. In an American skull of this size before me the ridges in question exist; but in the older and larger skulls they are strongly developed.

"6. The hook-formed process of the zygomatic process of the temporal bone lies with its anterior point, in the American beaver, hardly or only a little behind the anterior border of the temporal fossa, while in the European beaver it always lies more or less behind it. In the European beaver the end of the zygomatic process of the temporal bone appears on the whole more approached to the occiput and osseous auditory meatus."

According to my own observation, the hook-formed process referred to above is in the American beaver longer than in the European. We have but one or two skulls in which it appears somewhat shortened, without becoming as short as in the European variety. With respect to the relations of the zygomatic process and the auditory tube, the American skulls are variable, and strong resemblances could undoubtedly be found to the European form.

"7. In the American beaver there extends downward from the posterior angle of the posterior end of the parietal bone a more or less triangular, somewhat curved process, which proceeds between the posterior crucial process of the squamous portion of the temporal bone and the squamous portion of the occipital bone. In consequence of this but slightly indicated process in many European beavers, as in our Rolaer, the posterior and upper angle of the squamous portion of the temporal bone of the American beaver is generally more rounded, but in the European, triangular and shorter."

I have found but a single and partial exception to the above statement. In an American skull, No. 2031, S. I., there is an exact correspondence between the above-described processes and those of the European beaver, No. 6564, on the left side ; on the right side the American skull shows a faint indication of the uncial process of the parietal, and a slight but more obtuse development appears also in the European.

"8. In the beaver of the New World the end of the coronal process of the lower jaw is slightly or not at all hooked, at least not so strongly hooked as in several European. In all five lower jaws of the American beaver the anterior opening of the canalis infra-maxillaris lies under the alveolus of the anterior inferior molar, in the European beaver somewhat before the same."

In a large proportion of cases the coronal process of the lower jaw in the American beaver presents the hooked form. It is sometimes very much hooked. The description given of the anterior mental foramen corresponds with my observations.

"§ 4. Posterior aspect of the skull.

"The general form of the squamous portion of the occipital bone shows no essential variations. The middle portion of its posterior surface shows in the American as well as in the European a shallower or deeper, broader or narrower groove, or a single, sometimes even doubled longitudinal ridge.

"The occipital foramen, on the contrary, in all the European skulls, is narrower than in the American, but appears extended further upward than in the latter, so that its upper margin is nearly on a level with the base of the zygomatic process of the temporal bone, while in the American skulls the superior margin of the occipital foramen lies about opposite the inferior border of the zygomatic process. Correspondingly with the first-described relation of the occipital foramen the squamous portion of the occipital bone over the occipital foramen appears in the European skulls lower than in the American—an appearance especially striking in the two skulls of equal size with the American skull of Kuprianow"

If we examine a large number of skulls of the American beaver, the great variety of forms presented by the occipital foramen appears remarkable. It is sometimes low and broad, again a rounded arch, and in other instances shows the high triangular shape peculiar to the European variety. This form is found frequently in young, and occasionally in old skulls.

"§ 5. Inferior aspect of the European and American skulls.

"The groove occurring on the inferior surface of the base of the occiput so characteristic of the species *Castor*, from three to four lines deep, six to seven lines broad, posteriorly six to eight lines long, is in all the European skulls lying before me larger, deeper, and more rounded, and inclosed by rounded margins, posteriorly particularly strongly curved, so that it appears three to four lines deep, six to eight lines long, and posteriorly six to seven lines broad. In the same skulls we find it more or less widened back of its middle portion, while in the American skulls it appears smaller in comparison with its breadth, longer and narrower, not widened back of its middle point; at its posterior end even more or less narrowed; and possesses, in addition to its more lengthened form, nearly straight margins and less depth. Its longitudinal diameter is about six lines, its greater transverse diameter four to five lines, and its depth two and a half to three lines."

Brandt has well described the basilar cavity as it appears in the American, compared with the European beaver. Its form, however, in the American beaver, is subject to variation, being sometimes narrow and shallow, with its lateral borders nearly parallel, and in some cases it is more rounded—its length and breadth being equal—thus presenting an approximation to the European variety.

"The posterior processes of the inner sphenoidal wings proceeding to the osseous bullæ of the temporal bone, are in all the European shorter, and therefore the bullæ of the ossa temporum are moved further forward than in the American."

The European beaver skull before me presents the peculiarity named above, and the difference between the two varieties in this respect, is confirmed by my observations.

"The palate bones vary in the European and American skulls, both in length and breadth, as well as in the greater or less acuteness of their anterior extremity. In both there are skulls in which they agree or vary more or less."

Having but one European skull, I can only state that the palate bones in this skull, and in an American skull before me, agree perfectly in form, and in the position of the palatal foramina. There is undoubtedly some difference among American skulls as to the posterior width of the palate bones. The palatal foramina are sometimes opposite the space between the second and third molars, sometimes a little anterior to this.

"The malar arches often appear in the European beaver thicker, but in many individuals no thicker than in the American."

" The symphysis of the inferior maxillary is shorter and narrower in the European."

"In the structure of the molar teeth, I did not, in addition, succeed in finding any difference."

I have thus endeavored to show, from an examination of a large number of skulls of the American beaver, that a greater tendency to variation in these structures exists, than was observed by Dr. Brandt, in the smaller number (five American and eight European skulls) on which he based his differential characteristics.   It will be remembered that Brandt does not insist upon the most obvious feature which distinguishes the Old World beaver from that of the New World, viz., the greater lengthening posteriorly of the nasal bones, since it "cannot be rigorously proven in all cases."   Following out then the principle which guided his researches, many additional exceptional instances have been found to invalidate the conclusion that the European and the American beaver constitute different species.   The extremes of difference, in their aggregate, on the one side and the other, are sufficiently striking to justify us in regarding them as varieties of one and the same species; while the want of constancy in these peculiarities suggests the inference, that these variations are due to long separation of the races, and to accidental causes, rather than to original diversity of the stock.   It is conceded by the advocates of a diversity of species that the beavers of the Old and the New World cannot be distinguished by any external characteristic.   The same is true of their habits and instincts, except so far as they have evidently been controlled by external influences.   The castoreum secretion is variable, even in European beavers, and there are facts to show that the elements of the food of the animal are sometimes found in it.   The differences observed in it, being more of degree than of kind, are not of such a character as to render it improbable that they are due to the influence of climate, food, and accidental causes.   That the beavers of the Old and the New World would prove fertile *inter se*, is, from their great similarity, almost certain.   The beaver is a very old animal, as is proved by his fossil remains.   As an aquatic animal, and a vegetable feeder, it is probable that he lived at a very early epoch, perhaps before the present configuration of the continents, so that from his tendency to extensive distribution, and his prolific nature, there would be nothing to hinder the spread of a single species over both continents. That long separation should have developed certain peculiarities of structure might reasonably be expected. From the observed tendency to variation exhibited by the skulls of consanguinei, we should even expect to find these differences greater, in separated races, than actually occurs. There appears, therefore, to the writer, to be no necessity for assigning a separate and distinct origin to the beavers of the Old and the New World, in order to account for the differences which have thus far been observed between them.

III. Castoreum Organs, and Generative Organs

The beaver has long been celebrated for the peculiar secretion called castoreum, which has been much used in medicine. Other animals furnish highly odorous secretions, of which musk and civet are examples, the uses of which in relation to the animals are not well understood. Although much attention has been paid to the anatomy of the beaver, the organs furnishing the castoreum have not unfrequently been erroneously described. It will be seen in the descriptions and figures which follow, that the beaver has two sets of glandular organs, lying below the pubis, of which the upper pair furnish the castoreum, and the lower, an oily secretion. In the Leçons d'Anatomie Comparée (Cuvier), vol viii. p. 245, also in the Dictionnaire des Sciences Médicales, Art. Castor, and in the U. S. Dispensatory, by Wood & Bache, the castoreum is incorrectly referred to the lower pair of organs, and, again, both the upper and lower glands have been said to furnish this secretion.

The beaver has but a single orifice for the genito-urinary and the intestinal organs, and there is nothing in its external appearance by which its sex can be determined.

When the animal is laid on its back there is a space between the pubis and the scaly tail about seven inches long, covered with hair like the rest of the body. In the centre of this space is the upper margin of the cloacal orifice, which is one and a half inches in length, just within which, at the lower margin, is the orifice of the intestine. The width of the tail where the scales commence is about four inches.

On dissecting off the skin, the skin muscle is brought into view, and the forms of the sacs which it covers are recognized. The surface of this muscle next to the sacs is smooth and but slightly attached to them : with the underlying muscles it forms an envelope capable of compressing these sacs so as to expel their contents. The name given to these organs, in view of their supposed analogies, is preputial glands, though by Cuvier and others this term is applied to the lower sacs. I shall call the upper, the castoreum sacs, and the lower, oil sacs. By the trappers they are called the bark stone, and the oil stone.

FIG. 1.

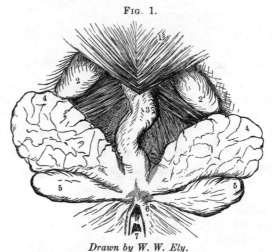

Drawn by W. W. Ely.

NOTE TO FIGURE 1.

1. Muscle covering pubis.
2. Testicles.
3. Penis.
4. Castoreum sacs.

5. Oil sacs.
6. Upper half of cloacal orifice.
7. End of rectum within the cloacal orifice.

Figs. 1 and 2 exhibit these organs in a male and a female beaver, the latter being a small-sized animal, weighing $29\frac{1}{2}$ lbs. The castoreum sacs, nearest the pubis, are oval, flattened, of a light color like parchment, and communicate freely with each other by their transverse portion. Linear marks and depressions on their surfaces correspond with membranous duplicatures within, which add largely to the internal surface, forming septa and cells covered and filled with castoreum. The larger folds have a general direction towards the outlet of the sacs. The sacs are formed of several layers of connective tissue, lined by a tender membrane, which is colored by the secretion, and exhibits minute follicular apertures.   The castoreum is light or dark yellow in different cases, viscid, adhesive, gritty from the presence of calcareous matter, and has a strong, peculiar odor.   Under the microscope, it shows granular and epithelial matter, and spherical crystals of

Fig. 2.

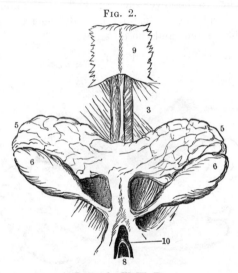

Drawn by W. W. Ely.

NOTE TO FIGURES 2 AND 3.

1. Uterus and Fallopian tubes.
2. Bladder and ureters.
3. Vagina.
4. Rectum.
5. Castoreum sacs.
6. Oil sacs.

7. Cloacal cavity laid open—above the figure are the vaginal and urethral orifices, the clitoris and nymphæ.
8. End of rectum.
9. Pubis, concealing the bladder and uterus.
10. Upper half of cloacal orifice.

carbonate of lime; these crystals are also found in the urine of the beaver. In the male, the castoreum sacs measured $4\frac{1}{4}''$ in length, $2''$ $10'''$ in width, with a circumference of $4\frac{3}{4}''$. Weight of one sac and contents, 900 grains. From both sacs 415 grains of pure castoreum was obtained, but the whole of the secretion could not be removed.

The oil sacs, or "preputial glands" (Cuvier), are connected

with the castoreum sacs, and are pyriform in shape. Each has a duct, which opens within, by the side of the cloacal orifice at its upper margin, surrounded by a dark areola. On everting the orifice of the duct, it appears to be a cul-de-sac, having three minute orifices at its bottom. Although each oil sac appears as one, there is, in addition to the principal gland, two smaller ones, which may be separated, each having its communication with the tube which furnishes the outlet; in each cavity are hairs loose or growing from its surface, and the smaller cavities are sometimes filled with them. The walls of the oil sacs are much thicker than the castoreum sacs, and contain many follicles of considerable size. The cavities contain a thick, oily, creamy fluid. From the larger cavity, about two drachms were obtained, having, when recent, a faint odor of castoreum. This secretion, after standing six months, is about half clear oil, and the remainder a whitish sediment. The whole is soluble in ether, except a small residue of epithelial matter, but the oil is sparingly soluble in strong alcohol. In a female beaver, Fig. 3, the castoreum sacs are $5\frac{1}{2}''$ long, and $3''$ broad. The oil sacs are $2\frac{1}{2}''$ long. The amount of castoreum in these sacs was small and dark colored.

The Rodents, as a class, are very prolific; this is true of the beaver. Their genital organs are consequently strongly developed. The statement of Cuvier, however, that the size of the testicles in the Rodents exceeds ordinarily that of the kidneys, is not true of this animal. Viii. 104.

In Fig. 1, the form of the penis is shown, curved and retracted. When extended it is five inches long, and $1\frac{3}{4}''$ in circumference. The glans is flattened, $1''\ 20'''$ in length, and covered with a rough integument. It contains a bone equal to its length, and largest at the base. The transverse communication of the castoreum sacs is behind the prepuce. The urethra has a spongy portion $3\frac{1}{2}''$ long, and a membranous one $2\frac{1}{2}''$. Cowper's glands lie behind the pubis. The prostate glands lie by the side of the urethra at its origin. The vesiculæ seminales are united, and lie behind the neck of the bladder, each being $1''\ 80'''$ long, $90'''$ wide, and $60'''$ thick. It is possible that these glands were hypertrophied, as their cavities contained a dense fibrous substance, a portion of which had escaped into the urethra, distending and obstructing its membranous portion. The testicles are contained in a sac projecting from the inguinal opening, and are $1\frac{1}{4}''$ in length.

The Weberian organ, or the uterus masculinus, is well developed in the beaver. It is triangular in shape, flattened and thin antero-posteriorly, and is connected by its edges with the vasa deferentiæ. It lies between the bladder and the vesiculæ seminales. Below it seems lost in the thin connective tissue. In the upper part, where it is $1\frac{1}{4}''$ in width, is a small cavity without any outlet. The filaments which extend from the superior angles lie upon the vasa deferentiæ, and disappear at the bottom of the testicles, being $6\frac{3}{4}''$ in length. The significance of this structure, so interesting to the philosophical anatomist, is but at present a matter of speculation. Homologous with the uterus, the vesicula prostatica, as it is sometimes called, like the mammæ of the male, suggests the idea of typical structures, or of organs of original utility, but dwarfed in the progress of development.

FIG. 3.

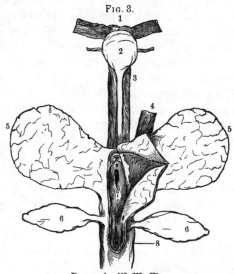

Drawn by W. W. Ely.

In Fig. 3, the genital organs of the female are represented. The parts being dissected from their connections, and laid on a flat surface before the drawing was made, their natural relations are somewhat altered. The oil sacs and castoreum sacs are disconnected. They are much larger than the other specimen, relatively to the size of the animal. The cloaca is laid open, and the vaginal orifice is higher than in the natural state ; this, and the urethral orifice, would be retracted and concealed by the nymphæ, which would be nearer the external orifice. The clitoris is small, dimpled, and surrounded with a prepuce, and the nymphæ are thin, composed of a membrane similar to that of the castoreum sacs, their lateral portions extending downward in the direction of the opening of the oil sacs R. Wagner asserts that the nymphæ are wanting in the inferior mammalia, but Cuvier says more correctly: "Le fait est que les nymphes existent chez plusieurs Rongeurs." Viii. 256.

The orifice of the urethra is half an inch behind the clitoris. The urethra and the vagina are each 4″ long. The latter is strongly muscular, and smooth within. The bladder, which lies in front of, and conceals the uterus, is contracted, thick, and rugose. The position of the ureters is seen in the figure. The uterus is 1½″ long, and its vaginal extremity is lobulated. It is divided into two cavities by a firm septum, each cavity opening into the vagina by a separate orifice. The Fallopian tubes are 9½″ long. The ovaries are small, oval, 67‴ long, 32‴ in width. It is probable, though I cannot affirm it, that pregnancy in the beaver is Fallopian, as in the rat and the rabbit.

CASTOREUM.—The difference in the castoreum as furnished by the European and the American beavers has long been known to chemists and physicians; the Russian castoreum being most esteemed as a medicine. The fresh specimens of American castoreum which I have seen, differ in amount, appearance, and consistence. The following are Brande's analyses of this substance :

CANADIAN CASTOR.		RUSSIAN CASTOR.	
Volatile oil	1·00	Volatile oil	2·0
Resin	13·85	Resin	58·6
Castorin	0·33	Castorin	2·5
Albumen	0·05	Cholesterin	1·2
Osmazome	0·20	Albumen	1·6
Carbonate of lime	33·62	Gelatin	10·4
Other salts	2·82	Osmazome	2·4
Mucus	2·30	Matter soluble in alcohol	1·6
Animal matter like horn	2·30	Carbonate of lime	2·6
Membrane	20·00	Other salts	2·4
Moisture and loss	22·83	Membrane	3·0
		Moisture and loss	11·7
	99·30		100·0

The European castoreum is supposed to contain a larger proportion of the volatile oil, castorin, and resin, and probably its superiority as a medicine depends upon the resinoid element. A specimen of castoreum which I obtained from a male American beaver more than a year ago was, at first, of a light yellow color, soft, and very adhesive. At the present time the color is the same except where it has had access to the air, which has changed the surface to a dark brown. One hundred parts of this castoreum lost fifty-six parts in boiling alcohol. Of the residuum, thirty-three parts dissolved with effervescence in diluted hydrochloric acid, affording evidence of a large amount of carbonate of lime. The remaining eleven parts appeared to be chiefly animal matter, but it was not critically examined. The alcoholic solution on cooling showed no trace of castorin. Mixed with water the alcoholic solution became milky. On filtration and thorough drying of the filter there resulted 41 parts of resin.

APPENDIX B.

Samuel Hearne's Article on the Beaver.

From Samuel Hearne's "Journey from Prince of Wales's Fort to the Northern Ocean." London: 4to., 1795, ch. vii. p. 226.

The beaver being so plentiful, the attention of my companions was chiefly engaged on them, as they not only furnished delicious food, but their skins proved a valuable acquisition, being a principal article of trade, as well as a serviceable one for clothing, etc.

The situation of the beaver houses is various; where the beavers are numerous, they are found to inhabit lakes, ponds, and rivers, as well as those narrow creeks which connect the numerous lakes with which this country abounds; but the latter are generally chosen by them where the depth of water and other circumstances are suitable, as they have then the advantage of a current to carry wood and other necessaries to their habitations, and because, in general, they are more difficult to be taken than those that are built in standing water.

There is no one particular part of a lake, pond, river, or creek, of which the beaver make choice for building their houses on in preference to another; for they sometimes build on points, sometimes in the hollow of a log, and often on small islands; they always choose, however, these parts that have such a depth of water as will resist the frost in winter, and prevent it from freezing to the bottom.

The beavers that build their houses on small rivers or creeks, in which the water is liable to be drained off when the back supplies are dried up by the frost, are wonderfully taught by instinct to provide against that evil by making a dam quite across the river, at a convenient distance from their houses. This I look upon as the most curious piece of workmanship that is performed by the beaver; not so much for the neatness of the work as for its strength and real service; and at the same time it discovers such a degree of sagacity and foresight in the animal of approaching evils, as is little inferior to that of the human species, and is certainly peculiar to these animals.

The beaver dams differ in shape according to the nature of the place in which they are built. If the water in the river or creek has but little motion, the dam is almost straight; but when the current is more rapid, it is always made with a considerable curve, convex toward the stream. The materials made use of in these dams are drift-wood, green willows, birch and poplar, if they can be got; also mud and stones, intermixed in such a manner as must evidently contribute to the strength of the dam; but in these dams there is no other order or method observed, except that of the work being carried on with regular success, and all the parts being made of equal strength.

In places which have been long frequented by beavers, undisturbed, their dam, by frequent repairing, becomes a solid bank, capable of resisting a great force both of water and ice; and as the willow, poplar, and birch generally take root and shoot up, they, by degrees, form a kind of regular-planted hedge, which I have seen in some places so tall, that birds have built their nests among the branches.

Though the beaver which build their houses in lakes, and other standing waters, may enjoy a sufficient quantity of their favorite element without the assistance of a dam, the trouble of getting wood and other necessaries to their habitation without the help of a current, must, in some measure, counterbalance the other advantages which are reaped from such a situation; for it must be observed that the beaver which build in rivers and creeks, always cut their wood above their houses, so that the current, with little trouble, conveys it to the place required.

The beaver houses are built of the same materials as their dams, and are always proportioned in size to the number of inhabitants, which seldom exceed four old, and six or eight young ones; though, by chance, I have seen above double that number.

These houses, though not altogether unworthy of admiration, fall very short of the general discription given of them; for instead of order or regulation being observed in rearing them, they are of a much ruder structure than their dams.

Those who have undertaken to describe the inside of beaver houses, as having several apartments appropriated to various uses, such as eating, sleeping, store-houses for provisions, and one for their natural occasions, etc., must have been very little acquainted with the subject; or, which is still worse, guilty of attempting to impose on the credulous by representing the greatest falsehoods as real facts. Many years constant residence among the Indians, during which I had an opportunity of seeing several hundreds of these houses, has enabled me to affirm that everything of the kind is entirely void of truth; for notwithstanding the sagacity of these animals, it has never been observed that they aim at any other conveniences in their houses than to have a dry place to lie on; and there they usually eat their victuals, which they occasionally take out of the water.

It frequently happens, that some of the large houses are found to have one or more partitions, if they deserve that appellation; but that is no more than a part of the main building, left by the sagacity of the beaver to support the roof. On such occasions it is common for these different apartments, as some are pleased to call them, to have no communication with each other but by water; so that, in fact, they may be called double or treble houses, rather than different apartments of the same house. I have seen a large beaver house built in a small island, that had near a dozen houses under one roof; and, two or three of these only excepted, none of them had any communication with each other but by water. As there were beavers enough to inhabit each apartment, it is more than probable that each family knew its own, and always entered at their own door without having any further connection with their neighbors than a friendly intercourse; and to join their united labors in erecting their separate habitations, and building their dams when required. It is difficult to say whether their interest on other occasions was any way reciprocal. The Indians of my party killed twelve old beavers, and twenty-five young and half-grown ones, out of the houses above mentioned; and on examination found that several had escaped their vigilance, and could not be taken but at the expense of more trouble than would be sufficient to take double the number in a less difficult situation.[1]

Travellers who assert that the beaver have had doors to their houses, one on the land side, and the other next the water, seem to be less acquainted with these animals than others who assign them an elegant suite of apartments. Such a proceeding would be quite contrary to their manner of life, and at the same time would render their houses of no use either to protect them from their enemies, or guard them against the extreme of cold in winter.

The quiquehatches or wolvereens, are great enemies to the beaver; and if there were a passage into their houses on the land side, would not leave one of them alive wherever they came.

I cannot refrain from smiling when I read the accounts of different authors who have written on the economy of these animals, as there seems to be a contest between them who shall most exceed in fiction. But the compiler of the "Wonders of Nature and Art" seems, in my opinion, to have succeeded less in this respect; as he has not only collected all the fictions into which other writers on the subject have run, but has so greatly improved on them, that little remains to be added to his account of the beaver besides a vocabulary of their language, a code of their laws, and a sketch of their religion, to make it the most complete natural history of that animal which can possibly be offered to the public.

There cannot be a greater imposition, or indeed a grosser insult on common understanding, than the wish to make us believe the

---

[1] The difficulty here alluded to was the numberless vaults the beaver had in the sides of the pond, and the immense thickness of the house in some parts.

stories of some of the works ascribed to the beaver; and though it is not to be supposed that the compiler of a general work can be intimately acquainted with every subject of which it may be necessary to treat, yet a very moderate share of understanding is surely sufficient to guard him against giving credit to such marvellous tales, however smoothly they may be told, or however boldly they may be asserted by the romancing traveller.

To deny that the beaver is possessed of a very considerable degree of sagacity would be as absurd in me as it is in these authors who think they cannot allow them too much. I shall willingly grant them their full share : but it is impossible for any one to conceive how, or by what means, a beaver whose full height when standing erect, does not exceed two feet and a half, or three feet at most, and whose fore paws are not much larger than a half-crown piece, can " drive stakes as thick as a man's leg into the ground three or four feet deep." Their "wattling these stakes with twigs," is equally absurd ; and their "plastering the inside of their houses with a composition of mud and straw, and swimming with mud and stones on their tails," are still more incredible. The form and size of the animal, notwithstanding all its sagacity, will not admit of its performing such feats ; and it would be as impossible for a beaver to use its tail as a trowel, except on the surface of the ground on which it walks, as it would have been for Sir James Thornhill to have painted the dome of St. Paul's Cathedral without the assistance of scaffolding. The joints of their tail will not admit of their turning it over their backs on any occasion whatever, as it has a natural inclination to bend downwards; and it is not without some considerable exertion that they can keep it from trailing on the ground. This being the case, they cannot sit erect like a squirrel, which is their common posture, particularly when eating, or when they are cleaning themselves, as a cat or squirrel does, without having their tails bent forward between their legs; and which may not improperly be called their trencher.

So far are the beaver from driving stakes into the ground when building their houses, that they lay most of the wood crosswise, and nearly horizontal, and without any other order than that of leaving a hollow or cavity in the middle ; when any unnecessary branches project inward, they cut them off with their teeth, and throw them in among the rest to prevent the mud from falling through the roof. It is a mistaken notion that the woodwork is first completed and then plastered; for the whole of their houses, as well as their dams, are from the foundation one mass of wood and mud mixed with stones, if they can be procured. The mud is always taken from the edge of the bank, or the bottom of the creek or pond, near the door of the house; and though their fore paws are so small, yet it is held close up between them under their throat, that they carry both mud and stones; while they always drag the wood with their teeth.

All their work is executed in the night, and they are so expeditious in completing it that in the course of one night I have known them to have collected as much mud at their houses as to have amounted to some thousands of their little handfuls; and when any mixture of grass or straw has appeared in it, it has been most assuredly mere chance, owing to the nature of the ground from which they had taken it. As to their designedly making a composition for that purpose it is entirely void of truth.

It is a great piece of policy in these animals to cover, or plaster, as it is usually called, the outside of their houses every fall with fresh mud, and as late as possible in the autumn, even when the frost becomes pretty severe; as by this means it soon freezes as hard as a stone, and prevents their common enemy, the quiquihatch, from disturbing them during the winter. And as they are frequently seen to walk over their work, and sometimes to give a flap with their tail, particularly when plunging into the water, this has, without doubt, given rise to the vulgar opinion that they use their tails as a trowel, with which they plaster their houses; whereas that flapping of the tail is no more than a custom, which they always preserve, even when they become tame and domestic, and more particularly so when they are startled.

Their food chiefly consists of a large root, something resembling a cabbage stalk, which grows at the bottom of the lakes and rivers. They eat also the bark of trees, particularly that of the poplar, birch, and willow; but the ice preventing them from getting to the land in winter, they have not any barks to feed upon during that season, except that of such sticks as they cut down in summer and throw into the water opposite the doors of their houses; and as they generally eat a great deal, the roots above mentioned constitute the chief part of their food during the winter. In summer they vary their diet by eating various kinds of herbage, and such berries as grow near their haunts during that season.

When the ice breaks up in the spring, the beaver always leave their houses, and rove about the whole summer, probably in search of a more commodious situation; but in case of not succeeding in their endeavors, they return again to their old habitations a little before the fall of the leaf, and lay in their winter stock of woods. They seldom begin to repair the houses till the frost commences, and never finish the outer coat till the cold is pretty severe, as has been already mentioned.

When they shift their habitations, or when the increase of their number render it necessary to make some addition to their houses, or to erect new ones, they begin felling the wood for these purposes early in the summer, but seldom begin to build till the middle or latter end of August, and never complete their houses till the cold weather be set in.

Notwithstanding what has been so repeatedly reported of these animals assembling in great bodies, and jointly erecting large towns, cities, and commonwealths, as they have sometimes been called, I am confident from many circumstances, that even where the greatest number of beaver are situated in the neighborhood of each other, their labors are not carried on jointly in the erection of their different habitations, nor have they any reciprocal interest except it be such as live immediately under the same roof; and then it extends no further than to build or keep a dam which is common to several houses. In such cases it is natural to think that every one who seemed benefited from such a dam, should assist in erecting it, being sensible of its utility to all.

Persons who attempt to take beaver in winter should be thoroughly acquainted with their manner of life; otherwise they will have endless trouble to effect their purpose, and probably without success in the end; because they always have a number of holes in the banks which serve them as places of retreat when any injury is offered to their houses, and in general it is in these holes that they are taken.

When the beaver which are situated in a small river or creek are to be taken, the Indians sometimes find it necessary to stake the river across, to prevent them from passing; after which they endeavor to find out all their holes or places of retreat in the banks. This requires much practice and experience to accomplish, and is performed in the following manner: every man being furnished with an ice chisel, lashes it to the end of a small staff, about four or five feet long; he then walks along the edge of the banks, and keeps knocking his chisel against the ice.   Those who are acquainted with that kind of work will know by the sound of the ice when they are opposite to any of the beaver holes or vaults.   As soon as they suspect any, they cut a hole through the ice big enough to admit an old beaver, and in this manner proceed until they have found out all their places of retreat, or at least as many of them as possible.   While the principal men are thus employed, some of the understrappers and the women are busy in breaking open the house, which at times is no easy task; for I have frequently known these houses to be five and six feet thick, and one in particular was more than eight feet thick on the crown.   When the beaver find that their habitations are invaded, they fly to their holes in the banks for shelter; and on being perceived by the Indians, which is easily done by attending to the motion of the water, they block up the entrance with stakes of wood, and then haul the beaver out of his hole either by hand if they can reach it, or with a large hook made for that purpose, which is fastened to the end of a long stick.

In this kind of hunting every man has the sole right to all the beaver caught by him in the holes or vaults; and as this is a constant rule, each person takes care to mark such as he discovers, by sticking up the branch of a tree or some other distinguishing post by which he may know them.   All that are caught in the house also are the property of the person who finds it.

The same regulations are observed, and the same process used in taking beaver that are found in lakes and other standing waters, except it be that of staking the lakes across, which would be both unnecessary and impossible.   Taking beaver houses in these situations is generally attended with less trouble and more success than in the former.

The beaver is an animal which cannot keep under water long at a time, so that when their houses are broken open, and all their places of retreat discovered, they have but one choice left, as it may be called, either to be taken in their houses or their vaults; in general they prefer the latter, for where there is one beaver caught in the house, many thousands are taken in their vaults in the banks.   Sometimes they are caught in nets, and in the summer very frequently in traps. In winter they are very fat and delicious; but the trouble of rearing their young, the thinness of their hair, and their constantly roving from place to place, with the trouble they have in providing against the approach of winter, generally keep them very poor during the summer season, at which time their flesh is but indifferent eating, and their skins of so little value that the Indians generally singe them, even to the amount of many thousands in one summer. They have from two to five young at a time. Mr. Dobbs, in his account of Hudson's Bay, enumerates no less than eight different kinds of beaver; but it must be understood that they are all of one kind and species; his distinctions arise wholly from the different seasons of the year in which they are killed, and the different uses to which their skins are applied, which is the sole reason that they vary so much in value.

* * * * * * *

Lefranc, as an Indian, must have known better than to have informed Mr. Dobbs that the beaver have from ten to fifteen young at a time; or if he did he must have deceived him willfully, for the Indians, by killing them in all stages of gestation, have abundant opportunities of ascertaining the usual number of their offspring. I have seen some hundreds of them killed at the season favorable for these observations, and never could discover more than six young in one female, and that only in two instances, for the usual number, as I have before observed, is from two to five.

Besides this unerring method of ascertaining the real number of young which any animal has at a time, there is another rule to go by with respect to the beaver, which experience has proved to the Indian never to vary or deceive them, that is by dissection; for on examining the womb of a beaver, even at a time when not with young, there is always found a hardish round for every young she had at the last litter. This is a circumstance I have been particularly careful to examine, and can affirm it to be true from real experience.

Most of the accounts, nay I may say all the accounts now extant respecting the beaver, are taken from the authority of the French, who have resided in Canada; but their accounts differ so much from the real state and economy of all the beaver to the north of that place, as to leave great room to suspect the truth of

them altogether.   In the first place, the assertion that they have two doors to their houses, one on the land side and the other next the water, is as I have before observed, quite contrary to fact and common sense, as it would render their houses of no use to them, either as places of shelter from the inclemency of the extreme cold in winter, or as a retreat from their common enemy the quiquehatch.   The only thing that could have made M. Du Pratz, and other French writers, conjecture that such a thing did exist, must have been from having seen some old beaver houses, which had been taken by the Indians; for they are always obliged to make a hole on one side of the house before they can drive them out; and it is more than probable that in so mild a climate as Canada the Indians do generally make these holes on the land side, which without doubt gave rise to the suggestion.

In respect to the beaver dunging in their houses, as some persons assert, it is quite wrong, as they always plunge into the water to do it.   I am the better enabled to make the assertion from having kept several of them till they became so domesticated as to answer to their name, and follow those to whom they were accustomed, in the same manner as a dog would do; and they were as much pleased at being fondled as any animal I ever saw; I had a house built for them, and a small piece of water before the door, into which they always plunged when they wanted to ease nature; and their dung being of a light substance, immediately rises and floats on the surface, then separates, and subsides to the bottom.   When the winter sets in so as to freeze the water solid, they still continue their custom of coming out of their houses and dunging and making water on the ice; and when the weather was so cold that I was obliged to take them into my house, they always went into a large tub of water which I set for that purpose, so that they made not the least dirt, though they are kept in my own sitting room, where they were the constant companions of the Indian women and children, and were so fond of their company, that when the Indians were absent for any considerable time, the beaver discovered great signs of uneasiness, and on their return showed equal marks of pleasure, by fondling on them, crawling into their laps, laying on their backs, sitting erect like a squirrel, and behaving to them like children who see their parents but seldom.   In general during the winter they lived on the same food as the women did, and were remark-

ably fond of rice and plumb-pudding; they could eat partridges and fresh venison very freely, but I never tried them with fish, though I have heard they will at times prey on them. In fact there are few of the graminivorous that may not be brought to be carnivorous. It is well known that our domestic poultry will eat animal food; thousands of geese that come to London market are fattened on tallow scraps; and our horses in Hudson's Bay would not only eat all kinds of animal food, but also drink freely of the wash or pot liquor intended for the hogs. And we are assured by the most authentic author, that in Iceland, not only black cattle, but also the sheep, are almost entirely fed on fish and fish-bones during the winter season. Even in the Isles of Orkney, and that in summer, the sheep attend the ebbing of the tide as regular as the Esquimaux curlew, and go down to the shore which the tide has left to feed on the sea-weed. This however is through necessity; for even the famous Island of Pomona will not afford them an existence above high water mark.

With respect to the inferior or slave beaver, of which some authors speak, it is in my opinion very difficult for those who are best acquainted with the economy of this animal, whether there are any that deserve that appellation. It sometimes happens that a beaver is caught which has but a very indifferent coat, and which has broad patches on the back and shoulders, almost wholly without hair. This is the only foundation for asserting that there is an inferior or slave beaver among them. And when one of the above description is taken, it is perhaps too hastily inferred, that the hair is worn off from these parts by carrying heavy loads; whereas it is most probable that it is caused by a disorder that attacks them somewhat similar to the mange, for were that falling off of the hair occasioned by performing extra labor, it is natural to think that instances of it would be more frequent than there are; as it is rare to see one of them in the course of seven or ten years. I have seen a whole house of these animals that had nothing on the surface of their bodies but the fine soft down, all the long hairs having molted off. This and every other deviation from the general run is undoubtedly owing to some particular disorder.

APPENDIX C.

Bennett's Article on the Beaver.

From "The Gardens and Menagerie of the Zoological Society Delineated."
Quadrupeds. Vol. i. p. 153. Published in 1835.

THE BEAVER.

(*Castor Fiber*, Linn.)

Among the numerous, widely dispersed, and prolific tribes of animals which compose the extremely natural order, called by Linnæus and the writers of his school Glires, there are none perhaps which possess so many claims on our attention as the well-marked and circumscribed little group on the history of which we are about to enter. The beavers, in fact, interest us not only as furnishing a most valuable fur, and producing a peculiar secretion occasionally and advantageously employed in medicine, but also as offering the most remarkable of the few instances occurring among quadrupeds of that architectural instinct, so remarkably prevalent in the inferior classes, which impels them to construct their own habitations with materials selected for the purpose, brought from a distance, and cemented together so as to form a regular and uniform structure.

The first and most essential character of the order to which they belong is obviously derived from the great development of their incisor teeth; and this peculiarity in structure, as might naturally be expected, is connected with a peculiarity in habits equally remarkable. So striking, indeed, is the propensity to gnawing, which distinguishes these animals, that many late zoologists, of the French school especially, have thrown aside the older designation applied to them by Linnæus, and adopted in its place the expressive name of Rongeurs or Rodentia. Of this faculty the beavers appear to exhibit the highest degree of development; their powerful incisor teeth not only serving them to strip off and divide the bark of trees, which forms their principal nutriment, but also enabling them, when urged by their instinct of construction, to gnaw through trunks of considerable thickness, and thus to obtain the timber of which they stand in need for the building of their habitations. These important organs contribute, therefore, in an especial manner, to supply them both with food and shelter.

The incisor teeth of the beavers are two in number in each jaw; they are broad, flat, and generally colored of a deep orange or almost chestnut brown anteriorly, and pass into acute angles on their posterior surface. Their extremities terminate externally in a cutting edge, and shelve considerably inward; for the anterior surface being alone coated with enamel, and consequently offering the greatest resistance, is less easily worn down by the action to which they are exposed. Those of either jaw correspond exactly with their opposites, and the form of the articulation of the lower jaw admitting of little or no lateral motion, their action is always from behind forward and *vice versa*. They have no true roots, but are of equal thickness throughout, and are implanted within the jaw in sacs or capsules, which reproduce them from the base as fast as they are worn down at the extremity. So strong a tendency have they to increase by this process, that whenever one of the incisors of either jaw has been accidentally injured or destroyed, the opposite tooth, meeting with no resistance from its antagonist, is propelled forward by a continual enlargement from the base to such an extent as to become at length perfectly monstrous. This mode of growth is common to the whole order, and the number of the incisor teeth is also the same in all the groups that compose it, with the exception of the family of which the hare forms the type.

The entire absence of canine teeth, leaving a vacant space of some extent between the incisors and the molars, is another character which the beavers have in common with all the Rodent animals; but the structure of their molar teeth differs from that of any other group. These latter organs furnish indeed the best characters that have yet been employed for the separation of the Rongeurs into distinct and natural genera. In the beavers they are four on each side in either jaw, and their crowns present a flattened surface on which the lines of enamel are so disposed as to form three folds on the outer side and one on the inner in those of the upper jaw, while those of the lower offer an arrangement directly the reverse. They were formerly suspected by M. F. Cuvier, who has paid particular attention to the teeth of the mammiferous quadrupeds, to be destitute of proper roots, and to increase from their base in the same manner as the incisors; but he has since candidly confessed the error into which he had been led by the inspection of a cranium in which they were not yet fully developed, and he now admits that in the adult animal they are furnished with true roots, and are consequently incapable of receiving any addition to their growth when once completely formed. Their flattened crowns sufficiently indicate that the food which they are intended to masticate is entirely vegetable.

In the regularity of their line of profile from the back of the head to the extremity of the nose, the lateral position of their diminutive eyes, the depth, obliquity, and obtuseness of their muscle, the vertical fissure of their upper lip, the softness and closeness of their fur, and the greater length and muscularity of their posterior limbs, the beavers may be regarded as almost typical of the order to which they belong. They exhibit, however, in their external form several striking modifications peculiar to themselves. Of these, the most remarkable consists in their tail, which differs in structure from that of every other quadruped. This organ, which is nearly half as long as the body, is broadly dilated, oval, flattened both above and below, covered at its thickened base alone with hair similar to that which invests the rest of the animal, but overlaid throughout the greater part of its extent with a peculiar incrustation which assumes the form of regular scales closely resembling those of fishes. The feet all terminate in five toes, those of the anterior extremities smaller and shorter than those of the posterior, and divided almost to the base, while the latter are united to their very tips by the intervention of a strong duplicature of the skin, which allows of their separation to a considerable extent, and forms a broad and palmated expansion, similar in form and serving for the same useful purpose with the webbed feet of the swimming birds. The nails are thick and strong; and that of the second toe of the hinder feet is remarkable for being formed of two portions, an upper one corresponding with those of the remaining toes, and an under, placed obliquely, and having a sharp cutting-edge directed downward.

The gait of the beavers is waddling and ungraceful, owing partly to the shortness and inequality of their limbs, and partly to the outward direction which is given to their heels to enable their feet more efficiently to fulfill the office of paddles in swimming. The toes alone of the anterior feet, but the whole of the under surface of the sole in the posterior, are applied to the ground in walking. The awkwardness of their appearance in this action is moreover heightened by the clumsiness of their figure, and by the difficulty which they seem to experience in dragging after them their cumbrous tail, which is generally suffered to trail upon the ground, but is sometimes slightly elevated or even curved upward, and is occasionally moved in a direction from side to side. In the water, however, this member becomes most useful, both as a paddle and a rudder, to urge them onward, and to direct them in their course.

It has often been questioned whether the beavers of Europe and America constitute two distinct species. M. F. Cuvier has lately pointed out some slight variations in the form and relative dimensions of different portions of the skulls which he had an opportunity of examining; but his observations cannot yet be regarded as conclusive. Other naturalists again have broadly maintained that the solitary and burrowing mode of life of the one, and the social and constructive propensities supposed to be peculiar to the other, alone afforded sufficient grounds of discrimination between them. But numberless instances have shown that these differences in their modes of life are the natural results of the circumstances in which the animals are respectively placed; and that the habits of each, in a situation favorable to the change, undergo a thorough revolution. Place the means within his reach, and the constructive instinct of the solitary beaver becomes fully developed; withdraw those means, and the once skillful builder degenerates into a burrowing hermit. Those of Europe are, for the most part, met with in the latter predicament, the neighborhood of civilized man having thinned their numbers and rendered their associations perilous. In America, on the contrary, they form populous villages; but only in the back and unsettled parts of the country; those which are found on the confines of the different settlements have precisely the same habits with the European animals.

That similar villages formerly existed in various parts of Europe, and more especially in the north, we have abundant proofs in the ruins of these ancient edifices. But it seems to have been too hastily taken for granted that none such are to be found at the present day. In the Transactions of the Berlin Natural

History Society for 1829, an extremely interesting account is given by M. de Meyerinck of a colony of beavers, which has been settled for upwards of a century on a little river called the Nuthe, about half a league above its confluence with the Elbe, in a desert and sequestered canton in the district of Magdeburg. Our author speaks of this little settlement as consisting, in the year 1822, of no more than from fifteen to twenty individuals; but few as they were they executed all the laborious tasks of a much more extensive society. They formed themselves burrows of thirty or forty paces in length, on a level with the stream, with one opening below the surface of the water, and another upon the land; built huts eight or ten feet in height, of branches and trunks of trees, laid without any regularity, and covered over with soft earth; and constructed of the same materials a dyke so perfect as to raise the level of the water more than a foot. All their habits indeed, as here described, coincide so exactly with those of the American beavers, that we should feel some surprise at M. de Meyerinck's assertion that they differed from them in several particulars, and especially in their manner of building, were it not manifest that his ideas of the transatlantic race were gleaned from the relations of those travellers who have indulged their imaginations, instead of relying upon their observations, in all that they have written concerning these singular animals.

The history of the beaver teems in fact with the most ridiculous exaggerations. Even the absurdities of the ancients have in this instance been exceeded by the credulity of the moderns. The former, indeed, knew the animal only in a state comparatively solitary, and could not therefore attribute to him those ideas of social policy and that settled system of government for which the latter have given him unbounded credit. This delusion, which was perhaps natural enough to those who took but a superficial view of the faculties of this almost mechanical animal, has now, however, passed away; and the intelligence of the beaver is recognized as nothing more than a remarkable instinct exerted upon one particular object, and upon that alone. In all respects, except as regards the skill with which he constructs his winter habitation, and the kind of combination into which he enters with his fellows for carrying their common purpose into effect, his intelligence is of the most limited description. He has, in fact, no need of those artful contrivances to which many animals are compelled to have recourse. His food is simple and easily procured. His enemies, man excepted, are few, and rarely of a formidable description; but if surprised by danger, he is quite unable to evade it by the exercise of cunning or sagacity, and his only hope of safety is in flight. It has been said that he is docile in captivity, and may be easily rendered obedient to the commands of his keeper; but it would appear that his docility is limited to a patient endurance of his condition, and his obedience to a simple recognition of those who take care of him, and whom he may be taught to follow from place to place.

His peculiar conformation renders the beaver what is commonly, although improperly, termed an amphibious animal, the greater part of his existence being passed in the water, in which he swims and dives with great dexterity. It is for this reason that he always selects for his dwelling-place the banks of rivers or lakes. Here he lives secluded during the summer in holes which he burrows in the earth, and which he quits only in search of his food, and to indulge himself with bathing. But as the autumn advances, he begins to look out for society, and to prepare against the rigors and the dearth of winter. With this view he associates himself with a band of his fellows, sometimes amounting in number to two or three hundred, and the whole body immediately set to work either to repair their old habitations, or if they have been compelled to desert their former place of abode, to construct new ones on the same plan.

The mode by which this is accomplished has been so repeatedly described by French and English travellers in the northern parts of America, that it might seem almost superfluous to enter into any details upon such a subject, were we not well assured that many of the facts vouched for in their relations, and most of the coloring which has been given to them, have been derived either from the warmth of their imaginations, from partial and imperfect observation, or from the credulous ignorance of their informants. Under these circumstances, we cannot do better than recur to the statements of one or two practical men, whose residence in the country, and close connection with the fur trade, gave them the best opportunities for obtaining correct information, and whose narratives bear in themselves the stamp of authenticity. Such were Hearne, one of the most intelligent and enterprising agents whom the Hudson's Bay Company ever employed; and

Cartwright, who resided for nearly sixteen years on the coast of Labrador for the sole purpose of procuring furs. From the journals of these two plain-dealing and matter-of-fact men we shall proceed to give the principal facts with which they furnish us relative to the habits of the beaver in its native state, and to the various modes adopted by the hunters for possessing themselves of its valuable skin.

The situations in which the beavers build are very various. Sometimes they take their abode in a pond or a lake, in which the water is tolerably uniform in height and pretty deep immediately under the bank; but they generally make choice of a running stream as more convenient for the conveyance of their materials. They are also said to select in preference the northern side for the advantage of the sun, and the bank of an island rather than that of the mainland, as affording them greater security from the attacks of their enemies. In this selection, however, their instinct frequently misleads them, for they have been known to build in situations where they have been unable to procure food, and where they have consequently perished from starvation, or to have fixed upon a stream which has been so swelled by the effects of a heavy thaw as to sweep away not only their magazine of provisions, but sometimes even their habitations.

When the water in the stream is not sufficiently deep for their purpose, or is liable to be diminished by the failure of the supply from above in consequence of frost, they commence their operations by throwing a dam across it below the part which they intend to occupy. In slow rivulets this is made nearly straight; but where the current is strong, it is formed with a curve of greater or less extent, the convexity of which is turned toward the stream. The materials of which this dam is constructed consist of drift-wood, and the branches of willows, birch, and poplars, compacted together by mud and stones. The work is raised in the form of a mound, of considerable thickness at the base, and gradually narrowing toward the summit, which is made perfectly level, and of the exact height of the body of water which it is intended to keep up. Cartwright adds that he has frequently crossed the rivers and creeks upon these dams with only slightly wetting his shoes. The sticks which are used in their construction vary in size from the thickness of a man's finger to that of his ankle, but are seldom larger unless where no others are to be procured. They are mostly obtained from the neighboring woods, where they are cut with a dexterity truly astonishing. A beaver, according to Cartwright, will lop off with its teeth at a single effort a stem of the thickness of a common walking-stick as cleanly as if it had been done by a gardener's pruning-knife. When compelled to have recourse to the larger trunks, they gnaw them round and round, always taking care that they shall fall in the direction of the water, in order as much as possible to save themselves carriage. Judging from the number of large trees sometimes cut down in a season, it would appear that the performance of this operation cannot occupy a very considerable time. As soon as the tree is felled they commence lopping off its branches, which, as well as the smaller trunks, they cut into lengths, according to their weight and thickness. These are dragged in their mouths, and sometimes on their shoulders, to the water side, where they are thrown into the stream, and towed with the current to their destination.

Exactly the same materials are employed in the construction of their habitations. These are built either immediately beneath the bank, or, if the pool be shallow, at some little distance from it. They begin by hollowing out the bottom, throwing up the mud and stones around it, and intermingling them with such sticks as they can procure. The walls having been thus raised to a sufficient height, the house is covered in with a roof in the shape of a dome, generally emerging about four feet, but sometimes as much as six or seven, from the water. The entrance is made beneath a projection which advances several feet into the stream with a regular descent, terminating at least three feet below the surface, to guard against its being frozen up. This is called by the hunters the angle, and a single dwelling is sometimes furnished with two or more. Near the entrance, and on the outside of their houses, the beavers store up the branches of trees, the bark of which forms their chief subsistence during the winter; and these magazines are sometimes so large as to rise above the surface of the water, and to contain more than a cart-load of provisions.

In all these operations there appears to be no other concert or combination among the beavers than that which results from a common instinct impelling them to the performance of a common task. The assertion that they are superintended in their labors by an overseer, who gives notice to his workmen when to be at their posts by flapping with his tail upon the water, divides them into parties for each several kinds of work, distributes their employments, assigns their stations, and superintends the execution of his commands, is too absurd to require refutation. But there are many other statements regarding them equally untrue, although not at first sight so palpably ridiculous. Thus it is said that their tails are used by them as sledges for the conveyance of their materials, a purpose for which the conformation of this appendage renders it highly improbable that it can serve, and which observation has proved to be performed in a very different manner. But not content with metamorphosing this organ into a sledge, our travellers have also made it a trowel, and have given very particular descriptions of the manner in which the beaver employs it in spreading the plaster, with which, according to their accounts, his work is overlaid. Unfortunately, however, it is equally unfitted by its structure for such an operation; and the only organs employed in mixing up the mud with the rest of the materials, are the fore paws and the mouth. These, in fact, are the instruments with which all the labors of the beavers are effected; and it is sufficiently obvious that neither with their assistance, nor indeed with the united powers of all their organs, could these animals drive stakes of the thickness of a man's leg three or four feet deep into the ground, or execute a variety or other feats for which they have obtained general credit.

The sticks and branches which they use, instead of being driven into the ground, are laid for the most part in a horizontal direction, and they are only prevented from floating away by the stones and mud which are brought up by the beavers in their paws from the bottom to be laid upon them, and which gradually become cemented into a firm and compact mass. All their work is performed during the night. Although the favorable nature or the situation may have induced many families to assemble in the same spot, they do not on that account carry on their operations in common; unless when a dam of large extent is to be built, when they usually unite their forces for its completion. Each family occupies itself exclusively on its own habitation, which has in general but one apartment. The idea of their houses being divided into several chambers, each allotted to its appropriate purpose, may have originated from the fact of their sometimes building by the side of a deserted dwelling, with which they occasionally open a communication. The families vary in the number of individuals of which they are composed, but seldom exceed two or four old ones, and twice as many young; the females producing once a year, from two to three or four at a birth, and the young ones generally quitting their parents at the age of three years, and seeking out or building a separate habitation for themselves.

In summer-time they feed either upon the bark of trees or upon the green herbage and the berries which grow in their neighborhood; but in winter their diet is almost restricted to the former article, of which they lay in a large stock previously to the setting in of the frost. From this store they cut away portions as their necessities require; and after tearing off the bark reject the wood, leaving it to float away with the current. Willow, poplar, and birch, are their favorite kinds, and the latter, according to Cartwright, renders their flesh "the most delicious eating of any animal in the known world." The root of the water-lily also affords them an occasional supply, and makes them very fat, but gives their flesh a strong and unpleasant flavor.

It is not, however, for the delicacy of their flesh, but for the peculiar closeness of their soft and glossy fur, that a war of extermination is carried on by man against these peaceful and innoxious beasts. That this fur was at an early period in great request for the manufacture of hats is proved by a proclamation issued in the year 1638, by which it was forbidden to make use of any materials therein except beaver stuff or beaver wool. From this time the attention of the North American Indians has been incessantly directed toward these poor animals, and vast quantities have in consequence been destroyed every year. Of the numbers thus sacrificed, and of the importance of the trade, some idea may be formed by the amount of the sales at various places and at different periods. In 1743 the Hudson's Bay Company alone sold 26,750 skins; and 127,080 were imported into Rochelle. Upwards of 170,000 were exported from Canada in 1788; and Quebec alone, in 1808, supplied this country with 126,927, which, at the estimated average of eighteen shillings and nine pence per skin, would produce no less a sum than £118,994.

The skin of the young or cub beaver is the most valuable, as being the darkest and the most glossy; and the winter coat is far superior to the summer.   The former season is consequently preferred for taking them, and various means are adopted for the purpose.   Sometimes the ice is cut through both above and below their dwellings, nets are thrown across, and the devoted animals are driven from their shelter by the breaking down of their houses, and compelled to enter the nets.   Sometimes a number of holes are made in the ice, and they are in like manner driven from their habitations; when, as they are unable to remain under water for any long time, they rise to the surface where the ice is broken, and are easily secured.   Under these circumstances they will frequently take refuge in the holes in the banks, which serve them for summer retreats; but the experienced hunters readily detect the situation of these vaults by striking with their chisels on the ice, and always select such spots for making their apertures, in which they seldom fail of capturing their victims. In summer it is more usual to take them in their houses by what is termed staking them.   For this purpose the hunters first make an aperture in the roof to ascertain the situation of the angle, and having adapted a number of stakes to the opening so as completely to blockade it, cover in the top, and leave the stakes on one side ready for use.   They then drive the beavers from all parts of the pond or river by means of dogs; and when the terrified animals have succeeded in reaching their home, they replace the stakes before the entry, remove the temporary covering from the roof, and either take them alive, or spear them in their house. When the sheet of water which they inhabit is merely kept up by a dam, they are still more easily taken by letting off the water and leaving their huts completely dry.   The gun is also sometimes, but not very commonly used; and log traps, baited with poplar sticks, occasionally add in a trifling degree to the havoc made among them.

So little is known of the manners of the beaver in a domesticated state, that we feel a peculiar gratification in having it in our power to give the extremely interesting history of an individual which belonged to Mr. Brodleip, to whose kindness we are indebted for the following statement:

"The animal arrived in this country in the winter of 1825, very young, being small and woolly, and without the covering of long hair which marks the adult beaver.   It was the sole survivor of five or six which were shipped at the same time, and it was in a very pitiable condition. Good treatment quickly restored it to health, and kindness soon made it familiar. When called by its name, 'Binny,' it generally answered with a little cry, and came to its owner. The hearth-rug was its favorite haunt, and thereon it would lie stretched out, sometimes on its back, sometimes on its side, and sometimes flat on its belly, but always near its master. The building instinct showed itself immediately it was let out of its cage and materials were placed in its way; and this before it had been a week in its new quarters. Its strength, even before it was half grown, was great. It would drag along a large sweeping-brush, or a warming-pan, grasping the handle with its teeth so that the load came over its shoulder, and advancing in an oblique direction till it arrived at the point where it wished to place it. The long and large materials were always taken first, and two of the longest were generally laid crosswise, with one of the ends of each touching the wall, and the other ends projecting out into the room. The area formed by the crossed brushes and the wall he would fill up with hand-brushes, rush baskets, books, boots, sticks, cloths, dried turf, or anything portable. As the work grew high, he supported himself on his tail, which propped him up admirably, and he would often, after laying on one of his building materials, sit up over against it, appearing to consider his work, or, as the country people say, 'judge it.' This pause was sometimes followed by changing the position of the material 'judged,' and sometimes it was left in its place. After he had piled up his materials in one part of the room (for he generally chose the same place), he proceeded to wall up the space between the feet of a chest of drawers, which stood, at a little distance from it, high enough on its legs to make the bottom a roof for him, using for this purpose dried turf and sticks, which he laid very even, and filling up the interstices with bits of coal, hay, cloth, or anything he could pick up. This last place he seemed to appropriate for his dwelling; the former work seemed to be intended for a dam. When he had walled up the space between the feet of the chest of drawers, he proceeded to carry in sticks, cloths, hay, cotton, and to make a nest; and when he had done he would sit up under the drawers and comb himself with the nails of his hind feet. In this operation, that which appeared at first to be a malformation was shown to be a beautiful adaptation to the necessities of the animal. The huge webbed hind feet of the beaver turn in so as to give the appearance of deformity; but if the toes were straight instead of being incurved, the animal could not use them for the purpose of keeping its fur in order and cleansing it from dirt and moisture.

"Binny generally carried small and light articles between his right fore leg and his chin, walking on the other three legs; and large masses, which he could not grasp readily with his teeth, he pushed forward, leaning against them with his right fore paw and his chin. He never carried anything on his tail, which he liked to dip in water, but he was not fond of plunging in the whole of his body. If his tail was kept moist, he never cared to drink; but if it was kept dry, it became hot, and the animal appeared distressed, and would drink a great deal. It is not impossible that the tail may have the power of absorbing water, like the skin of frogs, though it must be owned that the scaly integument which invests that member has not much of the character which generally belongs to absorbing surfaces.

"Bread, and bread and milk, and sugar, formed the principal part of Binny's food; but he was very fond of succulent fruits and roots. He was a most entertaining creature, and some highly comic scenes occurred between the worthy, but slow beaver, and a light and airy Macauco that was kept in the same apartment."

An animal so sociable in his habits ought to be affectionate; and very affectionate the beaver is said to be. Deage mentions two young ones which were taken alive and brought to a neighboring factory in Hudson's Bay, where they throve very fast until one of them was killed accidentally. The survivor instantly felt the loss, began to moan, and abstained from food until it died. Mr. Bullock mentioned to the narrator a similar instance which fell under his notice in North America. A male and female were kept together in a room, where they lived happily till the male was deprived of his partner by death. For a day or two he appeared to be hardly aware of his loss, and brought food and laid it before her. At last, finding that she did not stir, he covered her body with twigs and leaves, and was in a pining state when Mr. Bullock lost sight of him.

The specimens in the garden were sent to the Society from

Canada by Lord Dalhousie. They were partially deprived of sight before their arrival in this country, but one of them has still the use of one eye; and the other, although totally blind, dives most perseveringly for clay, and applies it to stop up every cranny in their common habitation that can admit "the winter's flaw." They both appear happy and contented.

FINIS.

A CATALOG OF
SELECTED DOVER BOOKS
IN ALL FIELDS OF INTEREST

A CATALOG OF SELECTED DOVER BOOKS IN ALL FIELDS OF INTEREST

CONCERNING THE SPIRITUAL IN ART, Wassily Kandinsky. Pioneering work by father of abstract art. Thoughts on color theory, nature of art. Analysis of earlier masters. 12 illustrations. 80pp. of text. 5⅜ × 8½. 23411-8 Pa. $2.50

LEONARDO ON THE HUMAN BODY, Leonardo da Vinci. More than 1200 of Leonardo's anatomical drawings on 215 plates. Leonardo's text, which accompanies the drawings, has been translated into English. 506pp. 8⅜ × 11¾. 24483-0 Pa. $10.95

GOBLIN MARKET, Christina Rossetti. Best-known work by poet comparable to Emily Dickinson, Alfred Tennyson. With 46 delightfully grotesque illustrations by Laurence Housman. 64pp. 4 × 6¾. 24516-0 Pa. $2.50

THE HEART OF THOREAU'S JOURNALS, edited by Odell Shepard. Selections from *Journal*, ranging over full gamut of interests. 228pp. 5⅜ × 8½. 20741-2 Pa. $4.50

MR. LINCOLN'S CAMERA MAN: MATHEW B. BRADY, Roy Meredith. Over 300 Brady photos reproduced directly from original negatives, photos. Lively commentary. 368pp. 8⅜ × 11¼. 23021-X Pa. $11.95

PHOTOGRAPHIC VIEWS OF SHERMAN'S CAMPAIGN, George N. Barnard. Reprint of landmark 1866 volume with 61 plates: battlefield of New Hope Church, the Etawah Bridge, the capture of Atlanta, etc. 80pp. 9 × 12. 23445-2 Pa. $6.00

A SHORT HISTORY OF ANATOMY AND PHYSIOLOGY FROM THE GREEKS TO HARVEY, Dr. Charles Singer. Thoroughly engrossing non-technical survey. 270 illustrations. 211pp. 5⅜ × 8½. 20389-1 Pa. $4.50

REDOUTE ROSES IRON-ON TRANSFER PATTERNS, Barbara Christopher. Redouté was botanical painter to the Empress Josephine; transfer his famous roses onto fabric with these 24 transfer patterns. 80pp. 8¼ × 10⅞. 24292-7 Pa. $3.50

THE FIVE BOOKS OF ARCHITECTURE, Sebastiano Serlio. Architectural milestone, first (1611) English translation of Renaissance classic. Unabridged reproduction of original edition includes over 300 woodcut illustrations. 416pp. 9⅜ × 12¼. 24349-4 Pa. $14.95

CARLSON'S GUIDE TO LANDSCAPE PAINTING, John F. Carlson. Authoritative, comprehensive guide covers, every aspect of landscape painting. 34 reproductions of paintings by author; 58 explanatory diagrams. 144pp. 8⅜ × 11. 22927-0 Pa. $4.95

101 PUZZLES IN THOUGHT AND LOGIC, C.R. Wylie, Jr. Solve murders, robberies, see which fishermen are liars—purely by reasoning! 107pp. 5⅜ × 8½. 20367-0 Pa. $2.00

TEST YOUR LOGIC, George J. Summers. 50 more truly new puzzles with new turns of thought, new subtleties of inference. 100pp. 5⅜ × 8½. 22877-0 Pa. $2.25

25 KITES THAT FLY, Leslie Hunt. Full, easy-to-follow instructions for kites made from inexpensive materials. Many novelties. 70 illustrations. 110pp. 5⅜ × 8½.
22550-X Pa. $2.25

PIANO TUNING, J. Cree Fischer. Clearest, best book for beginner, amateur. Simple repairs, raising dropped notes, tuning by easy method of flattened fifths. No previous skills needed. 4 illustrations. 201pp. 5⅜ × 8½. 23267-0 Pa. $3.50

EARLY AMERICAN IRON-ON TRANSFER PATTERNS, edited by Rita Weiss. 75 designs, borders, alphabets, from traditional American sources. 48pp. 8¼ × 11.
23162-3 Pa. $1.95

CROCHETING EDGINGS, edited by Rita Weiss. Over 100 of the best designs for these lovely trims for a host of household items. Complete instructions, illustrations. 48pp. 8¼ × 11. 24031-2 Pa. $2.25

FINGER PLAYS FOR NURSERY AND KINDERGARTEN, Emilie Poulsson. 18 finger plays with music (voice and piano); entertaining, instructive. Counting, nature lore, etc. Victorian classic. 53 illustrations. 80pp. 6½ × 9¼. 22588-7 Pa. $1.95

BOSTON THEN AND NOW, Peter Vanderwarker. Here in 59 side-by-side views are photographic documentations of the city's past and present. 119 photographs. Full captions. 122pp. 8¼ × 11. 24312-5 Pa. $6.95

CROCHETING BEDSPREADS, edited by Rita Weiss. 22 patterns, originally published in three instruction books 1939-41. 39 photos, 8 charts. Instructions. 48pp. 8¼ × 11. 23610-2 Pa. $2.00

HAWTHORNE ON PAINTING, Charles W. Hawthorne. Collected from notes taken by students at famous Cape Cod School; hundreds of direct, personal *apercus*, ideas, suggestions. 91pp. 5⅜ × 8½. 20653-X Pa. $2.50

THERMODYNAMICS, Enrico Fermi. A classic of modern science. Clear, organized treatment of systems, first and second laws, entropy, thermodynamic potentials, etc. Calculus required. 160pp. 5⅜ × 8½. 60361-X Pa. $4.00

TEN BOOKS ON ARCHITECTURE, Vitruvius. The most important book ever written on architecture. Early Roman aesthetics, technology, classical orders, site selection, all other aspects. Morgan translation. 331pp. 5⅜ × 8½. 20645-9 Pa. $5.50

THE CORNELL BREAD BOOK, Clive M. McCay and Jeanette B. McCay. Famed high-protein recipe incorporated into breads, rolls, buns, coffee cakes, pizza, pie crusts, more. Nearly 50 illustrations. 48pp. 8¼ × 11. 23995-0 Pa. $2.00

THE CRAFTSMAN'S HANDBOOK, Cennino Cennini. 15th-century handbook, school of Giotto, explains applying gold, silver leaf; gesso; fresco painting, grinding pigments, etc. 142pp. 6⅛ × 9¼. 20054-X Pa. $3.50

FRANK LLOYD WRIGHT'S FALLINGWATER, Donald Hoffmann. Full story of Wright's masterwork at Bear Run, Pa. 100 photographs of site, construction, and details of completed structure. 112pp. 9¼ × 10. 23671-4 Pa. $6.50

OVAL STAINED GLASS PATTERN BOOK, C. Eaton. 60 new designs framed in shape of an oval. Greater complexity, challenge with sinuous cats, birds, mandalas framed in antique shape. 64pp. 8¼ × 11. 24519-5 Pa. $3.50

THE MURDER BOOK OF J.G. REEDER, Edgar Wallace. Eight suspenseful stories by bestselling mystery writer of 20s and 30s. Features the donnish Mr. J.G. Reeder of Public Prosecutor's Office. 128pp. 5⅜ × 8½. (Available in U.S. only) 24374-5 Pa. $3.50

ANNE ORR'S CHARTED DESIGNS, Anne Orr. Best designs by premier needlework designer, all on charts: flowers, borders, birds, children, alphabets, etc. Over 100 charts, 10 in color. Total of 40pp. 8¼ × 11. 23704-4 Pa. $2.25

BASIC CONSTRUCTION TECHNIQUES FOR HOUSES AND SMALL BUILDINGS SIMPLY EXPLAINED, U.S. Bureau of Naval Personnel. Grading, masonry, woodworking, floor and wall framing, roof framing, plastering, tile setting, much more. Over 675 illustrations. 568pp. 6½ × 9¼. 20242-9 Pa. $8.95

MATISSE LINE DRAWINGS AND PRINTS, Henri Matisse. Representative collection of female nudes, faces, still lifes, experimental works, etc., from 1898 to 1948. 50 illustrations. 48pp. 8⅜ × 11¼. 23877-6 Pa. $2.50

HOW TO PLAY THE CHESS OPENINGS, Eugene Znosko-Borovsky. Clear, profound examinations of just what each opening is intended to do and how opponent can counter. Many sample games. 147pp. 5⅜ × 8½. 22795-2 Pa. $2.95

DUPLICATE BRIDGE, Alfred Sheinwold. Clear, thorough, easily followed account: rules, etiquette, scoring, strategy, bidding; Goren's point-count system, Blackwood and Gerber conventions, etc. 158pp. 5⅜ × 8½. 22741-3 Pa. $3.00

SARGENT PORTRAIT DRAWINGS, J.S. Sargent. Collection of 42 portraits reveals technical skill and intuitive eye of noted American portrait painter, John Singer Sargent. 48pp. 8¼ × 11⅛. 24524-1 Pa. $2.95

ENTERTAINING SCIENCE EXPERIMENTS WITH EVERYDAY OBJECTS, Martin Gardner. Over 100 experiments for youngsters. Will amuse, astonish, teach, and entertain. Over 100 illustrations. 127pp. 5⅜ × 8½. 24201-3 Pa. $2.50

TEDDY BEAR PAPER DOLLS IN FULL COLOR: A Family of Four Bears and Their Costumes, Crystal Collins. A family of four Teddy Bear paper dolls and nearly 60 cut-out costumes. Full color, printed one side only. 32pp. 9¼ × 12¼. 24550-0 Pa. $3.50

NEW CALLIGRAPHIC ORNAMENTS AND FLOURISHES, Arthur Baker. Unusual, multi-useable material: arrows, pointing hands, brackets and frames, ovals, swirls, birds, etc. Nearly 700 illustrations. 80pp. 8⅜ × 11¼. 24095-9 Pa. $3.75

DINOSAUR DIORAMAS TO CUT & ASSEMBLE, M. Kalmenoff. Two complete three-dimensional scenes in full color, with 31 cut-out animals and plants. Excellent educational toy for youngsters. Instructions; 2 assembly diagrams. 32pp. 9¼ × 12¼. 24541-1 Pa. $3.95

SILHOUETTES: A PICTORIAL ARCHIVE OF VARIED ILLUSTRATIONS, edited by Carol Belanger Grafton. Over 600 silhouettes from the 18th to 20th centuries. Profiles and full figures of men, women, children, birds, animals, groups and scenes, nature, ships, an alphabet. 144pp. 8⅜ × 11¼. 23781-8 Pa. $4.95

CATALOG OF DOVER BOOKS

THE BOOK OF WOOD CARVING, Charles Marshall Sayers. Still finest book for beginning student. Fundamentals, technique; gives 34 designs, over 34 projects for panels, bookends, mirrors, etc. 33 photos. 118pp. 7¾ × 10⅝. 23654-4 Pa. $3.95

CARVING COUNTRY CHARACTERS, Bill Higginbotham. Expert advice for beginning, advanced carvers on materials, techniques for creating 18 projects— mirthful panorama of American characters. 105 illustrations. 80pp. 8⅜ × 11. 24135-1 Pa. $2.50

300 ART NOUVEAU DESIGNS AND MOTIFS IN FULL COLOR, C.B. Grafton. 44 full-page plates display swirling lines and muted colors typical of Art Nouveau. Borders, frames, panels, cartouches, dingbats, etc. 48pp. 9⅜ × 12¼. 24354-0 Pa. $6.00

SELF-WORKING CARD TRICKS, Karl Fulves. Editor of *Pallbearer* offers 72 tricks that work automatically through nature of card deck. No sleight of hand needed. Often spectacular. 42 illustrations. 113pp. 5⅜ × 8½. 23334-0 Pa. $3.50

CUT AND ASSEMBLE A WESTERN FRONTIER TOWN, Edmund V. Gillon, Jr. Ten authentic full-color buildings on heavy cardboard stock in H-O scale. Sheriff's Office and Jail, Saloon, Wells Fargo, Opera House, others. 48pp. 9¼ × 12¼. 23736-2 Pa. $3.95

CUT AND ASSEMBLE AN EARLY NEW ENGLAND VILLAGE, Edmund V. Gillon, Jr. Printed in full color on heavy cardboard stock. 12 authentic buildings in H-O scale: Adams home in Quincy, Mass., Oliver Wight house in Sturbridge, smithy, store, church, others. 48pp. 9¼ × 12¼. 23536-X Pa. $3.95

THE TALE OF TWO BAD MICE, Beatrix Potter. Tom Thumb and Hunca Munca squeeze out of their hole and go exploring. 27 full-color Potter illustrations. 59pp. 4¼ × 5½. (Available in U.S. only) 23065-1 Pa. $1.50

CARVING FIGURE CARICATURES IN THE OZARK STYLE, Harold L. Enlow. Instructions and illustrations for ten delightful projects, plus general carving instructions. 22 drawings and 47 photographs altogether. 39pp. 8⅜ × 11. 23151-8 Pa. $2.50

A TREASURY OF FLOWER DESIGNS FOR ARTISTS, EMBROIDERERS AND CRAFTSMEN, Susan Gaber. 100 garden favorites lushly rendered by artist for artists, craftsmen, needleworkers. Many form frames, borders. 80pp. 8¼ × 11. 24096-7 Pa. $3.50

CUT & ASSEMBLE A TOY THEATER/THE NUTCRACKER BALLET, Tom Tierney. Model of a complete, full-color production of Tchaikovsky's classic. 6 backdrops, dozens of characters, familiar dance sequences. 32pp. 9⅜ × 12¼. 24194-7 Pa. $4.50

ANIMALS: 1,419 COPYRIGHT-FREE ILLUSTRATIONS OF MAMMALS, BIRDS, FISH, INSECTS, ETC., edited by Jim Harter. Clear wood engravings present, in extremely lifelike poses, over 1,000 species of animals. 284pp. 9 × 12. 23766-4 Pa. $9.95

MORE HAND SHADOWS, Henry Bursill. For those at their 'finger ends,'' 16 more effects—Shakespeare, a hare, a squirrel, Mr. Punch, and twelve more—each explained by a full-page illustration. Considerable period charm. 30pp. 6½ × 9¼. 21384-6 Pa. $1.95

SURREAL STICKERS AND UNREAL STAMPS, William Rowe. 224 haunting, hilarious stamps on gummed, perforated stock, with images of elephants, geisha girls, George Washington, etc. 16pp. one side. 8¼ × 11. 24371-0 Pa. $3.50

GOURMET KITCHEN LABELS, Ed Sibbett, Jr. 112 full-color labels (4 copies each of 28 designs). Fruit, bread, other culinary motifs. Gummed and perforated. 16pp. 8¼ × 11. 24087-8 Pa. $2.95

PATTERNS AND INSTRUCTIONS FOR CARVING AUTHENTIC BIRDS, H.D. Green. Detailed instructions, 27 diagrams, 85 photographs for carving 15 species of birds so life-like, they'll seem ready to fly! 8¼ × 11. 24222-6 Pa. $2.75

FLATLAND, E.A. Abbott. Science-fiction classic explores life of 2-D being in 3-D world. 16 illustrations. 103pp. 5⅜ × 8. 20001-9 Pa. $2.00

DRIED FLOWERS, Sarah Whitlock and Martha Rankin. Concise, clear, practical guide to dehydration, glycerinizing, pressing plant material, and more. Covers use of silica gel. 12 drawings. 32pp. 5⅜ × 8½. 21802-3 Pa. $1.00

EASY-TO-MAKE CANDLES, Gary V. Guy. Learn how easy it is to make all kinds of decorative candles. Step-by-step instructions. 82 illustrations. 48pp. 8¼ × 11. 23881-4 Pa. $2.50

SUPER STICKERS FOR KIDS, Carolyn Bracken. 128 gummed and perforated full-color stickers: GIRL WANTED, KEEP OUT, BORED OF EDUCATION, X-RATED, COMBAT ZONE, many others. 16pp. 8¼ × 11. 24092-4 Pa. $2.50

CUT AND COLOR PAPER MASKS, Michael Grater. Clowns, animals, funny faces...simply color them in, cut them out, and put them together, and you have 9 paper masks to play with and enjoy. 32pp. 8¼ × 11. 23171-2 Pa. $2.25

A CHRISTMAS CAROL: THE ORIGINAL MANUSCRIPT, Charles Dickens. Clear facsimile of Dickens manuscript, on facing pages with final printed text. 8 illustrations by John Leech, 4 in color on covers. 144pp. 8⅜ × 11¼. 20980-6 Pa. $5.95

CARVING SHOREBIRDS, Harry V. Shourds & Anthony Hillman. 16 full-size patterns (all double-page spreads) for 19 North American shorebirds with step-by-step instructions. 72pp. 9¼ × 12¼. 24287-0 Pa. $4.95

THE GENTLE ART OF MATHEMATICS, Dan Pedoe. Mathematical games, probability, the question of infinity, topology, how the laws of algebra work, problems of irrational numbers, and more. 42 figures. 143pp. 5⅜ × 8½. (EBE) 22949-1 Pa. $3.50

READY-TO-USE DOLLHOUSE WALLPAPER, Katzenbach & Warren, Inc. Stripe, 2 floral stripes, 2 allover florals, polka dot; all in full color. 4 sheets (350 sq. in.) of each, enough for average room. 48pp. 8¼ × 11. 23495-9 Pa. $2.95

MINIATURE IRON-ON TRANSFER PATTERNS FOR DOLLHOUSES, DOLLS, AND SMALL PROJECTS, Rita Weiss and Frank Fontana. Over 100 miniature patterns: rugs, bedspreads, quilts, chair seats, etc. In standard dollhouse size. 48pp. 8¼ × 11. 23741-9 Pa. $1.95

THE DINOSAUR COLORING BOOK, Anthony Rao. 45 renderings of dinosaurs, fossil birds, turtles, other creatures of Mesozoic Era. Scientifically accurate. Captions. 48pp. 8¼ × 11. 24022-3 Pa. $2.25

CATALOG OF DOVER BOOKS

JAPANESE DESIGN MOTIFS, Matsuya Co. Mon, or heraldic designs. Over 4000 typical, beautiful designs: birds, animals, flowers, swords, fans, geometrics; all beautifully stylized. 213pp. 11⅜ × 8¼. 22874-6 Pa. $7.95

THE TALE OF BENJAMIN BUNNY, Beatrix Potter. Peter Rabbit's cousin coaxes him back into Mr. McGregor's garden for a whole new set of adventures. All 27 full-color illustrations. 59pp. 4¼ × 5½. (Available in U.S. only) 21102-9 Pa. $1.50

THE TALE OF PETER RABBIT AND OTHER FAVORITE STORIES BOXED SET, Beatrix Potter. Seven of Beatrix Potter's best-loved tales including Peter Rabbit in a specially designed, durable boxed set. 4¼ × 5½. Total of 447pp. 158 color illustrations. (Available in U.S. only) 23903-9 Pa. $10.80

PRACTICAL MENTAL MAGIC, Theodore Annemann. Nearly 200 astonishing feats of mental magic revealed in step-by-step detail. Complete advice on staging, patter, etc. Illustrated. 320pp. 5⅜ × 8½. 24426-1 Pa. $5.95

CELEBRATED CASES OF JUDGE DEE (DEE GOONG AN), translated by Robert Van Gulik. Authentic 18th-century Chinese detective novel; Dee and associates solve three interlocked cases. Led to van Gulik's own stories with same characters. Extensive introduction. 9 illustrations. 237pp. 5⅜ × 8½.
23337-5 Pa. $4.50

CUT & FOLD EXTRATERRESTRIAL INVADERS THAT FLY, M. Grater. Stage your own lilliputian space battles. By following the step-by-step instructions and explanatory diagrams you can launch 22 full-color fliers into space. 36pp. 8¼ × 11. 24478-4 Pa. $2.95

CUT & ASSEMBLE VICTORIAN HOUSES, Edmund V. Gillon, Jr. Printed in full color on heavy cardboard stock, 4 authentic Victorian houses in H-O scale: Italian-style Villa, Octagon, Second Empire, Stick Style. 48pp. 9¼ × 12¼.
23849-0 Pa. $3.95

BEST SCIENCE FICTION STORIES OF H.G. WELLS, H.G. Wells. Full novel The Invisible Man, plus 17 short stories: "The Crystal Egg," "Aepyornis Island," "The Strange Orchid," etc. 303pp. 5⅜ × 8½. (Available in U.S. only)
21531-8 Pa. $4.95

TRADEMARK DESIGNS OF THE WORLD, Yusaku Kamekura. A lavish collection of nearly 700 trademarks, the work of Wright, Loewy, Klee, Binder, hundreds of others. 160pp. 8¾ × 8. (Available in U.S. only) 24191-2 Pa. $5.00

THE ARTIST'S AND CRAFTSMAN'S GUIDE TO REDUCING, ENLARGING AND TRANSFERRING DESIGNS, Rita Weiss. Discover, reduce, enlarge, transfer designs from any objects to any craft project. 12pp. plus 16 sheets special graph paper. 8¼ × 11. 24142-4 Pa. $3.25

TREASURY OF JAPANESE DESIGNS AND MOTIFS FOR ARTISTS AND CRAFTSMEN, edited by Carol Belanger Grafton. Indispensable collection of 360 traditional Japanese designs and motifs redrawn in clean, crisp black-and-white, copyright-free illustrations. 96pp. 8¼ × 11. 24435-0 Pa. $3.95

CHANCERY CURSIVE STROKE BY STROKE, Arthur Baker. Instructions and illustrations for each stroke of each letter (upper and lower case) and numerals. 54 full-page plates. 64pp. 8¼ × 11. 24278-1 Pa. $2.50

THE ENJOYMENT AND USE OF COLOR, Walter Sargent. Color relationships, values, intensities; complementary colors, illumination, similar topics. Color in nature and art. 7 color plates, 29 illustrations. 274pp. 5⅜ × 8½. 20944-X Pa. $4.50

SCULPTURE PRINCIPLES AND PRACTICE, Louis Slobodkin. Step-by-step approach to clay, plaster, metals, stone; classical and modern. 253 drawings, photos. 255pp. 8⅛ × 11. 22960-2 Pa. $7.50

VICTORIAN FASHION PAPER DOLLS FROM HARPER'S BAZAR, 1867-1898, Theodore Menten. Four female dolls with 28 elegant high fashion costumes, printed in full color. 32pp. 9¼ × 12¼. 23453-3 Pa. $3.50

FLOPSY, MOPSY AND COTTONTAIL: A Little Book of Paper Dolls in Full Color, Susan LaBelle. Three dolls and 21 costumes (7 for each doll) show Peter Rabbit's siblings dressed for holidays, gardening, hiking, etc. Charming borders, captions. 48pp. 4¼ × 5½. 24376-1 Pa. $2.25

NATIONAL LEAGUE BASEBALL CARD CLASSICS, Bert Randolph Sugar. 83 big-leaguers from 1909-69 on facsimile cards. Hubbell, Dean, Spahn, Brock plus advertising, info, no duplications. Perforated, detachable. 16pp. 8¼ × 11. 24308-7 Pa. $2.95

THE LOGICAL APPROACH TO CHESS, Dr. Max Euwe, et al. First-rate text of comprehensive strategy, tactics, theory for the amateur. No gambits to memorize, just a clear, logical approach. 224pp. 5⅜ × 8½. 24353-2 Pa. $4.50

MAGICK IN THEORY AND PRACTICE, Aleister Crowley. The summation of the thought and practice of the century's most famous necromancer, long hard to find. Crowley's best book. 436pp. 5⅜ × 8½. (Available in U.S. only) 23295-6 Pa. $6.50

THE HAUNTED HOTEL, Wilkie Collins. Collins' last great tale; doom and destiny in a Venetian palace. Praised by T.S. Eliot. 127pp. 5⅜ × 8½. 24333-8 Pa. $3.00

ART DECO DISPLAY ALPHABETS, Dan X. Solo. Wide variety of bold yet elegant lettering in handsome Art Deco styles. 100 complete fonts, with numerals, punctuation, more. 104pp. 8⅛ × 11. 24372-9 Pa. $4.00

CALLIGRAPHIC ALPHABETS, Arthur Baker. Nearly 150 complete alphabets by outstanding contemporary. Stimulating ideas; useful source for unique effects. 154 plates. 157pp. 8⅜ × 11¼. 21045-6 Pa. $4.95

ARTHUR BAKER'S HISTORIC CALLIGRAPHIC ALPHABETS, Arthur Baker. From monumental capitals of first-century Rome to humanistic cursive of 16th century, 33 alphabets in fresh interpretations. 88 plates. 96pp. 9 × 12. 24054-1 Pa. $4.50

LETTIE LANE PAPER DOLLS, Sheila Young. Genteel turn-of-the-century family very popular then and now. 24 paper dolls. 16 plates in full color. 32pp. 9¼ × 12¼. 24089-4 Pa. $3.50

KEYBOARD WORKS FOR SOLO INSTRUMENTS, G.F. Handel. 35 neglected works from Handel's vast oeuvre, originally jotted down as improvisations. Includes Eight Great Suites, others. New sequence. 174pp. 9⅜ × 12¼.
24338-9 Pa. $7.50

AMERICAN LEAGUE BASEBALL CARD CLASSICS, Bert Randolph Sugar. 82 stars from 1900s to 60s on facsimile cards. Ruth, Cobb, Mantle, Williams, plus advertising, info, no duplications. Perforated, detachable. 16pp. 8¼ × 11.
24286-2 Pa. $2.95

A TREASURY OF CHARTED DESIGNS FOR NEEDLEWORKERS, Georgia Gorham and Jeanne Warth. 141 charted designs: owl, cat with yarn, tulips, piano, spinning wheel, covered bridge, Victorian house and many others. 48pp. 8¼ × 11.
23558-0 Pa. $1.95

DANISH FLORAL CHARTED DESIGNS, Gerda Bengtsson. Exquisite collection of over 40 different florals: anemone, Iceland poppy, wild fruit, pansies, many others. 45 illustrations. 48pp. 8¼ × 11.
23957-8 Pa. $1.75

OLD PHILADELPHIA IN EARLY PHOTOGRAPHS 1839-1914, Robert F. Looney. 215 photographs: panoramas, street scenes, landmarks, President-elect Lincoln's visit, 1876 Centennial Exposition, much more. 230pp. 8⅜ × 11¾.
23345-6 Pa. $9.95

PRELUDE TO MATHEMATICS, W.W. Sawyer. Noted mathematician's lively, stimulating account of non-Euclidean geometry, matrices, determinants, group theory, other topics. Emphasis on novel, striking aspects. 224pp. 5⅜ × 8½.
24401-6 Pa. $4.50

ADVENTURES WITH A MICROSCOPE, Richard Headstrom. 59 adventures with clothing fibers, protozoa, ferns and lichens, roots and leaves, much more. 142 illustrations. 232pp. 5⅜ × 8½.
23471-1 Pa. $3.95

IDENTIFYING ANIMAL TRACKS: MAMMALS, BIRDS, AND OTHER ANIMALS OF THE EASTERN UNITED STATES, Richard Headstrom. For hunters, naturalists, scouts, nature-lovers. Diagrams of tracks, tips on identification. 128pp. 5⅜ × 8.
24442-3 Pa. $3.50

VICTORIAN FASHIONS AND COSTUMES FROM HARPER'S BAZAR, 1867-1898, edited by Stella Blum. Day costumes, evening wear, sports clothes, shoes, hats, other accessories in over 1,000 detailed engravings. 320pp. 9⅜ × 12¼.
22990-4 Pa. $9.95

EVERYDAY FASHIONS OF THE TWENTIES AS PICTURED IN SEARS AND OTHER CATALOGS, edited by Stella Blum. Actual dress of the Roaring Twenties, with text by Stella Blum. Over 750 illustrations, captions. 156pp. 9 × 12.
24134-3 Pa. $8.50

HALL OF FAME BASEBALL CARDS, edited by Bert Randolph Sugar. Cy Young, Ted Williams, Lou Gehrig, and many other Hall of Fame greats on 92 full-color, detachable reprints of early baseball cards. No duplication of cards with *Classic Baseball Cards.* 16pp. 8¼ × 11.
23624-2 Pa. $3.50

THE ART OF HAND LETTERING, Helm Wotzkow. Course in hand lettering, Roman, Gothic, Italic, Block, Script. Tools, proportions, optical aspects, individual variation. Very quality conscious. Hundreds of specimens. 320pp. 5⅜ × 8½.
21797-3 Pa. $4.95

HOW THE OTHER HALF LIVES, Jacob A. Riis. Journalistic record of filth, degradation, upward drive in New York immigrant slums, shops, around 1900. New edition includes 100 original Riis photos, monuments of early photography. 233pp. 10 × 7⅞. 22012-5 Pa. $7.95

CHINA AND ITS PEOPLE IN EARLY PHOTOGRAPHS, John Thomson. In 200 black-and-white photographs of exceptional quality photographic pioneer Thomson captures the mountains, dwellings, monuments and people of 19th-century China. 272pp. 9⅜ × 12¼. 24393-1 Pa. $12.95

GODEY COSTUME PLATES IN COLOR FOR DECOUPAGE AND FRAMING, edited by Eleanor Hasbrouk Rawlings. 24 full-color engravings depicting 19th-century Parisian haute couture. Printed on one side only. 56pp. 8¼ × 11. 23879-2 Pa. $3.95

ART NOUVEAU STAINED GLASS PATTERN BOOK, Ed Sibbett, Jr. 104 projects using well-known themes of Art Nouveau: swirling forms, florals, peacocks, and sensuous women. 60pp. 8¼ × 11. 23577-7 Pa. $3.50

QUICK AND EASY PATCHWORK ON THE SEWING MACHINE: Susan Aylsworth Murwin and Suzzy Payne. Instructions, diagrams show exactly how to machine sew 12 quilts. 48pp. of templates. 50 figures. 80pp. 8¼ × 11. 23770-2 Pa. $3.50

THE STANDARD BOOK OF QUILT MAKING AND COLLECTING, Marguerite Ickis. Full information, full-sized patterns for making 46 traditional quilts, also 150 other patterns. 483 illustrations. 273pp. 6⅞ × 9⅝. 20582-7 Pa. $5.95

LETTERING AND ALPHABETS, J. Albert Cavanagh. 85 complete alphabets lettered in various styles; instructions for spacing, roughs, brushwork. 121pp. 8¾ × 8. 20053-1 Pa. $3.75

LETTER FORMS: 110 COMPLETE ALPHABETS, Frederick Lambert. 110 sets of capital letters; 16 lower case alphabets; 70 sets of numbers and other symbols. 110pp. 8⅛ × 11. 22872-X Pa. $4.50

ORCHIDS AS HOUSE PLANTS, Rebecca Tyson Northen. Grow cattleyas and many other kinds of orchids—in a window, in a case, or under artificial light. 63 illustrations. 148pp. 5⅜ × 8½. 23261-1 Pa. $2.95

THE MUSHROOM HANDBOOK, Louis C.C. Krieger. Still the best popular handbook. Full descriptions of 259 species, extremely thorough text, poisons, folklore, etc. 32 color plates; 126 other illustrations. 560pp. 5⅜ × 8½. 21861-9 Pa. $8.50

THE DORÉ BIBLE ILLUSTRATIONS, Gustave Doré. All wonderful, detailed plates: Adam and Eve, Flood, Babylon, life of Jesus, etc. Brief King James text with each plate. 241 plates. 241pp. 9 × 12. 23004-X Pa. $8.95

THE BOOK OF KELLS: Selected Plates in Full Color, edited by Blanche Cirker. 32 full-page plates from greatest manuscript-icon of early Middle Ages. Fantastic, mysterious. Publisher's Note. Captions. 32pp. 9¾ × 12¼. 24345-1 Pa. $4.50

THE PERFECT WAGNERITE, George Bernard Shaw. Brilliant criticism of the Ring Cycle, with provocative interpretation of politics, economic theories behind the Ring. 136pp. 5⅜ × 8½. (Available in U.S. only) 21707-8 Pa. $3.00

CATALOG OF DOVER BOOKS

THE RIME OF THE ANCIENT MARINER, Gustave Doré, S.T. Coleridge. Doré's finest work, 34 plates capture moods, subtleties of poem. Full text. 77pp. 9¼ × 12. 22305-1 Pa. $4.95

SONGS OF INNOCENCE, William Blake. The first and most popular of Blake's famous "Illuminated Books," in a facsimile edition reproducing all 31 brightly colored plates. Additional printed text of each poem. 64pp. 5¼ × 7. 22764-2 Pa. $3.00

AN INTRODUCTION TO INFORMATION THEORY, J.R. Pierce. Second (1980) edition of most impressive non-technical account available. Encoding, entropy, noisy channel, related areas, etc. 320pp. 5⅜ × 8½. 24061-4 Pa. $4.95

THE DIVINE PROPORTION: A STUDY IN MATHEMATICAL BEAUTY, H.E. Huntley. "Divine proportion" or "golden ratio" in poetry, Pascal's triangle, philosophy, psychology, music, mathematical figures, etc. Excellent bridge between science and art. 58 figures. 185pp. 5⅜ × 8½. 22254-3 Pa. $3.95

THE DOVER NEW YORK WALKING GUIDE: From the Battery to Wall Street, Mary J. Shapiro. Superb inexpensive guide to historic buildings and locales in lower Manhattan: Trinity Church, Bowling Green, more. Complete Text; maps. 36 illustrations. 48pp. 3⅞ × 9¼. 24225-0 Pa. $2.50

NEW YORK THEN AND NOW, Edward B. Watson, Edmund V. Gillon, Jr. 83 important Manhattan sites: on facing pages early photographs (1875-1925) and 1976 photos by Gillon. 172 illustrations. 171pp. 9¼ × 10. 23361-8 Pa. $7.95

HISTORIC COSTUME IN PICTURES, Braun & Schneider. Over 1450 costumed figures from dawn of civilization to end of 19th century. English captions. 125 plates. 256pp. 8⅜ × 11¼. 23150-X Pa. $7.50

VICTORIAN AND EDWARDIAN FASHION: A Photographic Survey, Alison Gernsheim. First fashion history completely illustrated by contemporary photographs. Full text plus 235 photos, 1840-1914, in which many celebrities appear. 240pp. 6½ × 9¼. 24205-6 Pa. $6.00

CHARTED CHRISTMAS DESIGNS FOR COUNTED CROSS-STITCH AND OTHER NEEDLECRAFTS, Lindberg Press. Charted designs for 45 beautiful needlecraft projects with many yuletide and wintertime motifs. 48pp. 8¼ × 11. 24356-7 Pa. $1.95

101 FOLK DESIGNS FOR COUNTED CROSS-STITCH AND OTHER NEEDLE-CRAFTS, Carter Houck. 101 authentic charted folk designs in a wide array of lovely representations with many suggestions for effective use. 48pp. 8¼ × 11. 24369-9 Pa. $2.25

FIVE ACRES AND INDEPENDENCE, Maurice G. Kains. Great back-to-the-land classic explains basics of self-sufficient farming. The one book to get. 95 illustrations. 397pp. 5⅜ × 8½. 20974-1 Pa. $4.95

A MODERN HERBAL, Margaret Grieve. Much the fullest, most exact, most useful compilation of herbal material. Gigantic alphabetical encyclopedia, from aconite to zedoary, gives botanical information, medical properties, folklore, economic uses, and much else. Indispensable to serious reader. 161 illustrations. 888pp. 6½ × 9¼. (Available in U.S. only) 22798-7, 22799-5 Pa., Two-vol. set $16.45

DECORATIVE NAPKIN FOLDING FOR BEGINNERS, Lillian Oppenheimer and Natalie Epstein. 22 different napkin folds in the shape of a heart, clown's hat, love knot, etc. 63 drawings. 48pp. 8¼ × 11. 23797-4 Pa. $1.95

DECORATIVE LABELS FOR HOME CANNING, PRESERVING, AND OTHER HOUSEHOLD AND GIFT USES, Theodore Menten. 128 gummed, perforated labels, beautifully printed in 2 colors. 12 versions. Adhere to metal, glass, wood, ceramics. 24pp. 8¼ × 11. 23219-0 Pa. $2.95

EARLY AMERICAN STENCILS ON WALLS AND FURNITURE, Janet Waring. Thorough coverage of 19th-century folk art: techniques, artifacts, surviving specimens. 166 illustrations, 7 in color. 147pp. of text. 7⅞ × 10¾. 21906-2 Pa. $9.95

AMERICAN ANTIQUE WEATHERVANES, A.B. & W.T. Westervelt. Extensively illustrated 1883 catalog exhibiting over 550 copper weathervanes and finials. Excellent primary source by one of the principal manufacturers. 104pp. 6⅛ × 9¼. 24396-6 Pa. $3.95

ART STUDENTS' ANATOMY, Edmond J. Farris. Long favorite in art schools. Basic elements, common positions, actions. Full text, 158 illustrations. 159pp. 5⅜ × 8½. 20744-7 Pa. $3.95

BRIDGMAN'S LIFE DRAWING, George B. Bridgman. More than 500 drawings and text teach you to abstract the body into its major masses. Also specific areas of anatomy. 192pp. 6½ × 9¼. (EA) 22710-3 Pa. $4.50

COMPLETE PRELUDES AND ETUDES FOR SOLO PIANO, Frederic Chopin. All 26 Preludes, all 27 Etudes by greatest composer of piano music. Authoritative Paderewski edition. 224pp. 9 × 12. (Available in U.S. only) 24052-5 Pa. $7.50

PIANO MUSIC 1888-1905, Claude Debussy. Deux Arabesques, Suite Bergamesque, Masques, 1st series of Images, etc. 9 others, in corrected editions. 175pp. 9⅜ × 12¼. (ECE) 22771-5 Pa. $5.95

TEDDY BEAR IRON-ON TRANSFER PATTERNS, Ted Menten. 80 iron-on transfer patterns of male and female Teddys in a wide variety of activities, poses, sizes. 48pp. 8¼ × 11. 24596-9 Pa. $2.25

A PICTURE HISTORY OF THE BROOKLYN BRIDGE, M.J. Shapiro. Profusely illustrated account of greatest engineering achievement of 19th century. 167 rare photos & engravings recall construction, human drama. Extensive, detailed text. 122pp. 8¼ × 11. 24403-2 Pa. $7.95

NEW YORK IN THE THIRTIES, Berenice Abbott. Noted photographer's fascinating study shows new buildings that have become famous and old sights that have disappeared forever. 97 photographs. 97pp. 11⅜ × 10. 22967-X Pa. $6.50

MATHEMATICAL TABLES AND FORMULAS, Robert D. Carmichael and Edwin R. Smith. Logarithms, sines, tangents, trig functions, powers, roots, reciprocals, exponential and hyperbolic functions, formulas and theorems. 269pp. 5⅜ × 8½. 60111-0 Pa. $3.75

HANDBOOK OF MATHEMATICAL FUNCTIONS WITH FORMULAS, GRAPHS, AND MATHEMATICAL TABLES, edited by Milton Abramowitz and Irene A. Stegun. Vast compendium: 29 sets of tables, some to as high as 20 places. 1,046pp. 8 × 10½. 61272-4 Pa. $19.95

CATALOG OF DOVER BOOKS

REASON IN ART, George Santayana. Renowned philosopher's provocative, seminal treatment of basis of art in instinct and experience. Volume Four of *The Life of Reason.* 230pp. 5⅜ × 8. 24358-3 Pa. $4.50

LANGUAGE, TRUTH AND LOGIC, Alfred J. Ayer. Famous, clear introduction to Vienna, Cambridge schools of Logical Positivism. Role of philosophy, elimination of metaphysics, nature of analysis, etc. 160pp. 5⅜ × 8½. (USCO) 20010-8 Pa. $2.75

BASIC ELECTRONICS, U.S. Bureau of Naval Personnel. Electron tubes, circuits, antennas, AM, FM, and CW transmission and receiving, etc. 560 illustrations. 567pp. 6½ × 9¼. 21076-6 Pa. $8.95

THE ART DECO STYLE, edited by Theodore Menten. Furniture, jewelry, metalwork, ceramics, fabrics, lighting fixtures, interior decors, exteriors, graphics from pure French sources. Over 400 photographs. 183pp. 8⅜ × 11¼. 22824-X Pa. $6.95

THE FOUR BOOKS OF ARCHITECTURE, Andrea Palladio. 16th-century classic covers classical architectural remains, Renaissance revivals, classical orders, etc. 1738 Ware English edition. 216 plates. 110pp. of text. 9½ × 12¾. 21308-0 Pa. $11.50

THE WIT AND HUMOR OF OSCAR WILDE, edited by Alvin Redman. More than 1000 ripostes, paradoxes, wisecracks: Work is the curse of the drinking classes, I can resist everything except temptations, etc. 258pp. 5⅜ × 8½. (USCO) 20602-5 Pa. $3.50

THE DEVIL'S DICTIONARY, Ambrose Bierce. Barbed, bitter, brilliant witticisms in the form of a dictionary. Best, most ferocious satire America has produced. 145pp. 5⅜ × 8½. 20487-1 Pa. $2.50

ERTÉ'S FASHION DESIGNS, Erté. 210 black-and-white inventions from *Harper's Bazar*, 1918-32, plus 8pp. full-color covers. Captions. 88pp. 9 × 12. 24203-X Pa. $6.50

ERTÉ GRAPHICS, Erté. Collection of striking color graphics: *Seasons, Alphabet, Numerals, Aces* and *Precious Stones.* 50 plates, including 4 on covers. 48pp. 9⅜ × 12¼. 23580-7 Pa. $6.95

PAPER FOLDING FOR BEGINNERS, William D. Murray and Francis J. Rigney. Clearest book for making origami sail boats, roosters, frogs that move legs, etc. 40 projects. More than 275 illustrations. 94pp. 5⅜ × 8½. 20713-7 Pa. $2.25

ORIGAMI FOR THE ENTHUSIAST, John Montroll. Fish, ostrich, peacock, squirrel, rhinoceros, Pegasus, 19 other intricate subjects. Instructions. Diagrams. 128pp. 9 × 12. 23799-0 Pa. $4.95

CROCHETING NOVELTY POT HOLDERS, edited by Linda Macho. 64 useful, whimsical pot holders feature kitchen themes, animals, flowers, other novelties. Surprisingly easy to crochet. Complete instructions. 48pp. 8¼ × 11. 24296-X Pa. $1.95

CROCHETING DOILIES, edited by Rita Weiss. Irish Crochet, Jewel, Star Wheel, Vanity Fair and more. Also luncheon and console sets, runners and centerpieces. 51 illustrations. 48pp. 8¼ × 11. 23424-X Pa. $2.00

YUCATAN BEFORE AND AFTER THE CONQUEST, Diego de Landa. Only significant account of Yucatan written in the early post-Conquest era. Translated by William Gates. Over 120 illustrations. 162pp. 5⅜ × 8½.   23622-6 Pa. $3.50

ORNATE PICTORIAL CALLIGRAPHY, E.A. Lupfer. Complete instructions, over 150 examples help you create magnificent "flourishes" from which beautiful animals and objects gracefully emerge. 8⅛ × 11.   21957-7 Pa. $2.95

DOLLY DINGLE PAPER DOLLS, Grace Drayton. Cute chubby children by same artist who did Campbell Kids. Rare plates from 1910s. 30 paper dolls and over 100 outfits reproduced in full color. 32pp. 9¼ × 12¼.   23711-7 Pa. $3.50

CURIOUS GEORGE PAPER DOLLS IN FULL COLOR, H. A. Rey, Kathy Allert. Naughty little monkey-hero of children's books in two doll figures, plus 48 full-color costumes: pirate, Indian chief, fireman, more. 32pp. 9¼ × 12¼.
          24386-9 Pa. $3.50

GERMAN: HOW TO SPEAK AND WRITE IT, Joseph Rosenberg. Like *French, How to Speak and Write It.* Very rich modern course, with a wealth of pictorial material. 330 illustrations. 384pp. 5⅜ × 8½. (USUKO)   20271-2 Pa. $4.75

CATS AND KITTENS: 24 Ready-to-Mail Color Photo Postcards, D. Holby. Handsome collection; feline in a variety of adorable poses. Identifications. 12pp. on postcard stock. 8¼ × 11.   24469-5 Pa. $2.95

MARILYN MONROE PAPER DOLLS, Tom Tierney. 31 full-color designs on heavy stock, from *The Asphalt Jungle,Gentlemen Prefer Blondes,* 22 others.1 doll. 16 plates. 32pp. 9⅜ × 12¼.   23769-9 Pa. $3.50

FUNDAMENTALS OF LAYOUT, F.H. Wills. All phases of layout design discussed and illustrated in 121 illustrations. Indispensable as student's text or handbook for professional. 124pp. 8⅛.× 11.   21279-3 Pa. $4.50

FANTASTIC SUPER STICKERS, Ed Sibbett, Jr. 75 colorful pressure-sensitive stickers. Peel off and place for a touch of pizzazz: clowns, penguins, teddy bears, etc. Full color. 16pp. 8¼ × 11.   24471-7 Pa. $2.95

LABELS FOR ALL OCCASIONS, Ed Sibbett, Jr. 6 labels each of 16 different designs—baroque, art nouveau, art deco, Pennsylvania Dutch, etc.—in full color. 24pp. 8¼ × 11.   23688-9 Pa. $2.95

HOW TO CALCULATE QUICKLY: RAPID METHODS IN BASIC MATHE- MATICS, Henry Sticker. Addition, subtraction, multiplication, division, checks, etc. More than 8000 problems, solutions. 185pp. 5 × 7¼.   20295-X Pa. $2.95

THE CAT COLORING BOOK, Karen Baldauski. Handsome, realistic renderings of 40 splendid felines, from American shorthair to exotic types. 44 plates. Captions. 48pp. 8¼ × 11.   24011-8 Pa. $2.25

THE TALE OF PETER RABBIT, Beatrix Potter. The inimitable Peter's terrifying adventure in Mr. McGregor's garden, with all 27 wonderful, full-color Potter illustrations. 55pp. 4¼ × 5½. (Available in U.S. only)   22827-4 Pa. $1.60

BASIC ELECTRICITY, U.S. Bureau of Naval Personnel. Batteries, circuits, conductors, AC and DC, inductance and capacitance, generators, motors, trans- formers, amplifiers, etc. 349 illustrations. 448pp. 6½ × 9¼.   20973-3 Pa. $7.95

SOURCE BOOK OF MEDICAL HISTORY, edited by Logan Clendening, M.D. Original accounts ranging from Ancient Egypt and Greece to discovery of X-rays: Galen, Pasteur, Lavoisier, Harvey, Parkinson, others. 685pp. 5⅜ × 8½.
20621-1 Pa. $10.95

THE ROSE AND THE KEY, J.S. Lefanu. Superb mystery novel from Irish master. Dark doings among an ancient and aristocratic English family. Well-drawn characters; capital suspense. Introduction by N. Donaldson. 448pp. 5⅜ × 8½.
24377-X Pa. $6.95

SOUTH WIND, Norman Douglas. Witty, elegant novel of ideas set on languorous Mediterranean island of Nepenthe. Elegant prose, glittering epigrams, mordant satire. 1917 masterpiece. 416pp. 5⅜ × 8½. (Available in U.S. only)
24361-3 Pa. $5.95

RUSSELL'S CIVIL WAR PHOTOGRAPHS, Capt. A.J. Russell. 116 rare Civil War Photos: Bull Run, Virginia campaigns, bridges, railroads, Richmond, Lincoln's funeral car. Many never seen before. Captions. 128pp. 9⅜ × 12¼.
24283-8 Pa. $6.95

PHOTOGRAPHS BY MAN RAY: 105 Works, 1920-1934. Nudes, still lifes, landscapes, women's faces, celebrity portraits (Dali, Matisse, Picasso, others), rayographs. Reprinted from rare gravure edition. 128pp. 9⅜ × 12¼. (Available in U.S. only)
23842-3 Pa. $6.95

STAR NAMES: THEIR LORE AND MEANING, Richard H. Allen. Star names, the zodiac, constellations: folklore and literature associated with heavens. The basic book of its field, fascinating reading. 563pp. 5⅜ × 8½.   21079-0 Pa. $7.95

BURNHAM'S CELESTIAL HANDBOOK, Robert Burnham, Jr. Thorough guide to the stars beyond our solar system. Exhaustive treatment. Alphabetical by constellation: Andromeda to Cetus in Vol. 1; Chamaeleon to Orion in Vol. 2; and Pavo to Vulpecula in Vol. 3. Hundreds of illustrations. Index in Vol. 3. 2000pp. 6⅛ × 9¼.   23567-X, 23568-8, 23673-0 Pa. Three-vol. set $36.85

THE ART NOUVEAU STYLE BOOK OF ALPHONSE MUCHA, Alphonse Mucha. All 72 plates from Documents Decoratifs in original color. Stunning, essential work of Art Nouveau. 80pp. 9⅜ × 12¼.   24044-4 Pa. $7.95

DESIGNS BY ERTE; FASHION DRAWINGS AND ILLUSTRATIONS FROM "HARPER'S BAZAR," Erte. 310 fabulous line drawings and 14 Harper's Bazar covers, 8 in full color. Erte's exotic temptresses with tassels, fur muffs, long trains, coifs, more. 129pp. 9⅜ × 12¼.   23397-9 Pa. $6.95

HISTORY OF STRENGTH OF MATERIALS, Stephen P. Timoshenko. Excellent historical survey of the strength of materials with many references to the theories of elasticity and structure. 245 figures. 452pp. 5⅜ × 8½.   61187-6 Pa. $8.95

Prices subject to change without notice.
Available at your book dealer or write for free catalog to Dept. GI, Dover Publications, Inc., 31 East 2nd St. Mineola, N.Y. 11501. Dover publishes more than 175 books each year on science, elementary and advanced mathematics, biology, music, art, literary history, social sciences and other areas.